SELECTED POEMS

By W H. Auden

Collected Poems
Selected Poems
Collected Shorter Poems
Collected Longer Poems
The English Auden:
Poems, Essays & Dramatic Writings
1927-1939
Juvenilia
Look, Stranger
Another Time
Paul Bunyan
A Certain World
The Dyer's Hand
Prose 1926-1938
Lectures on Shakespeare
Essays & Reviews & Travel Books in
Prose & Verse
Tell Me the Truth About Love
As I Walked Out One Evening

with Christopher Isherwood
Plays and Other Dramatic Writings
1928-1938
The Dog Beneath the Skin
The Ascent of F6
and On The Frontier

with Chester Kallman
Libretti and Other Dramatic Writings
1939-1973

with Louis MacNeice
Letters from Iceland

with Paul Taylor
Norse Poems

with Leif Sjöberg
Markings by Dag Hammarskjöld

with Louis Kronenberger
The Faber Book of Aphorisms

By Alan Ansen
The Table Talk of W. H. Auden

W.H. AUDEN
Selected Poems

Edited by
Edward Mendelson

faber and faber

First published in the USA 1979
First published in Great Britain in 1979
by Faber and Faber Limited
3 Queen Square London WC1N 3AU

Printed in Italy

A CIP record for this book
is available from the British Library

ISBN 0–571–11396–6

20

Contents

Preface ix
1. Who stands, the crux left of the watershed 1
2. From the very first coming down 2
3. Control of the passes was, he saw, the key 3
4. Taller to-day, we remember similar evenings 3
5. Watch any day his nonchalant pauses, see 4
6. Will you turn a deaf ear 5
7. Sir, no man's enemy, forgiving all 7
8. It was Easter as I walked in the public gardens 7
9. Since you are going to begin to-day 12
10. Consider this and in our time 14
11. This lunar beauty 16
12. To ask the hard question is simple 17
13. Doom is dark and deeper than any sea-dingle 18
14. What's in your mind, my dove, my coney 19
15. "O where are you going?" said reader to rider 20
16. Though aware of our rank and alert to obey orders 20
17. O Love, the interest itself in thoughtless Heaven 25
18. O what is that sound which so thrills the ear 26
19. Hearing of harvests rotting in the valleys 28
20. Out on the lawn I lie in bed 29
21. A shilling life will give you all the facts 32
22. Our hunting fathers told the story 33
23. Easily, my dear, you move, easily your head 33
24. The Summer holds: upon its glittering lake 36
25. Now through night's caressing grip 41
26. O for doors to be open and an invite with gilded edges 42

27. Look, stranger, at this island now 43
28. Now the leaves are falling fast 43
29. Dear, though the night is gone 44
30. Casino 45
31. Journey to Iceland 46
32. "O who can ever gaze his fill" 48
33. Lay your sleeping head, my love 50
34. Spain 51
35. Orpheus 55
36. Miss Gee 55
37. Wrapped in a yielding air, beside 59
38. As I walked out one evening 60
39. Oxford 63
40. In Time of War 64
41. The Capital 78
42. Musée des Beaux Arts 79
43. Epitaph on a Tyrant 80
44. In Memory of W. B. Yeats 80
45. Refugee Blues 83
46. The Unknown Citizen 85
47. September 1, 1939 86
48. Law, say the gardeners, is the sun 89
49. In Memory of Sigmund Freud 91
50. Lady, weeping at the crossroads 95
51. Song for St. Cecilia's Day 96
52. The Quest 99
53. But I Can't 110
54. In Sickness and in Health 111
55. Jumbled in the common box 115
56. Atlantis 116
57. At the Grave of Henry James 119
58. Mundus et Infans 123
59. The Lesson 125
60. The Sea and the Mirror 127

61. Noon 175
62. Lament for a Lawgiver 176
63. Under Which Lyre 178
64. The Fall of Rome 183
65. In Praise of Limestone 184
66. Song 187
67. A Walk After Dark 188
68. Memorial for the City 190
69. Under Sirius 195
70. Fleet Visit 197
71. The Shield of Achilles 198
72. The Willow-Wren and the Stare 200
73. Nocturne 201
74. Bucolics 202
75. Horae Canonicae 216
76. Homage to Clio 232
77. First Things First 236
78. The More Loving One 237
79. Friday's Child 237
80. Good-bye to the Mezzogiorno 239
81. Dame Kind 242
82. You 245
83. After Reading a Child's Guide to Modern Physics 246
84. On the Circuit 248
85. Et in Arcadia Ego 250
86. Thanksgiving for a Habitat 252
87. Epithalamium 278
88. Fairground 280
89. River Profile 282
90. Prologue at Sixty 284
91. Forty Years On 287
92. Ode to Terminus 289
93. August 1968 291
94. A New Year Greeting 292

95. Moon Landing 294
96. Old People's Home 295
97. Talking to Myself 296
98. A Lullaby 299
99. A Thanksgiving 300
100. Archaeology 302
A Note on the Text 305
Index of Titles and First Lines 307

Preface

Auden was the first poet writing in English who felt at home in the twentieth century. He welcomed into his poetry all the disordered conditions of his time, all its variety of language and event. In this, as in almost everything else, he differed from his modernist predecessors such as Yeats, Lawrence, Eliot or Pound, who had turned nostalgically away from a flawed present to some lost illusory Eden where life was unified, hierarchy secure, and the grand style a natural extension of the vernacular. All of this Auden rejected. His continuing subject was the task of the present moment: erotic and political tasks in his early poems, ethical and religious ones later. When Auden looked back into history, it was to seek the causes of his present condition, that he might act better and more effectively in the future. The past his poems envisioned was never a southern classical domain of unreflective elegance, as it was for the modernists, but a past that had always been ruined, a northern industrial landscape marred by the same violence and sorrow that marred his own.

Everything that is most distinctive about Auden can be traced to his absorption in the present: even, in what might seem a paradox, his revival of the poetic forms and meters that modernism had pronounced dead a few years earlier. Auden was able to find them still alive and well, and as effective as they had always been. In Auden's unbroken vision of history, the ancient discontents survived in contemporary forms, but so did the ancient sources of personal and literary vitality. Modernism, disfranchised from the past by its own sense of isolated "modernity," could bring its literary tradition into the present only as battered ironic fragments (as in Eliot) or by visionary heroic efforts (like Pound's) to "make it new." For Auden, it had never grown old. A laconic Old English toughness thrived in his poetry, as did an Augustan civility. One might even find, in the shape of Auden's career, traces of an ambitious recapitulation of a thousand years of European literary history: his earliest poems use the Icelandic sagas as their major source; then in the thirties Dante is heard insistently in the background of his work; followed by Shakespeare in the forties; and in the sixties, Goethe.

Modernism tended to look back toward the lost reigns of a native aristocracy; too often, it found the reflected glory of ancient "tradition" in political leaders who promised to restore social grandeur and unity through coercive force. Auden's refusal to idealize the past saved him from comparable fits of mistaken generosity. His poems and essays present the idea of the good society as, at best, a possibility, never actually to be achieved, but towards which one must always work. In Auden's poems from the thirties, this idea took form in a vision of history as the product of unconscious but purposive forces, of which social-democratic movements were potentially the conscious agents; one was free either to reject these forces or to ally oneself with them, but the choice was less a moral one than a choice between ultimate victory and ultimate defeat. Auden later renounced this view—which in any case he held less as a personal belief than as a scaffolding on which to build his poetry—and disowned the poems that expressed it. He came to understand history as the realm of conscious ethical choices, made personally and deliberately, and, if at all possible, in full awareness of their consequences. Whichever of these views Auden's political poems assumed, the poems consistently used the same basic technique. From the exhortatory "Spain" to the meditative "Vespers," Auden dramatized the unresolvable tension between personal wishes or fantasies (apocalytic fantasies in his early years, arcadian ones afterwards) and the claims and obligations of the social realm (which he designated "history" in the early poems, "the city" in the later ones). This drama of public responsibility and private desire is part of a tradition that extends back to Virgil and beyond, but by the early part of this century it had disappeared from English poetry. Auden revived it with the same confidence and exuberance he had brought to his revival of traditional poetic forms.

In short, the surest way to misunderstand Auden is to read him as the modernists' heir. Except in his very earliest and latest poems, there is virtually nothing modernist about him. From the viewpoint of literary history, this is the most important aspect of his work. Most critics of twentieth-century poetry, however, still judge poems by their conformity to modernist norms; consequently, a myth has grown up around Auden to the effect that he fell into a decline almost as soon as he began writing. Critics who give credence to this myth mean, in fact, that Auden stopped writing the sort of poems they know how to read: poems written in a subjective voice, in tones of imaginative superiority and regretful isolation. Auden's poems speak instead in a voice almost unknown to English poetry since the end of the eighteenth century: the voice of a citizen who knows the obligations of his citizenship.

Like Brecht in Germany, whose career offers the closest parallels with his own, Auden began with a brashly threatening manner that grew into an ironic didactic one. Both Auden and Brecht started out as amoral romantic anarchists; and both, around the age of thirty, adopted a chastening public orthodoxy—Christianity in Auden's case, Communism in Brecht's. Both came to prefer mixed styles and miscellaneous influences to the purity of the lyric or the intensity of the visionary tradition. Both collaborated with other writers (once even with each other) as no poet had done since the start of the romantic era. Unlike the modernists, both adopted popular forms without the disclaimer of an ironic tone. Each exploited the didactic powers of literature, but rejected the reigning modernist assumptions that granted primacy to the creative imagination or asserted the writing of poetry to be the central human act. Neither was afraid to be vulgar, and neither would entrust serious issues to the inflation of the grand style. Modernism was a movement populated by exiles, at home only in their art. Auden and Brecht were exiles who returned.

The poem that opens this selection (dating from 1927, when Auden was twenty) is the first that Auden wrote in the voice he came to recognize as his own. For about five years afterwards, his voice retained something of the modernist accent he had learned from Eliot, and his poems used the free verse he had learned at the same school. These first poems often have the air of gnomic fragments; they seem to be elements of some hidden private myth whose individual details never quite resolve themselves into a unified narrative. The same qualities of division and irresolution that mark the poems also mark the world they describe, a world where doomed heroes look down in isolation on an equally doomed society. There is division also between the poems and their readers; the poems not only refuse to yield up any cohesive meanings, but adopt a recurrent tone of foreboding and threat: "It is time for the destruction of error," "It is later than you think." Auden's early readers missed the point when they inferred from the poems' elusive privacy the existence of a coterie who shared the meanings and got the jokes; Auden's friends were as much in the dark as everyone else. The elusiveness and indecipherability of the early poems are part of their meaning: they enact the isolation they describe.

The turn away from this early style, and from the manner and subjects of modernism, can be dated precisely. Auden prepared for it in the late spring of 1933, in a series of poems that expressed first the hope of a release from isolation and from the delusive wish for an innocent place elsewhere, and, finally, asked for the will and strength to "rebuild our cities, not dream of islands." Then, in June 1933, Auden experienced what he later called a "Vision of Agape." He was sitting on a lawn with three colleagues from the school where he was teaching, when, he wrote, "quite suddenly and unexpectedly, something happened. I felt myself invaded by a power which, though I consented to it, was irresistible and certainly not mine. For the first time in my life I knew exactly—because, thanks to the power, I was doing it—what it meant to love one's neighbor as oneself." Before this, his poems had only been able to celebrate moments of impersonal erotic intensity, which he called "love." Now, in the poem "Out on the lawn I lie in bed," prompted by his vision, he had praise for everything around him. He described as "lucky" ("luck" in Auden's vocabulary has almost the force of religious "grace") "this point in time and space"—that is, the immediate moment and his "chosen . . . working-place" where he had both friends and responsibilities. His earlier forebodings are transformed into a hymn of renewal; the mutual affections of his friends will have effects beyond the privacy of their English garden and will share in the strength that can rebuild the ruined city.

This jubilant tone could not last, but Auden's sense of public responsibility did. He now began to address his audience, rather than withdraw from it or threaten it; and his audience, amid the discontents of the thirties, was eager to listen. No English poet since Byron achieved fame so quickly. In plays that borrowed their techniques from the music-hall and the cabaret, in poems written in stirring rhythms with memorable rhymes, he hoped to "make action urgent and its nature clear." This proved to be less simple than he imagined. The urgency was vivid enough in his political poems, but the exact nature of the actions urged was never as clear as he might have wished. Readers felt free to find their own actions and attitudes endorsed in these poems, and Auden, recognizing this, began to face his own increasing scruples over his easy relations with his audience. He began to use "vague" as a strong moral pejorative; and the word seemed to apply to many of his own public statements, whose resonance and rhetorical force tended to overwhelm any objections that readers, or Auden's conscience, might raise against their content or their imprecision. In his most politically active years, in the mid-thirties, Auden constantly maintained an inward debate that led him to answer a public exhortation like "Spain" with the hermetic mysteries of a poem like "Orpheus," written at about the same moment. His love poems insisted on the fragility and transience of personal relations, while at the same time his public poems proclaimed a hope for universal harmony. Auden was never altogether happy in his role as poetic prophet to the English Left, and he was often most divided when he appeared most committed. As early as 1936 he sensed that if he were ever to escape the temptations to fame and to the power to shape opinion that led him to accept his role, he would have to leave England. His work in the later thirties records a series of exploratory voyages from England to Spain, Iceland, China, across Europe, finally to America, where, in 1938, he made his decision to leave both England and the role it offered, and to leave, he thought, forever.

When he arrived in America to stay, early in 1939, he set to work on what was virtually a new career, recapitulating his earlier one in a drastically different manner. He began to explore once again the same thematic and formal territory he had covered in his English years, but with a maturer vision, and no longer distracted by the claims of a public. Whether or not by conscious intention, each of the longer poems he wrote during his first years in America served, in effect, as a replacement for a long poem he had written earlier in England. Thus in 1928 he had written a Christmas charade, "Paid on Both Sides"; now, in 1941–42, he wrote a Christmas oratorio, "For the Time Being." In place of his 1936 verse-epistle to a dead poet, "Letter to Lord Byron," he wrote in 1940 a verse-epistle to a living friend, "New Year Letter." In 1931 he had invented a form for *The Orators*, a three-part structure, framed by a prologue and epilogue, with the first part spoken by a series of voices, the second by a single voice, and the third again by multiple voices; in 1943–44 he used the same form, with the central sequence inverted, for "The Sea and the Mirror." When he published the first of his collected editions in 1945, the later poems were all present and complete, while the earlier ones had been either dismembered into their component parts or dropped entirely. Similarly, the inconclusive ending of his 1938 sonnet sequence "In Time of War"—"Wandering lost upon the mountains of our choice"—

was resolved at the close of his 1940 sonnet sequence, "The Quest," in the recovered peace of "The Garden." Even the way he made his living in America repeated a pattern he had followed in the thirties: in England he had taught at various schools until 1935 when he left to work as a free-lance writer; in America he taught at various colleges and universities until 1945, then once again took up his free lance.

His shorter poems emerged from the same process of remaking that gave form to the longer ones. Shortly after he reached New York he began to write in a compressed introspective style that corresponded to the gnomic privacy of his earliest poems but transformed the old aggressiveness into self-reproach. Auden's poems passed judgement on his earlier self and work with a severity that disconcerted his admirers (who complained only of his departure from England, which he seemed to think was the best thing he had done). But the change in his life was as deep and extensive as the change in his work. The restrained and chastened intensity of his first American poems was a sign of his newly discovered commitment to the Anglican faith he once thought he had outgrown in adolescence. In his first year in America he began attending church; he returned to communion late in 1940. The equivocal political commitments of a few years earlier proved to have been rehearsals for a religious commitment that was permanent and undivided, even if its later expression became considerably more relaxed. The last of his longer poems, "The Age of Anxiety" (1944–46), celebrates the personal triumph of his faith, against all odds. There was a corresponding change in the commitments of his love poems. In the thirties he had written of the transience of eros: "Lay your sleeping head, my love," this century's most famous love lyric, praises a faithless and unequal relationship, its inequality signaled by the very act of the conscious lover's address to his unconscious partner. In the forties Auden wrote of a love that was spousal and permanent, whose responsibility endured—as one title put it, in a phrase from the marriage service—"In Sickness and in Health."

The shift from private to public concerns that occurred in Auden's work in the early thirties occurred again in the mid-forties, although now he was without ambition for social influence and lived in a country where poets traditionally had none. His departure from England proved not to have been a rejection of all public roles, as he thought at the time, but a rejection of the wrong ones. He now became an interpreter of his society, not its scourge or prophet. Once again, as in England, he began collaborating on works for the stage. From the late forties onwards he wrote moral parables in the form of opera libretti, as in the thirties he had written political propaganda in the form of musical plays. His greatest works in the late forties and fifties were his extended meditations on the city, its historical origins and present complexities. An initial exploration of the subject, "Memorial for the City," a poem prompted in part by his experience of Germany in 1945, led to the extraordinary sequence of "Horae Canonicae," where the events of a single day, among various urban roles and personalities, are set within a framework encompassing vast reaches of time. The sequence's passage from dawn to dusk corresponds to passages from birth to death, from the rise to the fall of a city, and from the creation to the second coming. Parallel with these urban poems are a group set in rural landscapes: "In Praise of Limestone" establishes the theme, and the sequence of "Bucolics" extends and develops it.

In the late fifties and sixties Auden turned to the more local significance of a single dwelling place. In 1957, he bought a farmhouse in Austria as a summer home (the first home he had ever owned) and began the poems that grew into the sequence "Thanksgiving for a Habitat." While narrowing his focus to his private hearth he retained his sense of historical and social extension; each room of the house, like each landscape in "Bucolics," has its moral and political analogues, and more often than not, is the occasion for a meditation on history.

In his final years his subjects narrowed still further, and he returned to a transformed version of the privacy of his first poems. He left America to return to England. A nostalgic note, absent since his earliest poems, began to enter his work once more. Still, as he had denied his earlier nostalgic longings by recalling the evidence of history ("The pillar dug from the desert recorded only / The sack of a city"), now he emphasized the imaginary quality of the past whose image he evoked by writing about it in the language of folk tales. He wrote again of a doomed landscape: not an external one, but the microcosmos of his own aging body. He directed his meditations on history to thanksgiving rather than analysis: if his last poems concern his doomed flesh they also celebrate the family and the age from which it sprang. He made explicit his gratitude to his literary sources. At the end, in "Archaeology," his last completed poem, he delved into an unknowably remote past, yet —as he prepared for his own exit from the world of time into an unknowable future—he concluded with an affirmation. History, he wrote, is made "by the criminal in us: / goodness is timeless."

In preparing the text of a selection of Auden's work, an editor must make his own decision between the claims of errant history and those of timeless goodness. Auden applied a moral standard to his earlier poems—and, some critics have charged, tried to rewrite his own history in the process—when he revised or discarded some of his most famous work, either in an effort to make it conform to his later standards of precision and clarity, or, more notoriously, to rid it of statements he had come to regard as hateful and false. All the collected and selected editions he prepared, and that are currently available on either side of the Atlantic, reflect his later judgements. Yet the claims of history, and of readers who want the discarded poems, are strong, and the present selection acknowledges them by reprinting the texts of the early editions and by including poems Auden rejected. A historical edition of this kind, reflecting the author's work as it first appeared in public rather than his final vision of it, should not be taken as implying that Auden's revisions or rejections were in any way misguided; they were logical and consistent, and in almost every instance produced versions that were more coherent and complex than the originals. Probably the best way to get to know Auden's work is to read the early versions first for their greater immediate impact, and the revised versions afterwards for their greater subtlety and depth. For most readers this book will be a First Auden, and the later collections are recommended as a Second.

Most criticism, however, has taken a censorious view of Auden's revisions, and the issue is an important one because behind it is a larger dispute about Auden's theory of poetry. In making his revisions, and in justifying them as he did, Auden was systematically rejecting a whole range of modernist assumptions about poetic form, the nature of poetic language, and the effects of poetry on its audience. Critics who find the changes deplorable generally argue, in effect, that a poet loses his right to revise or reject his work after he publishes it—as if the skill with which he brought his poems from their early drafts to the point of publication somehow left him at the moment they appeared, making him a trespasser on his own work thereafter. This argument presupposes the romantic notion that poetic form is, or ought to be, "organic," that an authentic poem is shaped by its own internal forces rather than by the external effects of craft; versions of this idea survived as central tenets of modernism. In revising his poems, Auden opened his workshop to the public, and the spectacle proved unsettling, especially as his revisions, unlike Yeats', moved against the current of literary fashion. In the later part of his career, he increasingly called attention in his essays to the technical aspects of verse, the details of metrical and stanzaic construction—much as Brecht had brought his stagehands into the full view of the audience. The goal in each case was to remove the mystery that surrounds works of art, to explode the myth of poetic inspiration, and to deny any special privileges to poetry in the realm of language or to artists in the realm of ethics.

Critics mistook this attitude as a "rejection" of poetry,

when in fact it was a recognition of its potential effects. The most notorious aspect of Auden's revisions, as of his whole poetic theory, was his insistence that a poem must not be "dishonest," must not express beliefs that a poet does not actually hold, no matter how rhetorically effective he finds them. In Auden's view, poetry could not be exempted from ethical standards of truth or falsehood: a poem could be a lie, and what was more serious, a poetic lie could be more persuasive in the public realm than lies less eloquently expressed. Words had the potential to do good or evil, whether their source was political discourse or the ordered images of a poem. Auden's sense of the effect of poetic language—like Brecht's sense of the effect of stage performance—differs entirely from the modernist theory that sets poetry apart from the world, either in an interior psychological arena or in the enclosed garden of reflexivity where poems refer only to themselves. Already in the thirties, Auden's political poems assumed they had the power to affect attitudes, and therefore indirectly to affect action; his later judgements on those poems made the same assumption, but from a very different moral perspective. In the first version of "In Memory of W. B. Yeats" Auden had written that time would pardon writers like Kipling and Claudel for their right-wing views; the implication was that the left-wing views held by Auden and his audience were consonant with the force of history and would need no forgiveness whatever. Auden soon found this less easy to believe than he did when he wrote it, and was less willing to encourage such complacency in his readers. He dropped the stanzas about Kipling and Claudel, and dropped entirely such poems as "Spain" where the "struggle" is more important than its consequences and goodness is equated with victory, or "September 1, 1939" where a rhetorical sleight-of-hand grants the moral value of just actions to the ironic "messages" of the isolated just. These poems are memorable enough to survive all of Auden's interference, and there are ancient and vigorous critical standards by which they must be judged great art; still, when Auden called them "trash which he is ashamed to have written" he was taking them far more seriously—and taking poetic language far more seriously—than his critics ever did.

Too seriously, most readers would argue. Yet the revisions Auden made in the forties, like the changes in his life and work, effectively put into practice the doubts he had experienced earlier. He had embedded an allegory of his mixed feelings into *The Ascent of F6*, a play written with Christopher Isherwood in 1936. The play traces the destruction of a mountain climber (Auden's dramatic representative), at the moment of his greatest triumph, as a result of the conflicts inherent in a public role his private terrors tempted him to accept. Auden avoided a parallel fate by leaving England for America at the height of his fame, and by working to expunge from his poetry the tendencies that he sensed might otherwise have destroyed him and his poetry together. Later he could write more tolerantly of the temptation to "ruin a fine tenor voice / For effects that bring down the house," but by that time, having defeated his public temptations, he had set out to conquer his private ones also. The poems he wrote in this period, in the forties and after, are less immediately compelling than his earlier ones, but more profound and more rewarding in the long term. His masterpiece is arguably "The Sea and the Mirror" (its nearest rivals may be "New Year Letter" and "Horae Canonicae"), whose longest section, "Caliban to the Audience," is the work he preferred to all his others. It had been the most recalcitrant in conception—he was stalled six months before he could work out its form—and the most pleasurable in the writing; and it confronted most directly and comprehensively the limits and powers of his art, and its temptations and possibilities.

This selection includes poems chosen from all of Auden's books of verse; a note on sources may be found at the back. The texts are those of first publication in book form, modified only by the rare minor revisions Auden made within a few months of publication, and by the correction of misprints.

The arrangement is chronological, except where Auden arranged a group of poems written at different times into a single sequence; dates of composition are appended to each poem. I have tried to include examples from the full range of Auden's work in all its enormous variety of form, rhetoric and content; the only major formal omission, I believe, results from the impossibility of including either of the two long verse-letters, which took up too many pages to reprint in full and proved unamenable to abridgment. One long poem, "The Sea and the Mirror," is printed complete, and excerpts from other longer works are included only in cases where Auden printed the same excerpts as separate poems. The titles, or lack of titles in the early work, correspond to the usage in the first editions; the titles used for excerpts from "The Age of Anxiety" are those Auden used when he printed them in periodicals. No selection from a great poet has ever been satisfactory—a rule I know has not been broken by this one.

E.M.

1

Who stands, the crux left of the watershed,
On the wet road between the chafing grass
Below him sees dismantled washing-floors,
Snatches of tramline running to the wood,
An industry already comatose,
Yet sparsely living. A ramshackle engine
At Cashwell raises water; for ten years
It lay in flooded workings until this,
Its latter office, grudgingly performed,
And further here and there, though many dead
Lie under the poor soil, some acts are chosen
Taken from recent winters; two there were
Cleaned out a damaged shaft by hand, clutching
The winch the gale would tear them from; one died
During a storm, the fells impassable,
Not at his village, but in wooden shape
Through long abandoned levels nosed his way
And in his final valley went to ground.

Go home, now, stranger, proud of your young stock,
Stranger, turn back again, frustrate and vexed:
This land, cut off, will not communicate,
Be no accessory content to one
Aimless for faces rather there than here.
Beams from your car may cross a bedroom wall,
They wake no sleeper; you may hear the wind
Arriving driven from the ignorant sea
To hurt itself on pane, on bark of elm
Where sap unbaffled rises, being Spring;
But seldom this. Near you, taller than grass,
Ears poise before decision, scenting danger.

August 1927

2

From the very first coming down
Into a new valley with a frown
Because of the sun and a lost way,
You certainly remain: to-day
I, crouching behind a sheep-pen, heard
Travel across a sudden bird,
Cry out against the storm, and found
The year's arc a completed round
And love's worn circuit re-begun,
Endless with no dissenting turn.
Shall see, shall pass, as we have seen
The swallow on the tile, Spring's green
Preliminary shiver, passed
A solitary truck, the last
Of shunting in the Autumn. But now
To interrupt the homely brow,
Thought warmed to evening through and through
Your letter comes, speaking as you,
Speaking of much but not to come.

Nor speech is close nor fingers numb,
If love not seldom has received
An unjust answer, was deceived.
I, decent with the seasons, move
Different or with a different love,
Nor question overmuch the nod,
The stone smile of this country god
That never was more reticent,
Always afraid to say more than it meant.

December 1927

3

Control of the passes was, he saw, the key
To this new district, but who would get it?
He, the trained spy, had walked into the trap
For a bogus guide, seduced with the old tricks.

At Greenhearth was a fine site for a dam
And easy power, had they pushed the rail
Some stations nearer. They ignored his wires.
The bridges were unbuilt and trouble coming.

The street music seemed gracious now to one
For weeks up in the desert. Woken by water
Running away in the dark, he often had
Reproached the night for a companion
Dreamed of already. They would shoot, of course,
Parting easily who were never joined.

January 1928

4

Taller to-day, we remember similar evenings,
Walking together in the windless orchard
Where the brook runs over the gravel, far from the glacier.

Again in the room with the sofa hiding the grate,
Look down to the river when the rain is over,
See him turn to the window, hearing our last
Of Captain Ferguson.

It is seen how excellent hands have turned to commonness.
One staring too long, went blind in a tower,
One sold all his manors to fight, broke through, and faltered.

Nights come bringing the snow, and the dead howl
Under the headlands in their windy dwelling
Because the Adversary put too easy questions
On lonely roads.

But happy now, though no nearer each other,
We see the farms lighted all along the valley;
Down at the mill-shed the hammering stops
And men go home.

Noises at dawn will bring
Freedom for some, but not this peace
No bird can contradict: passing, but is sufficient now
For something fulfilled this hour, loved or endured.

March 1928

5

Watch any day his nonchalant pauses, see
His dextrous handling of a wrap as he
Steps after into cars, the beggar's envy.

"There is a free one," many say, but err.
He is not that returning conqueror,
Nor ever the poles' circumnavigator.

But poised between shocking falls on razor-edge
Has taught himself this balancing subterfuge
Of the accosting profile, the erect carriage.

The song, the varied action of the blood
Would drown the warning from the iron wood
Would cancel the inertia of the buried:

Travelling by daylight on from house to house
The longest way to the intrinsic peace,
With love's fidelity and with love's weakness.

March 1929

6

Will you turn a deaf ear
To what they said on the shore,
Interrogate their poises
In their rich houses;

Of stork-legged heaven-reachers
Of the compulsory touchers
The sensitive amusers
And masked amazers?

Yet wear no ruffian badge
Nor lie behind the hedge
Waiting with bombs of conspiracy
In arm-pit secrecy;

Carry no talisman
For germ or the abrupt pain
Needing no concrete shelter
Nor porcelain filter.

Will you wheel death anywhere
In his invalid chair,
With no affectionate instant
But his attendant?

For to be held for friend
By an undeveloped mind
To be joke for children is
Death's happiness:

Whose anecdotes betray
His favourite colour as blue
Colour of distant bells
And boys' overalls.

His tales of the bad lands
Disturb the sewing hands;
Hard to be superior
On parting nausea;

To accept the cushions from
Women against martyrdom,
Yet applauding the circuits
Of racing cyclists.

Never to make signs
Fear neither maelstrom nor zones
Salute with soldiers' wives
When the flag waves;

Remembering there is
No recognised gift for this;
No income, no bounty,
No promised country.

But to see brave sent home
Hermetically sealed with shame
And cold's victorious wrestle
With molten metal.

A neutralising peace
And an average disgrace
Are honour to discover
For later other.

September 1929

7

Sir, no man's enemy, forgiving all
But will his negative inversion, be prodigal:
Send to us power and light, a sovereign touch
Curing the intolerable neural itch,
The exhaustion of weaning, the liar's quinsy,
And the distortions of ingrown virginity.
Prohibit sharply the rehearsed response
And gradually correct the coward's stance;
Cover in time with beams those in retreat
That, spotted, they turn though the reverse were great;
Publish each healer that in city lives
Or country houses at the end of drives;
Harrow the house of the dead; look shining at
New styles of architecture, a change of heart.

October 1929

8

I

It was Easter as I walked in the public gardens
Hearing the frogs exhaling from the pond,
Watching traffic of magnificent cloud
Moving without anxiety on open sky—
Season when lovers and writers find
An altering speech for altering things,
An emphasis on new names, on the arm
A fresh hand with fresh power.
But thinking so I came at once
Where solitary man sat weeping on a bench,
Hanging his head down, with his mouth distorted
Helpless and ugly as an embryo chicken.

So I remember all of those whose death
Is necessary condition of the season's setting forth,
Who sorry in this time look only back
To Christmas intimacy, a winter dialogue
Fading in silence, leaving them in tears.
And recent particulars come to mind:
The death by cancer of a once hated master,
A friend's analysis of his own failure,
Listened to at intervals throughout the winter
At different hours and in different rooms.
But always with success of others for comparison,
The happiness, for instance, of my friend Kurt Groote,
Absence of fear in Gerhart Meyer
From the sea, the truly strong man.

A 'bus ran home then, on the public ground
Lay fallen bicycles like huddled corpses:
No chattering valves of laughter emphasised
Nor the swept gown ends of a gesture stirred
The sessile hush; until a sudden shower
Fell willing into grass and closed the day,
Making choice seem a necessary error.

April 1929

II

Coming out of me living is always thinking,
Thinking changing and changing living,
Am feeling as it was seeing—
In city leaning on harbour parapet
To watch a colony of duck below
Sit, preen, and doze on buttresses
Or upright paddle on flickering stream,
Casually fishing at a passing straw.
Those find sun's luxury enough,
Shadow know not of homesick foreigner
Nor restlessness of intercepted growth.

All this time was anxiety at night,
Shooting and barricade in street.
Walking home late I listened to a friend
Talking excitedly of final war
Of proletariat against police—
That one shot girl of nineteen through the knees,
They threw that one down concrete stair—
Till I was angry, said I was pleased.

Time passes in Hessen, in Gutensberg,
With hill-top and evening holds me up,
Tiny observer of enormous world.
Smoke rises from factory in field,
Memory of fire: On all sides heard
Vanishing music of isolated larks:
From village square voices in hymn,
Men's voices, an old use.
And I above standing, saying in thinking:

"Is first baby, warm in mother,
Before born and is still mother,
Time passes and now is other,
Is knowledge in him now of other,
Cries in cold air, himself no friend.
In grown man also, may see in face
In his day-thinking and in his night-thinking
Is wareness and is fear of other,
Alone in flesh, himself no friend.

"He say 'We must forgive and forget,'
Forgetting saying but is unforgiving
And unforgiving is in his living;
Body reminds in him to loving,
Reminds but takes no further part,
Perfunctorily affectionate in hired room
But takes no part and is unloving
But loving death. May see in dead,
In face of dead that loving wish,

As one returns from Africa to wife
And his ancestral property in Wales."

Yet sometimes man look and say good
At strict beauty of locomotive,
Completeness of gesture or unclouded eye;
In me so absolute unity of evening
And field and distance was in me for peace,
Was over me in feeling without forgetting
Those ducks' indifference, that friend's hysteria,
Without wishing and with forgiving,
To love my life, not as other,
Not as bird's life, not as child's,
"Cannot," I said, "being no child now nor a bird."

May 1929

III

Order to stewards and the study of time,
Correct in books, was earlier than this
But joined this by the wires I watched from train,
Slackening of wire and posts' sharp reprimand,
In month of August to a cottage coming.

Being alone, the frightened soul
Returns to this life of sheep and hay
No longer his: he every hour
Moves further from this and must so move,
As child is weaned from his mother and leaves home
But taking the first steps falters, is vexed,
Happy only to find home, a place
Where no tax is levied for being there.

So, insecure, he loves and love
Is insecure, gives less than he expects.
He knows not if it be seed in time to display
Luxuriantly in a wonderful fructification
Or whether it be but a degenerate remnant
Of something immense in the past but now

Surviving only as the infectiousness of disease
Or in the malicious caricature of drunkenness;
Its end glossed over by the careless but known long
To finer perception of the mad and ill.

Moving along the track which is himself,
He loves what he hopes will last, which gone,
Begins the difficult work of mourning,
And as foreign settlers to strange country come,
By mispronunciation of native words
And by intermarriage create a new race
And a new language, so may the soul
Be weaned at last to independent delight.

Startled by the violent laugh of a jay
I went from wood, from crunch underfoot,
Air between stems as under water;
As I shall leave the summer, see autumn come
Focusing stars more sharply in the sky,
See frozen buzzard flipped down the weir
And carried out to sea, leave autumn,
See winter, winter for earth and us,
A forethought of death that we may find ourselves at death
Not helplessly strange to the new conditions.

August 1929

IV

It is time for the destruction of error.
The chairs are being brought in from the garden,
The summer talk stopped on that savage coast
Before the storms, after the guests and birds:
In sanatoriums they laugh less and less,
Less certain of cure; and the loud madman
Sinks now into a more terrible calm.

The falling leaves know it, the children,
At play on the fuming alkali-tip
Or by the flooded football ground, know it—

This is the dragon's day, the devourer's:
Orders are given to the enemy for a time
With underground proliferation of mould,
With constant whisper and the casual question,
To haunt the poisoned in his shunned house,
To destroy the efflorescence of the flesh,
To censor the play of the mind, to enforce
Conformity with the orthodox bone,
With organised fear, the articulated skeleton.

You whom I gladly walk with, touch,
Or wait for as one certain of good,
We know it, we know that love
Needs more than the admiring excitement of union,
More than the abrupt self-confident farewell,
The heel on the finishing blade of grass,
The self-confidence of the falling root,
Needs death, death of the grain, our death,
Death of the old gang; would leave them
In sullen valley where is made no friend,
The old gang to be forgotten in the spring,
The hard bitch and the riding-master,
Stiff underground; deep in clear lake
The lolling bridegroom, beautiful, there.

October 1929

9

Since you are going to begin to-day
Let us consider what it is you do.
You are the one whose part it is to lean,
For whom it is not good to be alone.
Laugh warmly turning shyly in the hall
Or climb with bare knees the volcanic hill,
Acquire that flick of wrist and after strain

Relax in your darling's arms like a stone
Remembering everything you can confess,
Making the most of firelight, of hours of fuss;
But joy is mine not yours—to have come so far,
Whose cleverest invention was lately fur;
Lizards my best once who took years to breed,
Could not control the temperature of blood.
To reach that shape for your face to assume,
Pleasure to many and despair to some,
I shifted ranges, lived epochs handicapped
By climate, wars, or what the young men kept,
Modified theories on the types of dross,
Altered desire and history of dress.

You in the town now call the exile fool
That writes home once a year as last leaves fall,
Think—Romans had a language in their day
And ordered roads with it, but it had to die:
Your culture can but leave—forgot as sure
As place-name origins in favourite shire—
Jottings for stories, some often-mentioned Jack,
And references in letters to a private joke,
Equipment rusting in unweeded lanes,
Virtues still advertised on local lines;
And your conviction shall help none to fly,
Cause rather a perversion on next floor.

Nor even is despair your own, when swiftly
Comes general assault on your ideas of safety:
That sense of famine, central anguish felt
For goodness wasted at peripheral fault,
Your shutting up the house and taking prow
To go into the wilderness to pray,
Means that I wish to leave and to pass on,
Select another form, perhaps your son;
Though he reject you, join opposing team
Be late or early at another time,

My treatment will not differ—he will be tipped,
Found weeping, signed for, made to answer, topped.
Do not imagine you can abdicate;
Before you reach the frontier you are caught;
Others have tried it and will try again
To finish that which they did not begin:
Their fate must always be the same as yours,
To suffer the loss they were afraid of, yes,
Holders of one position, wrong for years.

November 1929

10

Consider this and in our time
As the hawk sees it or the helmeted airman:
The clouds rift suddenly—look there
At cigarette-end smouldering on a border
At the first garden party of the year.
Pass on, admire the view of the massif
Through plate-glass windows of the Sport Hotel;
Join there the insufficient units
Dangerous, easy, in furs, in uniform
And constellated at reserved tables
Supplied with feelings by an efficient band
Relayed elsewhere to farmers and their dogs
Sitting in kitchens in the stormy fens.

Long ago, supreme Antagonist,
More powerful than the great northern whale
Ancient and sorry at life's limiting defect,
In Cornwall, Mendip, or the Pennine moor
Your comments on the highborn mining-captains,
Found they no answer, made them wish to die
—Lie since in barrows out of harm.
You talk to your admirers every day
By silted harbours, derelict works,

In strangled orchards, and the silent comb
Where dogs have worried or a bird was shot.
Order the ill that they attack at once:
Visit the ports and, interrupting
The leisurely conversation in the bar
Within a stone's throw of the sunlit water,
Beckon your chosen out. Summon
Those handsome and diseased youngsters, those women
Your solitary agents in the country parishes;
And mobilise the powerful forces latent
In soils that make the farmer brutal
In the infected sinus, and the eyes of stoats.
Then, ready, start your rumour, soft
But horrifying in its capacity to disgust
Which, spreading magnified, shall come to be
A polar peril, a prodigious alarm,
Scattering the people, as torn-up paper
Rags and utensils in a sudden gust,
Seized with immeasurable neurotic dread.

Financier, leaving your little room
Where the money is made but not spent,
You'll need your typist and your boy no more;
The game is up for you and for the others,
Who, thinking, pace in slippers on the lawns
Of College Quad or Cathedral Close,
Who are born nurses, who live in shorts
Sleeping with people and playing fives.
Seekers after happiness, all who follow
The convolutions of your simple wish,
It is later than you think; nearer that day
Far other than that distant afternoon
Amid rustle of frocks and stamping feet
They gave the prizes to the ruined boys.
You cannot be away, then, no
Not though you pack to leave within an hour,
Escaping humming down arterial roads:

The date was yours; the prey to fugues,
Irregular breathing and alternate ascendancies
After some haunted migratory years
To disintegrate on an instant in the explosion of mania
Or lapse for ever into a classic fatigue.

March 1930

11

This lunar beauty
Has no history
Is complete and early;
If beauty later
Bear any feature
It had a lover
And is another.

This like a dream
Keeps other time
And daytime is
The loss of this;
For time is inches
And the heart's changes
Where ghost has haunted
Lost and wanted.

But this was never
A ghost's endeavour
Nor finished this,
Was ghost at ease;
And till it pass
Love shall not near
The sweetness here
Nor sorrow take
His endless look.

April 1930

12

To ask the hard question is simple;
Asking at meeting
With the simple glance of acquaintance
To what these go
And how these do:
To ask the hard question is simple,
The simple act of the confused will.

But the answer
Is hard and hard to remember:
On steps or on shore
The ears listening
To words at meeting,
The eyes looking
At the hands helping,
Are never sure
Of what they learn
From how these things are done.
And forgetting to listen or see
Makes forgetting easy;
Only remembering the method of remembering,
Remembering only in another way,
Only the strangely exciting lie,
Afraid
To remember what the fish ignored,
How the bird escaped, or if the sheep obeyed.

Till, losing memory,
Bird, fish, and sheep are ghostly,
And ghosts must do again
What gives them pain.
Cowardice cries
For windy skies,
Coldness for water,
Obedience for a master.

Shall memory restore
The steps and the shore,
The face and the meeting place;
Shall the bird live,
Shall the fish dive,
And sheep obey
In a sheep's way;
Can love remember
The question and the answer,
For love recover
What has been dark and rich and warm all over?

? August 1930

13

Doom is dark and deeper than any sea-dingle.
Upon what man it fall
In spring, day-wishing flowers appearing,
Avalanche sliding, white snow from rock-face,
That he should leave his house,
No cloud-soft hand can hold him, restraint by women;
But ever that man goes
Through place-keepers, through forest trees,
A stranger to strangers over undried sea,
Houses for fishes, suffocating water,
Or lonely on fell as chat,
By pot-holed becks
A bird stone-haunting, an unquiet bird.

There head falls forward, fatigued at evening,
And dreams of home,
Waving from window, spread of welcome,
Kissing of wife under single sheet;
But waking sees
Bird-flocks nameless to him, through doorway voices
Of new men making another love.

Save him from hostile capture,
From sudden tiger's spring at corner;
Protect his house,
His anxious house where days are counted
From thunderbolt protect,
From gradual ruin spreading like a stain;
Converting number from vague to certain,
Bring joy, bring day of his returning,
Lucky with day approaching, with leaning dawn.

August 1930

14

What's in your mind, my dove, my coney;
Do thoughts grow like feathers, the dead end of life;
Is it making of love or counting of money,
Or raid on the jewels, the plans of a thief?

Open your eyes, my dearest dallier;
Let hunt with your hands for escaping me;
Go through the motions of exploring the familiar;
Stand on the brink of the warm white day.

Rise with the wind, my great big serpent;
Silence the birds and darken the air;
Change me with terror, alive in a moment;
Strike for the heart and have me there.

November 1930

15

"O where are you going?" said reader to rider,
"That valley is fatal where furnaces burn,
  Yonder's the midden whose odours will madden,
  That gap is the grave where the tall return."

"O do you imagine," said fearer to farer,
"That dusk will delay on your path to the pass,
  Your diligent looking discover the lacking
  Your footsteps feel from granite to grass?"

"O what was that bird," said horror to hearer,
"Did you see that shape in the twisted trees?
  Behind you swiftly the figure comes softly,
  The spot on your skin is a shocking disease?"

"Out of this house"—said rider to reader
"Yours never will"—said farer to fearer
"They're looking for you"—said hearer to horror
  As he left them there, as he left them there.

from "The Orators": October 1931

16

(TO MY PUPILS)

Though aware of our rank and alert to obey orders,
Watching with binoculars the movement of the grass for an
ambush,
The pistol cocked, the code-word committed to memory;
    The youngest drummer
Knows all the peace-time stories like the oldest soldier,
    Though frontier-conscious,

About the tall white gods who landed from their open boat,
Skilled in the working of copper, appointing our feast-days,
Before the islands were submerged, when the
weather was calm,
The maned lion common,
An open wishing-well in every garden;
When love came easy.

Perfectly certain, all of us, but not from the records,
Not from the unshaven agent who returned to the camp;
The pillar dug from the desert recorded only
The sack of a city,
The agent clutching his side collapsed at our feet,
"Sorry! They got me!"

Yes, they were living here once but do not now,
Yes, they are living still but do not here;
Lying awake after Lights Out a recruit may speak up:
"Who told you all this?"
The tent-talk pauses a little till a veteran answers
"Go to sleep, Sonny!"

Turning over he closes his eyes, and then in a moment
Sees the sun at midnight bright over cornfield and pasture,
Our hope. . . . Someone jostles him, fumbling for boots,
Time to change guard:
Boy, the quarrel was before your time, the aggressor
No one you know.

Your childish moments of awareness were all of our world,
At five you sprang, already a tiger in the garden,
At night your mother taught you to pray for our Daddy
Far away fighting,
One morning you fell off a horse and your brother mocked you:
"Just like a girl!"

You've got their names to live up to and questions won't help,
You've a very full programme, first aid, gunnery, tactics,
The technique to master of raids and hand-to-hand fighting;
Are you in training?
Are you taking care of yourself? Are you sure of passing
The endurance test?

Now we're due to parade on the square in front of the
Cathedral,
When the bishop has blessed us, to file in after the choir-boys,
To stand with the wine-dark conquerors in the roped-off pews,
Shout ourselves hoarse:
"They ran like hares; we have broken them up like firewood;
They fought against God."

While in a great rift in the limestone miles away
At the same hour they gather, tethering their horses
beside them;
A scarecrow prophet from a boulder foresees our judgement,
Their oppressors howling;
And the bitter psalm is caught by the gale from the rocks:
"How long shall they flourish?"

What have we all been doing to have made from Fear
That laconic war-bitten captain addressing them now
"Heart and head shall be keener, mood the more
As our might lessens":
To have caused their shout "We will fight till
we lie down beside
The Lord we have loved"?

There's Wrath who has learnt every trick of guerilla warfare,
The shamming dead, the night-raid, the feinted retreat;
Envy their brilliant pamphleteer, to lying
As husband true,
Expert impersonator and linguist, proud of his power
To hoodwink sentries.

Gluttony living alone, austerer than us,
Big simple Greed, Acedia famed with them all
For her stamina, keeping the outposts, and somewhere Lust
With his sapper's skill,
Muttering to his fuses in a tunnel "Could I meet here with Love,
I would hug him to death."

There are faces there for which for a very long time
We've been on the look-out, though often at home we imagined,
Catching sight of a back or hearing a voice through a doorway,
We had found them at last;
Put our arms round their necks
and looked in their eyes and discovered
We were unlucky.

And some of them, surely, we seem to have seen before:
Why, that girl who rode off on her bicycle one fine
summer evening
And never returned, she's there; and the banker we'd noticed
Worried for weeks;
Till he failed to arrive one morning and his room was empty,
Gone with a suitcase.

They speak of things done on the frontier we were never told,
The hidden path to their squat Pictish tower
They will never reveal though kept without
sleep, for their code is
"Death to the squealer":
They are brave, yes, though our newspapers
mention their bravery
In inverted commas.

But careful; back to our lines; it is unsafe there,
Passports are issued no longer; that area is closed;
There's no fire in the waiting-room now
at the climbers' junction,
And all this year

Work has been stopped on the power-house;
the wind whistles under
The half-built culverts.

Do you think that because you have heard that on
Christmas Eve
In a quiet sector they walked about on the skyline,
Exchanged cigarettes, both learning the words for "I love you"
In either language,
You can stroll across for a smoke and a chat any evening?
Try it and see.

That rifle-sight you're designing; is it ready yet?
You're holding us up; the office is getting impatient;
The square munition works out on the old allotments
Needs stricter watching;
If you see any loiterers there you may shoot without warning,
We must stop that leakage.

All leave is cancelled to-night; we must say good-bye.
We entrain at once for the North; we shall see in the morning
The headlands we're doomed to attack; snow
down to the tide-line:
Though the bunting signals
"Indoors before it's too late; cut peat for your fires,"
We shall lie out there.

from "The Orators": November 1931

17

O Love, the interest itself in thoughtless Heaven,
Make simpler daily the beating of man's heart; within,
There in the ring where name and image meet,

Inspire them with such a longing as will make his thought
Alive like patterns a murmuration of starlings
Rising in joy over wolds unwittingly weave;

Here too on our little reef display your power,
This fortress perched on the edge of the Atlantic scarp,
The mole between all Europe and the exile-crowded sea;

And make us as Newton was, who in his garden watching
The apple falling towards England, became aware
Between himself and her of an eternal tie.

For now that dream which so long has contented our will,
I mean, of uniting the dead into a splendid empire,
Under whose fertilising flood the Lancashire moss

Sprouted up chimneys, and Glamorgan hid a life
Grim as a tidal rock-pool's in its glove-shaped valleys,
Is already retreating into her maternal shadow;

Leaving the furnaces gasping in the impossible air,
The flotsam at which Dumbarton gapes and hungers;
While upon wind-loved Rowley no hammer shakes

The cluster of mounds like a midget golf course, graves
Of some who created these intelligible dangerous marvels;
Affectionate people, but crude their sense of glory.

Far-sighted as falcons, they looked down another future;
For the seed in their loins were hostile, though
afraid of their pride,
And, tall with a shadow now, inertly wait.

In bar, in netted chicken-farm, in lighthouse,
Standing on these impoverished constricting acres,
The ladies and gentlemen apart, too much alone,

Consider the years of the measured world begun,
The barren spiritual marriage of stone and water.
Yet, O, at this very moment of our hopeless sigh

When inland they are thinking their thoughts but are
watching these islands,
As children in Chester look to Moel Fammau to decide
On picnics by the clearness or withdrawal of her
treeless crown,

Some possible dream, long coiled in the ammonite's slumber
Is uncurling, prepared to lay on our talk and kindness
Its military silence, its surgeon's idea of pain;

And out of the Future into actual History,
As when Merlin, tamer of horses, and his lords to whom
Stonehenge was still a thought, the Pillars passed

And into the undared ocean swung north their prow,
Drives through the night and star-concealing dawn
For the virgin roadsteads of our hearts an unwavering keel.

May 1932

18

O what is that sound which so thrills the ear
Down in the valley drumming, drumming?
Only the scarlet soldiers, dear,
The soldiers coming.

O what is that light I see flashing so clear
  Over the distance brightly, brightly?
Only the sun on their weapons, dear,
    As they step lightly.

O what are they doing with all that gear;
  What are they doing this morning, this morning?
Only the usual manoeuvres, dear,
    Or perhaps a warning.

O why have they left the road down there;
  Why are they suddenly wheeling, wheeling?
Perhaps a change in the orders, dear;
    Why are you kneeling?

O haven't they stopped for the doctor's care;
  Haven't they reined their horses, their horses?
Why, they are none of them wounded, dear,
    None of these forces.

O is it the parson they want with white hair;
  Is it the parson, is it, is it?
No, they are passing his gateway, dear,
    Without a visit.

O it must be the farmer who lives so near;
  It must be the farmer so cunning, so cunning?
They have passed the farm already, dear,
    And now they are running.

O where are you going? stay with me here!
  Were the vows you swore me deceiving, deceiving?
No, I promised to love you, dear,
    But I must be leaving.

O it's broken the lock and splintered the door,
  O it's the gate where they're turning, turning;
Their feet are heavy on the floor
    And their eyes are burning.

October 1932

19

Hearing of harvests rotting in the valleys,
Seeing at end of street the barren mountains,
Round corners coming suddenly on water,
Knowing them shipwrecked who were launched for islands,
We honour founders of these starving cities,
Whose honour is the image of our sorrow.

Which cannot see its likeness in their sorrow
That brought them desperate to the brink of valleys;
Dreaming of evening walks through learned cities,
They reined their violent horses on the mountains,
Those fields like ships to castaways on islands,
Visions of green to them that craved for water.

They built by rivers and at night the water
Running past windows comforted their sorrow;
Each in his little bed conceived of islands
Where every day was dancing in the valleys,
And all the year trees blossomed on the mountains,
Where love was innocent, being far from cities.

But dawn came back and they were still in cities;
No marvellous creature rose up from the water,
There was still gold and silver in the mountains,
And hunger was a more immediate sorrow;
Although to moping villagers in valleys
Some waving pilgrims were describing islands.

"The gods," they promised, "visit us from islands,
Are stalking head-up, lovely through the cities;
Now is the time to leave your wretched valleys
And sail with them across the lime-green water;
Sitting at their white sides, forget your sorrow,
The shadow cast across your lives by mountains."

So many, doubtful, perished in the mountains
Climbing up crags to get a view of islands;
So many, fearful, took with them their sorrow
Which stayed them when they reached unhappy cities;
So many, careless, dived and drowned in water;
So many, wretched, would not leave their valleys.

It is the sorrow; shall it melt? Ah, water
Would gush, flush, green these mountains and these valleys,
And we rebuild our cities, not dream of islands.

May 1933

20

(TO GEOFFREY HOYLAND)

Out on the lawn I lie in bed,
Vega conspicuous overhead
In the windless nights of June;
Forests of green have done complete
The day's activity; my feet
Point to the rising moon.

Lucky, this point in time and space
Is chosen as my working place;
Where the sexy airs of summer,
The bathing hours and the bare arms,
The leisured drives through a land of farms,
Are good to the newcomer.

Equal with colleagues in a ring
I sit on each calm evening,
Enchanted as the flowers
The opening light draws out of hiding
From leaves with all its dove-like pleading
Its logic and its powers.

That later we, though parted then
May still recall these evenings when
Fear gave his watch no look;
The lion griefs loped from the shade
And on our knees their muzzles laid,
And Death put down his book.

Moreover, eyes in which I learn
That I am glad to look, return
My glances every day;
And when the birds and rising sun
Waken me, I shall speak with one
Who has not gone away.

Now North and South and East and West
Those I love lie down to rest;
The moon looks on them all:
The healers and the brilliant talkers,
The eccentrics and the silent walkers,
The dumpy and the tall.

She climbs the European sky;
Churches and power stations lie
Alike among earth's fixtures:
Into the galleries she peers,
And blankly as an orphan stares
Upon the marvellous pictures.

To gravity attentive, she
Can notice nothing here; though we
Whom hunger cannot move,
From gardens where we feel secure
Look up, and with a sigh endure
The tyrannies of love:

And, gentle, do not care to know,
Where Poland draws her Eastern bow,
What violence is done;

Nor ask what doubtful act allows
Our freedom in this English house,
  Our picnics in the sun.

The creepered wall stands up to hide
The gathering multitudes outside
  Whose glances hunger worsens;
Concealing from their wretchedness
Our metaphysical distress,
  Our kindness to ten persons.

And now no path on which we move
But shows already traces of
  Intentions not our own,
Thoroughly able to achieve
What our excitement could conceive,
  But our hands left alone.

For what by nature and by training
We loved, has little strength remaining.
  Though we would gladly give
The Oxford colleges, Big Ben,
And all the birds in Wicken Fen,
  It has no wish to live.

Soon through the dykes of our content
The crumpling flood will force a rent,
  And, taller than a tree,
Hold sudden death before our eyes
Whose river-dreams long hid the size
  And vigours of the sea.

But when the waters make retreat
And through the black mud first the wheat
  In shy green stalks appears;
When stranded monsters gasping lie,
And sounds of riveting terrify
  Their whorled unsubtle ears:

May this for which we dread to lose
Our privacy, need no excuse
  But to that strength belong;
As through a child's rash happy cries
The drowned voices of his parents rise
  In unlamenting song.

After discharges of alarm,
All unpredicted may it calm
  The pulse of nervous nations;
Forgive the murderer in his glass,
Tough in its patience to surpass
  The tigress her swift motions.

June 1933

21

A shilling life will give you all the facts:
How Father beat him, how he ran away,
What were the struggles of his youth, what acts
Made him the greatest figure of his day:
Of how he fought, fished, hunted, worked all night,
Though giddy, climbed new mountains; named a sea:
Some of the last researchers even write
Love made him weep his pints like you and me.

With all his honours on, he sighed for one
Who, say astonished critics, lived at home;
Did little jobs about the house with skill
And nothing else; could whistle; would sit still
Or potter round the garden; answered some
Of his long marvellous letters but kept none.

? 1934

22

Our hunting fathers told the story
  Of the sadness of the creatures,
Pitied the limits and the lack
  Set in their finished features;
Saw in the lion's intolerant look,
Behind the quarry's dying glare,
Love raging for the personal glory
  That reason's gift would add,
The liberal appetite and power,
  The rightness of a god.

Who nurtured in that fine tradition
  Predicted the result,
Guessed love by nature suited to
  The intricate ways of guilt?
That human ligaments could so
His southern gestures modify,
And make it his mature ambition
  To think no thought but ours,
To hunger, work illegally,
  And be anonymous?

? May 1934

23

Easily, my dear, you move, easily your head
And easily as through the leaves of a photograph album I'm led
Through the night's delights and the day's impressions,
Past the tall tenements and the trees in the wood;
Though sombre the sixteen skies of Europe
    And the Danube flood.

Looking and loving our behaviours pass
The stones, the steels and the polished glass;
Lucky to Love the new pansy railway,
The sterile farms where his looks are fed,
And in the policed unlucky city
        Lucky his bed.

He from these lands of terrifying mottoes
Makes worlds as innocent as Beatrix Potter's;
Through bankrupt countries where they mend the roads
Along the endless plains his will is
Intent as a collector to pursue
        His greens and lilies.

Easy for him to find in your face
The pool of silence and the tower of grace,
To conjure a camera into a wishing rose;
Simple to excite in the air from a glance
The horses, the fountains, the sidedrum, the trombone
        And the dance, the dance.

Summoned by such a music from our time,
Such images to audience come
As vanity cannot dispel nor bless:
Hunger and love in their variations
Grouped invalids watching the flight of the birds
        And single assassins.

Ten thousand of the desperate marching by
Five feet, six feet, seven feet high:
Hitler and Mussolini in their wooing poses
Churchill acknowledging the voters' greeting
Roosevelt at the microphone, Van der Lubbe laughing
        And our first meeting.

But love, except at our proposal,
Will do no trick at his disposal;
Without opinions of his own, performs

The programme that we think of merit,
And through our private stuff must work
        His public spirit.

Certain it became while we were still incomplete
There were certain prizes for which we would never compete;
A choice was killed by every childish illness,
The boiling tears among the hothouse plants,
The rigid promise fractured in the garden,
        And the long aunts.

And every day there bolted from the field
Desires to which we could not yield;
Fewer and clearer grew the plans,
Schemes for a life and sketches for a hatred,
And early among my interesting scrawls
        Appeared your portrait.

You stand now before me, flesh and bone
These ghosts would like to make their own.
Are they your choices? O, be deaf
When hatred would proffer her immediate pleasure,
And glory swap her fascinating rubbish
        For your one treasure.

Be deaf too, standing uncertain now,
A pine tree shadow across your brow,
To what I hear and wish I did not:
The voice of love saying lightly, brightly—
"Be Lubbe, be Hitler, but be my good
        Daily, nightly."

The power that corrupts, that power to excess
The beautiful quite naturally possess:
To them the fathers and the children turn:
And all who long for their destruction,
The arrogant and self-insulted, wait
        The looked instruction.

Shall idleness ring then your eyes like the pest?
O will you unnoticed and mildly like the rest,
Will you join the lost in their sneering circles,
Forfeit the beautiful interest and fall
Where the engaging face is the face of the betrayer,
And the pang is all?

Wind shakes the tree; the mountains darken;
And the heart repeats though we would not hearken:
"Yours is the choice, to whom the gods awarded
The language of learning and the language of love,
Crooked to move as a moneybug or a cancer
Or straight as a dove."

November 1934

24

The Summer holds: upon its glittering lake
Lie Europe and the islands; many rivers
Wrinkling its surface like a ploughman's palm.
Under the bellies of the grazing horses
On the far side of posts and bridges
The vigorous shadows dwindle; nothing wavers.
Calm at this moment the Dutch sea so shallow
That sunk St. Paul's would ever show its golden cross
And still the deep water that divides us still from Norway.

We would show you at first an English village: You shall choose its location
Wherever your heart directs you most longingly to look; you are loving towards it:
Whether north to Scots Gap and Bellingham where the black rams defy the panting engine:
Or west to the Welsh Marches; to the lilting speech and the magicians' faces:

Wherever you were a child or had your first affair
There it stands amidst your darling scenery:
A parish bounded by the wreckers' cliff; or meadows where
browse the Shorthorn and maplike Frisian
As at Trent Junction where the Soar comes gliding; out of
green Leicestershire to swell the ampler current.

Hiker with sunburn blisters on your office pallor,
Cross-country champion with corks in your hands,
When you have eaten
your sandwich, your salt and your apple,
When you have begged
your glass of milk from the ill-kept farm,
What is it you see?

I see barns falling, fences broken,
Pasture not ploughland, weeds not wheat.
The great houses remain but only half are inhabited,
Dusty the gunrooms and the stable clocks stationary.
Some have been turned into prep-schools where the diet is in
the hands of an experienced matron,
Others into club-houses for the golf-bore and the top-hole.
Those who sang in the inns at evening have departed; they
saw their hope in another country,
Their children have entered the service of the suburban areas;
they have become typists, mannequins and factory
operatives; they desired a different rhythm of life.
But their places are taken by another population, with views
about nature,
Brought in charabanc and saloon along arterial roads;
Tourists to whom the Tudor cafés
Offer Bovril and buns upon Breton ware
With leather-work as a sideline: Filling stations
Supplying petrol from rustic pumps.
Those who fancy themselves as foxes or desire a
special setting for spooning
Erect their villas at the right places,
Airtight, lighted, elaborately warmed;

And nervous people who will never marry
Live upon dividends in the old-world cottages
With an animal for a friend or a volume of memoirs.

Man is changed by his living; but not fast enough.
His concern to-day is for that which yesterday did not occur.
In the hour of the Blue Bird and the Bristol Bomber, his
thoughts are appropriate to the years of the
Penny Farthing:
He tosses at night who at noonday found no truth.

Stand aside now: The play is beginning
In the village of which we have spoken; called Pressan Ambo:
Here too corruption spreads its peculiar and emphatic odours
And Life lurks, evil, out of its epoch.

The young men in Pressan to-night
Toss on their beds
Their pillows do not comfort
Their uneasy heads.
The lot that decides their fate
Is cast to-morrow,
One must depart and face
Danger and sorrow.

Is it me? Is it me? Is it . . . me?

Look in your heart and see:
There lies the answer.
Though the heart like a clever
Conjuror or dancer
Deceive you often into many
A curious sleight
And motives like stowaways
Are found too late.

What shall he do, whose heart
Chooses to depart?

He shall against his peace
  Feel his heart harden,
Envy the heavy birds
  At home in a garden.
For walk he must the empty
  Selfish journey
Between the needless risk
  And the endless safety.

Will he safe and sound
  Return to his own ground?

Clouds and lions stand
  Before him dangerous
And the hostility of dreams.
  O let him honour us
Lest he should be ashamed
  In the hour of crisis,
In the valleys of corrosion
  Tarnish his brightness.

Who are you, whose speech
  Sounds far out of reach?

You are the town and we are the clock.
We are the guardians of the gate in the rock,
          The Two.
On your left and on your right
In the day and in the night,
          We are watching you.

Wiser not to ask just what has occurred
To them who disobeyed our word;
          To those
We were the whirlpool, we were the reef,
We were the formal nightmare, grief
          And the unlucky rose.

Climb up the crane, learn the sailors' words
When the ships from the islands laden with birds
Come in.
Tell your stories of fishing and other men's wives:
The expansive moments of constricted lives
In the lighted inn.

But do not imagine we do not know
Nor that what you hide with such care won't show
At a glance.
Nothing is done, nothing is said,
But don't make the mistake of believing us dead:
I shouldn't dance.

We're afraid in that case you'll have a fall.
We've been watching you over the garden wall
For hours.
The sky is darkening like a stain,
Something is going to fall like rain
And it won't be flowers.

When the green field comes off like a lid
Revealing what was much better hid:
Unpleasant.
And look, behind you without a sound
The woods have come up and are standing round
In deadly crescent.

The bolt is sliding in its groove,
Outside the window is the black remov-
ers van.
And now with sudden swift emergence
Come the women in dark glasses and the
humpbacked surgeons
And the scissor man.

This might happen any day
So be careful what you say
Or do.

Be clean, be tidy, oil the lock,
Trim the garden, wind the clock,
Remember the Two.

from "The Dog Beneath the Skin": 1932, ? 1934

25

Now through night's caressing grip
Earth and all her oceans slip,
Capes of China slide away
From her fingers into day
And the Americas incline
Coasts towards her shadow line.
Now the ragged vagrants creep
Into crooked holes to sleep:
Just and unjust, worst and best,
Change their places as they rest:
Awkward lovers lie in fields
Where disdainful beauty yields:
While the splendid and the proud
Naked stand before the crowd
And the losing gambler gains
And the beggar entertains:
May sleep's healing power extend
Through these hours to our friend.
Unpursued by hostile force,
Traction engine, bull or horse
Or revolting succubus;
Calmly till the morning break
Let him lie, then gently wake.

from "The Dog Beneath the Skin": ? 1935

26

O for doors to be open and an invite with gilded edges
To dine with Lord Lobcock and Count Asthma on the
platinum benches,
With the somersaults and fireworks, the roast and the
smacking kisses—
Cried the six cripples to the silent statue,
The six beggared cripples.

And Garbo's and Cleopatra's wits to go astraying,
In a feather ocean with me to go fishing and playing
Still jolly when the cock has burst himself with crowing—
Cried the six cripples to the silent statue,
The six beggared cripples.

And to stand on green turf among the craning yellow faces,
Dependent on the chestnut, the sable, and Arabian horses,
And me with a magic crystal to foresee their places—
Cried the six cripples to the silent statue,
The six beggared cripples.

And this square to be a deck, and these pigeons sails to rig
And to follow the delicious breeze like a tantony pig
To the shaded feverless islands where the melons are big—
Cried the six cripples to the silent statue,
The six beggared cripples.

And these shops to be turned to tulips in a garden bed,
And me with my stick to thrash each merchant dead
As he pokes from a flower his bald and wicked head—
Cried the six cripples to the silent statue,
The six beggared cripples.

And a hole in the bottom of heaven, and Peter and Paul
And each smug surprised saint like parachutes to fall,
And every one-legged beggar to have no legs at all—
Cried the six cripples to the silent statue,
The six beggared cripples.

? Spring 1935

27

Look, stranger, at this island now
The leaping light for your delight discovers,
Stand stable here
And silent be,
That through the channels of the ear
May wander like a river
The swaying sound of the sea.

Here at the small field's ending pause
Where the chalk wall falls to the foam, and its tall ledges
Oppose the pluck
And knock of the tide,
And the shingle scrambles after the suck-
ing surf, and the gull lodges
A moment on its sheer side.

Far off like floating seeds the ships
Diverge on urgent voluntary errands;
And the full view
Indeed may enter
And move in memory as now these clouds do,
That pass the harbour mirror
And all the summer through the water saunter.

November 1935

28

Now the leaves are falling fast,
Nurse's flowers will not last;
Nurses to the graves are gone,
And the prams go rolling on.

Whispering neighbours, left and right,
Pluck us from the real delight;
And the active hands must freeze
Lonely on the separate knees.

Dead in hundreds at the back
Follow wooden in our track,
Arms raised stiffly to reprove
In false attitudes of love.

Starving through the leafless wood
Trolls run scolding for their food;
And the nightingale is dumb,
And the angel will not come.

Cold, impossible, ahead
Lifts the mountain's lovely head
Whose white waterfall could bless
Travellers in their last distress.

March 1936

29

Dear, though the night is gone,
The dream still haunts to-day
That brought us to a room,
Cavernous, lofty as
A railway terminus,
And crowded in that gloom
Were beds, and we in one
In a far corner lay.

Our whisper woke no clocks,
We kissed and I was glad
At everything you did,

Indifferent to those
Who sat with hostile eyes
In pairs on every bed,
Arms round each other's necks,
Inert and vaguely sad.

O but what worm of guilt
Or what malignant doubt
Am I the victim of;
That you then, unabashed,
Did what I never wished,
Confessed another love;
And I, submissive, felt
Unwanted and went out?

March 1936

30

Casino

Only the hands are living; to the wheel attracted,
Are moved, as deer trek desperately towards a creek
  Through the dust and scrub of the desert, or gently
  As sunflowers turn to the light.

And as the night takes up the cries of feverish children,
The cravings of lions in dens, the loves of dons,
  Gathers them all and remains the night, the
  Great room is full of their prayers.

To the last feast of isolation, self-invited,
They flock, and in the rite of disbelief are joined;
  From numbers all their stars are recreated,
  The enchanted, the world, the sad.

Without, the rivers flow among the wholly living,
Quite near their trysts; and the mountains part them;
and the bird,
Deep in the greens and moistures of summer,
Sings towards their work.

But here no nymph comes naked to the youngest shepherd,
The fountain is deserted, the laurel will not grow;
The labyrinth is safe but endless, and broken
Is Ariadne's thread.

As deeper in these hands is grooved their fortune: "Lucky
Were few, and it is possible that none were loved;
And what was godlike in this generation
Was never to be born."

April 1936

31

Journey to Iceland

And the traveller hopes: "Let me be far from any
Physician"; and the ports have names for the sea;
The citiless, the corroding, the sorrow;
And North means to all: "Reject!"

And the great plains are for ever where the cold fish is hunted,
And everywhere; the light birds flicker and flaunt;
Under the scolding flag the lover
Of islands may see at last,

Faintly, his limited hope; and he nears the glitter
Of glaciers, the sterile immature mountains intense
In the abnormal day of this world, and a river's
Fan-like polyp of sand.

Then let the good citizen here find natural marvels:
The horse-shoe ravine, the issue of steam from a cleft
    In the rock, and rocks, and waterfalls brushing the
    Rocks, and among the rocks birds.

And the student of prose and conduct, places to visit;
The site of a church where a bishop was put in a bag,
    The bath of a great historian, the rock where
    An outlaw dreaded the dark.

Remember the doomed man thrown by his horse and crying:
"Beautiful is the hillside, I will not go";
    The old woman confessing: "He that I loved the
    Best, to him I was worst,"

For Europe is absent. This is an island and therefore
Unreal. And the steadfast affections of its dead may be bought
    By those whose dreams accuse them of being
    Spitefully alive, and the pale

From too much passion of kissing feel pure in its deserts.
Can they? For the world is, and the present, and the lie.
    And the narrow bridge over the torrent,
    And the small farm under the crag

Are the natural setting for the jealousies of a province;
And the weak vow of fidelity is formed by the cairn;
    And within the indigenous figure on horseback
    On the bridle path down by the lake

The blood moves also by crooked and furtive inches,
Asks all your questions: "Where is the homage? When
    Shall justice be done? O who is against me?
    Why am I always alone?"

Present then the world to the world with its mendicant shadow;
Let the suits be flash, the Minister of Commerce insane;
    Let jazz be bestowed on the huts, and the beauty's
    Set cosmopolitan smile.

For our time has no favourite suburb; no local features
Are those of the young for whom all wish to care;
    The promise is only a promise, the fabulous
    Country impartially far.

Tears fall in all the rivers. Again the driver
Pulls on his gloves and in a blinding snowstorm starts
    Upon his deadly journey; and again the writer
    Runs howling to his art.

July 1936

32

"O who can ever gaze his fill,"
    Farmer and fisherman say,
"On native shore and local hill,
Grudge aching limb or callus on the hand?
Fathers, grandfathers stood upon this land,
And here the pilgrims from our loins shall stand."
    So farmer and fisherman say
    In their fortunate heyday:
    But Death's soft answer drifts across
    Empty catch or harvest loss
      Or an unlucky May:
The earth is an oyster with nothing inside it
    Not to be born is the best for man
The end of toil is a bailiff's order
    Throw down the mattock and dance while you can.

"O life's too short for friends who share,"
    Travellers think in their hearts,
"The city's common bed, the air,
The mountain bivouac and the bathing beach,
Where incidents draw every day from each
Memorable gesture and witty speech."

So travellers think in their hearts,
Till malice or circumstance parts
Them from their constant humour:
And slyly Death's coercive rumour
In the silence starts:
A friend is the old tale of Narcissus
Not to be born is the best for man
An active partner in something disgraceful
Change your partner, dance while you can.

"O stretch your hands across the sea,"
The impassioned lover cries,
"Stretch them towards your harm and me.
Our grass is green, and sensual our brief bed,
The stream sings at its foot, and at its head
The mild and vegetarian beasts are fed."
So the impassioned lover cries
Till his storm of pleasure dies:
From the bedpost and the rocks
Death's enticing echo mocks,
And his voice replies:
The greater the love, the more false to its object
Not to be born is the best for man
After the kiss comes the impulse to throttle
Break the embraces, dance while you can.

"I see the guilty world forgiven,"
Dreamer and drunkard sing,
"The ladders let down out of heaven;
The laurel springing from the martyr's blood;
The children skipping where the weepers stood;
The lovers natural, and the beasts all good."
So dreamer and drunkard sing
Till day their sobriety bring:
Parrotwise with death's reply
From whelping fear and nesting lie,
Woods and their echoes ring:

The desires of the heart are as crooked as corkscrews
Not to be born is the best for man
The second best is a formal order
The dance's pattern, dance while you can.
Dance, dance, for the figure is easy
The tune is catching and will not stop
Dance till the stars come down with the rafters
Dance, dance, dance till you drop.

September 1936

33

Lay your sleeping head, my love,
Human on my faithless arm;
Time and fevers burn away
Individual beauty from
Thoughtful children, and the grave
Proves the child ephemeral:
But in my arms till break of day
Let the living creature lie,
Mortal, guilty, but to me
The entirely beautiful.

Soul and body have no bounds:
To lovers as they lie upon
Her tolerant enchanted slope
In their ordinary swoon,
Grave the vision Venus sends
Of supernatural sympathy,
Universal love and hope;
While an abstract insight wakes
Among the glaciers and the rocks
The hermit's sensual ecstasy.

Certainty, fidelity
On the stroke of midnight pass
Like vibrations of a bell,
And fashionable madmen raise
Their pedantic boring cry:
Every farthing of the cost,
All the dreaded cards foretell,
Shall be paid, but from this night
Not a whisper, not a thought,
Not a kiss nor look be lost.

Beauty, midnight, vision dies:
Let the winds of dawn that blow
Softly round your dreaming head
Such a day of sweetness show
Eye and knocking heart may bless,
Find the mortal world enough;
Noons of dryness see you fed
By the involuntary powers,
Nights of insult let you pass
Watched by every human love.

January 1937

34

Spain

Yesterday all the past. The language of size
Spreading to China along the trade-routes; the diffusion
        Of the counting-frame and the cromlech;
Yesterday the shadow-reckoning in the sunny climates.

Yesterday the assessment of insurance by cards,
The divination of water; yesterday the invention
        Of cartwheels and clocks, the taming of
Horses. Yesterday the bustling world of the navigators.

Yesterday the abolition of fairies and giants,
The fortress like a motionless eagle eyeing the valley,
    The chapel built in the forest;
Yesterday the carving of angels and alarming gargoyles;

The trial of heretics among the columns of stone;
Yesterday the theological feuds in the taverns
    And the miraculous cure at the fountain;
Yesterday the Sabbath of witches; but to-day the struggle.

Yesterday the installation of dynamos and turbines,
The construction of railways in the colonial desert;
    Yesterday the classic lecture
On the origin of Mankind. But to-day the struggle.

Yesterday the belief in the absolute value of Greek,
The fall of the curtain upon the death of a hero;
    Yesterday the prayer to the sunset
And the adoration of madmen. But to-day the struggle.

As the poet whispers, startled among the pines,
Or where the loose waterfall sings compact, or upright
    On the crag by the leaning tower:
"O my vision. O send me the luck of the sailor."

And the investigator peers through his instruments
At the inhuman provinces, the virile bacillus
    Or enormous Jupiter finished:
"But the lives of my friends. I inquire. I inquire."

And the poor in their fireless lodgings, dropping the sheets
Of the evening paper: "Our day is our loss, O show us
    History the operator, the
Organiser, Time the refreshing river."

And the nations combine each cry, invoking the life
That shapes the individual belly and orders
    The private nocturnal terror:
"Did you not found the city state of the sponge,

"Raise the vast military empires of the shark
And the tiger, establish the robin's plucky canton?
Intervene. O descend as a dove or
A furious papa or a mild engineer, but descend."

And the life, if it answers at all, replies from the heart
And the eyes and the lungs, from the
shops and squares of the city:
"O no, I am not the mover;
Not to-day; not to you. To you, I'm the

"Yes-man, the bar-companion, the easily-duped;
I am whatever you do. I am your vow to be
Good, your humorous story.
I am your business voice. I am your marriage.

"What's your proposal? To build the just city? I will.
I agree. Or is it the suicide pact, the romantic
Death? Very well, I accept, for
I am your choice, your decision. Yes, I am Spain."

Many have heard it on remote peninsulas,
On sleepy plains, in the aberrant fishermen's islands
Or the corrupt heart of the city,
Have heard and migrated like gulls or the seeds of a flower.

They clung like burrs to the long expresses that lurch
Through the unjust lands, through the night,
through the alpine tunnel;
They floated over the oceans;
They walked the passes. All presented their lives.

On that arid square, that fragment nipped off from hot
Africa, soldered so crudely to inventive Europe;
On that tableland scored by rivers,
Our thoughts have bodies; the menacing shapes of our fever

Are precise and alive. For the fears which made us respond
To the medicine ad. and the brochure of winter cruises
        Have become invading battalions;
And our faces, the institute-face, the chain-store, the ruin

Are projecting their greed as the firing squad and the bomb.
Madrid is the heart. Our moments of tenderness blossom
        As the ambulance and the sandbag;
Our hours of friendship into a people's army.

To-morrow, perhaps the future. The research on fatigue
And the movements of packers; the gradual exploring of all the
        Octaves of radiation;
To-morrow the enlarging of consciousness by diet and
                                                        breathing.

To-morrow the rediscovery of romantic love,
The photographing of ravens; all the fun under
        Liberty's masterful shadow;
To-morrow the hour of the pageant-master and the musician,

The beautiful roar of the chorus under the dome;
To-morrow the exchanging of tips on the breeding of terriers,
        The eager election of chairmen
By the sudden forest of hands. But to-day the struggle.

To-morrow for the young the poets exploding like bombs,
The walks by the lake, the weeks of perfect communion;
        To-morrow the bicycle races
Through the suburbs on summer evenings. But to-day the
                                                        struggle.

To-day the deliberate increase in the chances of death,
The conscious acceptance of guilt in the necessary murder;
        To-day the expending of powers
On the flat ephemeral pamphlet and the boring meeting.

To-day the makeshift consolations: the shared cigarette,
The cards in the candlelit barn, and the scraping concert,
        The masculine jokes; to-day the
Fumbled and unsatisfactory embrace before hurting.

The stars are dead. The animals will not look.
We are left alone with our day, and the time is short, and
        History to the defeated
May say Alas but cannot help nor pardon.

April 1937

35

Orpheus

What does the song hope for? And the moved hands
A little way from the birds, the shy, the delightful?
        To be bewildered and happy,
        Or most of all the knowledge of life?

But the beautiful are content with the sharp notes of the air;
The warmth is enough. O if winter really
        Oppose, if the weak snowflake,
        What will the wish, what will the dance do?

April 1937

36

Miss Gee

Let me tell you a little story
    About Miss Edith Gee;
She lived in Clevedon Terrace
    At Number 83.

She'd a slight squint in her left eye,
  Her lips they were thin and small,
She had narrow sloping shoulders
  And she had no bust at all.

She'd a velvet hat with trimmings,
  And a dark-grey serge costume;
She lived in Clevedon Terrace
  In a small bed-sitting room.

She'd a purple mac for wet days,
  A green umbrella too to take,
She'd a bicycle with shopping basket
  And a harsh back-pedal brake.

The Church of Saint Aloysius
  Was not so very far;
She did a lot of knitting,
  Knitting for that Church Bazaar.

Miss Gee looked up at the starlight
  And said: "Does anyone care
That I live in Clevedon Terrace
  On one hundred pounds a year?"

She dreamed a dream one evening
  That she was the Queen of France
And the Vicar of Saint Aloysius
  Asked Her Majesty to dance.

But a storm blew down the palace,
  She was biking through a field of corn,
And a bull with the face of the Vicar
  Was charging with lowered horn.

She could feel his hot breath behind her,
  He was going to overtake;
And the bicycle went slower and slower
  Because of that back-pedal brake.

Summer made the trees a picture,
Winter made them a wreck;
She bicycled to the evening service
With her clothes buttoned up to her neck.

She passed by the loving couples,
She turned her head away;
She passed by the loving couples
And they didn't ask her to stay.

Miss Gee sat down in the side-aisle,
She heard the organ play;
And the choir it sang so sweetly
At the ending of the day.

Miss Gee knelt down in the side-aisle,
She knelt down on her knees;
"Lead me not into temptation
But make me a good girl, please."

The days and nights went by her
Like waves round a Cornish wreck;
She bicycled down to the doctor
With her clothes buttoned up to her neck.

She bicycled down to the doctor,
And rang the surgery bell;
"O, doctor, I've a pain inside me,
And I don't feel very well."

Doctor Thomas looked her over,
And then he looked some more;
Walked over to his wash-basin,
Said: "Why didn't you come before?"

Doctor Thomas sat over his dinner,
Though his wife was waiting to ring;
Rolling his bread into pellets,
Said: "Cancer's a funny thing.

"Nobody knows what the cause is,
Though some pretend they do;
It's like some hidden assassin
Waiting to strike at you.

"Childless women get it,
And men when they retire;
It's as if there had to be some outlet
For their foiled creative fire."

His wife she rang for the servant,
Said: "Don't be so morbid, dear";
He said: "I saw Miss Gee this evening
And she's a goner, I fear."

They took Miss Gee to the hospital,
She lay there a total wreck,
Lay in the ward for women
With the bedclothes right up to her neck.

They laid her on the table,
The students began to laugh;
And Mr. Rose the surgeon
He cut Miss Gee in half.

Mr. Rose he turned to his students,
Said: "Gentlemen, if you please,
We seldom see a sarcoma
As far advanced as this."

They took her off the table,
They wheeled away Miss Gee
Down to another department
Where they study Anatomy.

They hung her from the ceiling,
Yes, they hung up Miss Gee;
And a couple of Oxford Groupers
Carefully dissected her knee.

April 1937

37

Wrapped in a yielding air, beside
The flower's soundless hunger,
Close to the tree's clandestine tide,
Close to the bird's high fever,
Loud in his hope and anger,
Erect about his skeleton,
Stands the expressive lover,
Stands the deliberate man.

Beneath the hot incurious sun,
Past stronger beasts and fairer
He picks his way, a living gun,
With gun and lens and bible,
A militant enquirer,
The friend, the rash, the enemy,
The essayist, the able,
Able at times to cry.

The friendless and unhated stone
Lies everywhere about him,
The Brothered-One, the Not-Alone,
The brothered and the hated
Whose family have taught him
To set against the large and dumb,
The timeless and the rooted,
His money and his time.

For mother's fading hopes become
Dull wives to his dull spirits
Soon dulled by nurse's moral thumb,
That dullard fond betrayer,
And, childish, he inherits,
So soon by legal father tricked,
The tall and gorgeous tower,
Gorgeous but locked, but locked.

And ruled by dead men never met,
By pious guess deluded,
Upon the stool of madness set
Or stool of desolation,
Sits murderous and clear-headed;
Enormous beauties round him move,
For grandiose is his vision
And grandiose his love.

Determined on Time's honest shield
The lamb must face the tigress,
Their faithful quarrel never healed
Though, faithless, he consider
His dream of vaguer ages,
Hunter and victim reconciled,
The lion and the adder,
The adder and the child.

Fresh loves betray him, every day
Over his green horizon
A fresh deserter rides away,
And miles away birds mutter
Of ambush and of treason;
To fresh defeats he still must move,
To further griefs and greater,
And the defeat of grief.

May 1937

38

As I walked out one evening,
Walking down Bristol Street,
The crowds upon the pavement
Were fields of harvest wheat.

And down by the brimming river
I heard a lover sing
Under an arch of the railway:
"Love has no ending.

"I'll love you, dear, I'll love you
Till China and Africa meet
And the river jumps over the mountain
And the salmon sing in the street.

"I'll love you till the ocean
Is folded and hung up to dry
And the seven stars go squawking
Like geese about the sky.

"The years shall run like rabbits
For in my arms I hold
The Flower of the Ages
And the first love of the world."

But all the clocks in the city
Began to whirr and chime:
"O let not Time deceive you,
You cannot conquer Time.

"In the burrows of the Nightmare
Where Justice naked is,
Time watches from the shadow
And coughs when you would kiss.

"In headaches and in worry
Vaguely life leaks away,
And Time will have his fancy
To-morrow or to-day.

"Into many a green valley
Drifts the appalling snow;
Time breaks the threaded dances
And the diver's brilliant bow.

"O plunge your hands in water,
    Plunge them in up to the wrist;
Stare, stare in the basin
    And wonder what you've missed.

"The glacier knocks in the cupboard,
    The desert sighs in the bed,
And the crack in the tea-cup opens
    A lane to the land of the dead.

"Where the beggars raffle the banknotes
    And the Giant is enchanting to Jack,
And the Lily-white Boy is a Roarer
    And Jill goes down on her back.

"O look, look in the mirror,
    O look in your distress;
Life remains a blessing
    Although you cannot bless.

"O stand, stand at the window
    As the tears scald and start;
You shall love your crooked neighbour
    With your crooked heart."

It was late, late in the evening,
    The lovers they were gone;
The clocks had ceased their chiming
    And the deep river ran on.

November 1937

39

Oxford

Nature is so near: the rooks in the college garden
Like agile babies still speak the language of feeling;
By the tower the river still runs to the sea and will run,
And the stones in that tower are utterly
Satisfied still with their weight.

And the minerals and creatures, so deeply
in love with their lives
Their sin of accidie excludes all others,
Challenge the nervous students with a careless beauty,
Setting a single error
Against their countless faults.

O in these quadrangles where Wisdom honours herself
Does the original stone merely echo that praise
Shallowly, or utter a bland hymn of comfort,
The founder's equivocal blessing
On all who worship Success?

Promising to the sharp sword all the glittering prizes,
The cars, the hotels, the service, the boisterous bed,
Then power to silence outrage with a testament,
The widow's tears forgotten,
The fatherless unheard.

Whispering to chauffeurs and little girls, to tourists and dons,
That Knowledge is conceived in the hot womb of Violence
Who in a late hour of apprehension and exhaustion
Strains to her weeping breast
That blue-eyed darling head.

And is that child happy with his box of lucky books
And all the jokes of learning? Birds cannot grieve:
Wisdom is a beautiful bird; but to the wise
Often, often is it denied
To be beautiful or good.

Without are the shops, the works, the whole green county
Where a cigarette comforts the guilty and a kiss the weak;
There thousands fidget and poke and spend their money:
Eros Paidagogos
Weeps on his virginal bed.

Ah, if that thoughtless almost natural world
Would snatch his sorrow to her loving sensual heart!
But he is Eros and must hate what most he loves;
And she is of Nature; Nature
Can only love herself.

And over the talkative city like any other
Weep the non-attached angels. Here too the knowledge of death
Is a consuming love: And the natural heart refuses
The low unflattering voice
That rests not till it find a hearing.

December 1937

40

In Time of War

I

So from the years the gifts were showered; each
Ran off with his at once into his life:
Bee took the politics that make a hive,
Fish swam as fish, peach settled into peach.

And were successful at the first endeavour;
The hour of birth their only time at college,
They were content with their precocious knowledge,
And knew their station and were good for ever.

Till finally there came a childish creature
On whom the years could model any feature,
And fake with ease a leopard or a dove;

Who by the lightest wind was changed and shaken,
And looked for truth and was continually mistaken,
And envied his few friends and chose his love.

II

They wondered why the fruit had been forbidden;
It taught them nothing new. They hid their pride,
But did not listen much when they were chidden;
They knew exactly what to do outside.

They left: immediately the memory faded
Of all they'd learnt; they could not understand
The dogs now who, before, had always aided;
The stream was dumb with whom they'd always planned.

They wept and quarrelled: freedom was so wild.
In front, maturity, as he ascended,
Retired like a horizon from the child;

The dangers and the punishments grew greater;
And the way back by angels was defended
Against the poet and the legislator.

III

Only a smell had feelings to make known,
Only an eye could point in a direction;
The fountain's utterance was itself alone;
The bird meant nothing: that was his projection

Who named it as he hunted it for food.
He felt the interest in his throat, and found
That he could send his servant to the wood,
Or kiss his bride to rapture with a sound.

They bred like locusts till they hid the green
And edges of the world: and he was abject,
And to his own creation became subject;

And shook with hate for things he'd never seen,
And knew of love without love's proper object,
And was oppressed as he had never been.

IV

He stayed: and was imprisoned in possession.
The seasons stood like guards about his ways,
The mountains chose the mother of his children,
And like a conscience the sun ruled his days.

Beyond him his young cousins in the city
Pursued their rapid and unnatural course,
Believed in nothing but were easy-going,
And treated strangers like a favourite horse.

And he changed little,
But took his colour from the earth,
And grew in likeness to his sheep and cattle.

The townsman thought him miserly and simple,
The poet wept and saw in him the truth,
And the oppressor held him up as an example.

V

His generous bearing was a new invention:
For life was slow; earth needed to be careless:
With horse and sword he drew the girls' attention;
He was the Rich, the Bountiful, the Fearless.

And to the young he came as a salvation;
They needed him to free them from their mothers,
And grew sharp-witted in the long migration,
And round his camp fires learnt all men are brothers.

But suddenly the earth was full: he was not wanted.
And he became the shabby and demented,
And took to drink to screw his nerves to murder;

Or sat in offices and stole,
And spoke approvingly of Law and Order,
And hated life with all his soul.

VI

He watched the stars and noted birds in flight;
The rivers flooded or the Empire fell:
He made predictions and was sometimes right;
His lucky guesses were rewarded well.

And fell in love with Truth before he knew her,
And rode into imaginary lands,
With solitude and fasting hoped to woo her,
And mocked at those who served her with their hands.

But her he never wanted to despise,
But listened always for her voice; and when
She beckoned to him, he obeyed in meekness,

And followed her and looked into her eyes;
Saw there reflected every human weakness,
And saw himself as one of many men.

VII

He was their servant—some say he was blind—
And moved among their faces and their things;
Their feeling gathered in him like a wind
And sang: they cried—"It is a God that sings"—

And worshipped him and set him up apart,
And made him vain, till he mistook for song
The little tremors of his mind and heart
At each domestic wrong.

Songs came no more: he had to make them.
With what precision was each strophe planned.
He hugged his sorrow like a plot of land,

And walked like an assassin through the town,
And looked at men and did not like them,
But trembled if one passed him with a frown.

VIII

He turned his field into a meeting-place,
And grew the tolerant ironic eye,
And formed the mobile money-changer's face,
And found the notion of equality.

And strangers were as brothers to his clocks,
And with his spires he made a human sky;
Museums stored his learning like a box,
And paper watched his money like a spy.

It grew so fast his life was overgrown,
And he forgot what once it had been made for,
And gathered into crowds and was alone,

And lived expensively and did without,
And could not find the earth which he had paid for,
Nor feel the love that he knew all about.

IX

They died and entered the closed life like nuns:
Even the very poor lost something; oppression
Was no more a fact; and the self-centred ones
Took up an even more extreme position.

And the kingly and the saintly also were
Distributed among the woods and oceans,
And touch our open sorrow everywhere,
Airs, waters, places, round our sex and reasons;

Are what we feed on as we make our choice.
We bring them back with promises to free them,
But as ourselves continually betray them:

They hear their deaths lamented in our voice,
But in our knowledge know we could restore them;
They could return to freedom; they would rejoice.

X

As a young child the wisest could adore him;
He felt familiar to them like their wives:
The very poor saved up their pennies for him,
And martyrs brought him presents of their lives.

But who could sit and play with him all day?
Their other needs were pressing, work, and bed:
The beautiful stone courts were built where they
Could leave him to be worshipped and well fed.

But he escaped. They were too blind to tell
That it was he who came with them to labour,
And talked and grew up with them like a neighbour:

To fear and greed those courts became a centre;
The poor saw there the tyrant's citadel,
And martyrs the lost face of the tormentor.

XI

He looked in all His wisdom from the throne
Down on the humble boy who kept the sheep,
And sent a dove; the dove returned alone:
Youth liked the music, but soon fell asleep.

But He had planned such future for the youth:
Surely His duty now was to compel;
For later he would come to love the truth,
And own his gratitude. The eagle fell.

It did not work: His conversation bored
The boy who yawned and whistled and made faces,
And wriggled free from fatherly embraces;

But with the eagle he was always willing
To go where it suggested, and adored
And learnt from it the many ways of killing.

XII

And the age ended, and the last deliverer died
In bed, grown idle and unhappy; they were safe:
The sudden shadow of the giant's enormous calf
Would fall no more at dusk across the lawn outside.

They slept in peace: in marshes here and there no doubt
A sterile dragon lingered to a natural death,
But in a year the spoor had vanished from the heath;
The kobold's knocking in the mountain petered out.

Only the sculptors and the poets were half sad,
And the pert retinue from the magician's house
Grumbled and went elsewhere. The vanquished powers were glad

To be invisible and free: without remorse
Struck down the sons who strayed into their course,
And ravished the daughters, and drove the fathers mad.

XIII

Certainly praise: let the song mount again and again
For life as it blossoms out in a jar or a face,
For the vegetable patience, the animal grace;
Some people have been happy; there have been great men.

But hear the morning's injured weeping, and know why:
Cities and men have fallen; the will of the Unjust
Has never lost its power; still, all princes must
Employ the Fairly-Noble unifying Lie.

History opposes its grief to our buoyant song:
The Good Place has not been; our star has warmed to birth
A race of promise that has never proved its worth;

The quick new West is false; and prodigious, but wrong
This passive flower-like people who for so long
In the Eighteen Provinces have constructed the earth.

XIV

Yes, we are going to suffer, now; the sky
Throbs like a feverish forehead; pain is real;
The groping searchlights suddenly reveal
The little natures that will make us cry,

Who never quite believed they could exist,
Not where we were. They take us by surprise
Like ugly long-forgotten memories,
And like a conscience all the guns resist.

Behind each sociable home-loving eye
The private massacres are taking place;
All Women, Jews, the Rich, the Human Race.

The mountains cannot judge us when we lie:
We dwell upon the earth; the earth obeys
The intelligent and evil till they die.

XV

Engines bear them through the sky: they're free
And isolated like the very rich;
Remote like savants, they can only see
The breathing city as a target which

Requires their skill; will never see how flying
Is the creation of ideas they hate,
Nor how their own machines are always trying
To push through into life. They chose a fate

The islands where they live did not compel.
Though earth may teach our proper discipline,
At any time it will be possible

To turn away from freedom and become
Bound like the heiress in her mother's womb,
And helpless as the poor have always been.

XVI

Here war is simple like a monument:
A telephone is speaking to a man;
Flags on a map assert that troops were sent;
A boy brings milk in bowls. There is a plan

For living men in terror of their lives,
Who thirst at nine who were to thirst at noon,
And can be lost and are, and miss their wives,
And, unlike an idea, can die too soon.

But ideas can be true although men die,
And we can watch a thousand faces
Made active by one lie:

And maps can really point to places
Where life is evil now:
Nanking; Dachau.

XVII

They are and suffer; that is all they do:
A bandage hides the place where each is living,
His knowledge of the world restricted to
The treatment that the instruments are giving.

And lie apart like epochs from each other
—Truth in their sense is how much they can bear;
It is not talk like ours, but groans they smother—
And are remote as plants; we stand elsewhere.

For who when healthy can become a foot?
Even a scratch we can't recall when cured,
But are boisterous in a moment and believe

In the common world of the uninjured, and cannot
Imagine isolation. Only happiness is shared,
And anger, and the idea of love.

XVIII

Far from the heart of culture he was used:
Abandoned by his general and his lice,
Under a padded quilt he closed his eyes
And vanished. He will not be introduced

When this campaign is tidied into books:
No vital knowledge perished in his skull;
His jokes were stale; like wartime, he was dull;
His name is lost for ever like his looks.

He neither knew nor chose the Good, but taught us,
And added meaning like a comma, when
He turned to dust in China that our daughters

Be fit to love the earth, and not again
Disgraced before the dogs; that, where are waters,
Mountains and houses, may be also men.

XIX

But in the evening the oppression lifted;
The peaks came into focus; it had rained:
Across the lawns and cultured flowers drifted
The conversation of the highly trained.

The gardeners watched them pass and priced their shoes;
A chauffeur waited, reading in the drive,
For them to finish their exchange of views;
It seemed a picture of the private life.

Far off, no matter what good they intended,
The armies waited for a verbal error
With all the instruments for causing pain:

And on the issue of their charm depended
A land laid waste, with all its young men slain,
The women weeping, and the towns in terror.

XX

They carry terror with them like a purse,
And flinch from the horizon like a gun;
And all the rivers and the railways run
Away from Neighbourhood as from a curse.

They cling and huddle in the new disaster
Like children sent to school, and cry in turn;
For Space has rules they cannot hope to learn,
Time speaks a language they will never master.

We live here. We lie in the Present's unopened
Sorrow; its limits are what we are.
The prisoner ought never to pardon his cell.

Can future ages ever escape so far,
Yet feel derived from everything that happened,
Even from us, that even this was well?

XXI

The life of man is never quite completed;
The daring and the chatter will go on:
But, as an artist feels his power gone,
These walk the earth and know themselves defeated.

Some could not bear nor break the young and mourn for
The wounded myths that once made nations good,
Some lost a world they never understood,
Some saw too clearly all that man was born for.

Loss is their shadow-wife, Anxiety
Receives them like a grand hotel; but where
They may regret they must; their life, to hear

The call of the forbidden cities, see
The stranger watch them with a happy stare,
And Freedom hostile in each home and tree.

XXII

Simple like all dream wishes, they employ
The elementary language of the heart,
And speak to muscles of the need for joy:
The dying and the lovers soon to part

Hear them and have to whistle. Always new,
They mirror every change in our position;
They are our evidence of what we do;
They speak directly to our lost condition.

Think in this year what pleased the dancers best:
When Austria died and China was forsaken,
Shanghai in flames and Teruel re-taken,

France put her case before the world: "Partout
Il y a de la joie." America addressed
The earth: "Do you love me as I love you?"

XXIII

When all the apparatus of report
Confirms the triumph of our enemies;
Our bastion pierced, our army in retreat,
Violence successful like a new disease,

And Wrong a charmer everywhere invited;
When we regret that we were ever born:
Let us remember all who seemed deserted.
To-night in China let me think of one,

Who through ten years of silence worked and waited,
Until in Muzot all his powers spoke,
And everything was given once for all:

And with the gratitude of the Completed
He went out in the winter night to stroke
That little tower like a great animal.

XXIV

No, not their names. It was the others who built
Each great coercive avenue and square,
Where men can only recollect and stare,
The really lonely with the sense of guilt

Who wanted to persist like that for ever;
The unloved had to leave material traces:
But these need nothing but our better faces,
And dwell in them, and know that we shall never

Remember who we are nor why we're needed.
Earth grew them as a bay grows fishermen
Or hills a shepherd; they grew ripe and seeded;

And the seeds clung to us; even our blood
Was able to revive them; and they grew again;
Happy their wish and mild to flower and flood.

XXV

Nothing is given: we must find our law.
Great buildings jostle in the sun for domination;
Behind them stretch like sorry vegetation
The low recessive houses of the poor.

We have no destiny assigned us:
Nothing is certain but the body; we plan
To better ourselves; the hospitals alone remind us
Of the equality of man.

Children are really loved here, even by police:
They speak of years before the big were lonely,
And will be lost.

And only
The brass bands throbbing in the parks foretell
Some future reign of happiness and peace.

We learn to pity and rebel.

XXVI

Always far from the centre of our names,
The little workshop of love: yes, but how wrong
We were about the old manors and the long
Abandoned Folly and the children's games.

Only the acquisitive expects a quaint
Unsaleable product, something to please
An artistic girl; it's the selfish who sees
In every impractical beggar a saint.

We can't believe that we ourselves designed it,
A minor item of our daring plan
That caused no trouble; we took no notice of it.

Disaster comes, and we're amazed to find it
The single project that since work began
Through all the cycle showed a steady profit.

XXVII

Wandering lost upon the mountains of our choice,
Again and again we sigh for an ancient South,
For the warm nude ages of instinctive poise,
For the taste of joy in the innocent mouth.

Asleep in our huts, how we dream of a part
In the glorious balls of the future; each intricate maze
Has a plan, and the disciplined movements of the heart
Can follow for ever and ever its harmless ways.

We envy streams and houses that are sure:
But we are articled to error; we
Were never nude and calm like a great door,

And never will be perfect like the fountains;
We live in freedom by necessity,
A mountain people dwelling among mountains.

1938 (except XII, 1936)

41

The Capital

Quarter of pleasures where the rich are always waiting,
Waiting expensively for miracles to happen,
O little restaurant where the lovers eat each other,
Café where exiles have established a malicious village;

You with your charm and your apparatus have abolished
The strictness of winter and the spring's compulsion;
Far from your lights the outraged punitive father,
The dullness of mere obedience here is apparent.

Yet with orchestras and glances, O, you betray us
To belief in our infinite powers; and the innocent
Unobservant offender falls in a moment
Victim to the heart's invisible furies.

In unlighted streets you hide away the appalling;
Factories where lives are made for a temporary use
Like collars or chairs, rooms where the lonely are battered
Slowly like pebbles into fortuitous shapes.

But the sky you illumine, your glow is visible far
Into the dark countryside, the enormous, the frozen,
Where, hinting at the forbidden like a wicked uncle,
Night after night to the farmer's children you beckon.

December 1938

42

Musée des Beaux Arts

About suffering they were never wrong,
The Old Masters: how well they understood
Its human position; how it takes place
While someone else is eating or opening a window or just
walking dully along;
How, when the aged are reverently, passionately waiting
For the miraculous birth, there always must be
Children who did not specially want it to happen, skating
On a pond at the edge of the wood:
They never forgot
That even the dreadful martyrdom must run its course
Anyhow in a corner, some untidy spot
Where the dogs go on with their doggy
life and the torturer's horse
Scratches its innocent behind on a tree.

In Brueghel's *Icarus*, for instance: how everything turns away
Quite leisurely from the disaster; the ploughman may
Have heard the splash, the forsaken cry,
But for him it was not an important failure; the sun shone
As it had to on the white legs disappearing into the green
Water; and the expensive delicate ship that must have seen
Something amazing, a boy falling out of the sky,
Had somewhere to get to and sailed calmly on.

December 1938

43

Epitaph on a Tyrant

Perfection, of a kind, was what he was after,
And the poetry he invented was easy to understand;
He knew human folly like the back of his hand,
And was greatly interested in armies and fleets;
When he laughed, respectable senators burst with laughter,
And when he cried the little children died in the streets.

January 1939

44

In Memory of W. B. Yeats

(d. January 1939)

I

He disappeared in the dead of winter:
The brooks were frozen, the air-ports almost deserted,
And snow disfigured the public statues;
The mercury sank in the mouth of the dying day.
O all the instruments agree
The day of his death was a dark cold day.

Far from his illness
The wolves ran on through the evergreen forests,
The peasant river was untempted by the fashionable quays;
By mourning tongues
The death of the poet was kept from his poems.

But for him it was his last afternoon as himself,
An afternoon of nurses and rumours;
The provinces of his body revolted,
The squares of his mind were empty,
Silence invaded the suburbs,
The current of his feeling failed: he became his admirers.

Now he is scattered among a hundred cities
And wholly given over to unfamiliar affections;
To find his happiness in another kind of wood
And be punished under a foreign code of conscience.
The words of a dead man
Are modified in the guts of the living.

But in the importance and noise of to-morrow
When the brokers are roaring like beasts on the
floor of the Bourse,
And the poor have the sufferings to which
they are fairly accustomed,
And each in the cell of himself is almost
convinced of his freedom;
A few thousand will think of this day
As one thinks of a day when one did something
slightly unusual.

O all the instruments agree
The day of his death was a dark cold day.

II

You were silly like us: your gift survived it all;
The parish of rich women, physical decay,
Yourself; mad Ireland hurt you into poetry.

Now Ireland has her madness and her weather still,
For poetry makes nothing happen: it survives
In the valley of its saying where executives
Would never want to tamper; it flows south
From ranches of isolation and the busy griefs,
Raw towns that we believe and die in; it survives,
A way of happening, a mouth.

III

Earth, receive an honoured guest;
William Yeats is laid to rest:
Let the Irish vessel lie
Emptied of its poetry.

Time that is intolerant
Of the brave and innocent,
And indifferent in a week
To a beautiful physique,

Worships language and forgives
Everyone by whom it lives;
Pardons cowardice, conceit,
Lays its honours at their feet.

Time that with this strange excuse
Pardoned Kipling and his views,
And will pardon Paul Claudel,
Pardons him for writing well.

In the nightmare of the dark
All the dogs of Europe bark,
And the living nations wait,
Each sequestered in its hate;

Intellectual disgrace
Stares from every human face,
And the seas of pity lie
Locked and frozen in each eye.

Follow, poet, follow right
To the bottom of the night,
With your unconstraining voice
Still persuade us to rejoice;

With the farming of a verse
Make a vineyard of the curse,
Sing of human unsuccess
In a rapture of distress;

In the deserts of the heart
Let the healing fountain start,
In the prison of his days
Teach the free man how to praise.

February 1939

45

Refugee Blues

Say this city has ten million souls,
Some are living in mansions, some are living in holes:
Yet there's no place for us, my dear, yet there's no place for us.

Once we had a country and we thought it fair,
Look in the atlas and you'll find it there:
We cannot go there now, my dear, we cannot go there now.

In the village churchyard there grows an old yew,
Every spring it blossoms anew:
Old passports can't do that, my dear, old passports can't do that.

The consul banged the table and said,
"If you've got no passport you're officially dead":
But we are still alive, my dear, but we are still alive.

Went to a committee; they offered me a chair;
Asked me politely to return next year:
But where shall we go to-day, my dear, but where shall we go to-day?

Came to a public meeting; the speaker got up and said;
"If we let them in, they will steal our daily bread":
He was talking of you and me, my dear, he was talking of you and me.

Thought I heard the thunder rumbling in the sky;
It was Hitler over Europe, saying, "They must die":
O we were in his mind, my dear, O we were in his mind.

Saw a poodle in a jacket fastened with a pin,
Saw a door opened and a cat let in:
But they weren't German Jews, my dear, but they weren't German Jews.

Went down the harbour and stood upon the quay,
Saw the fish swimming as if they were free:
Only ten feet away, my dear, only ten feet away.

Walked through a wood, saw the birds in the trees;
They had no politicians and sang at their ease:
They weren't the human race, my dear, they weren't the human race.

Dreamed I saw a building with a thousand floors,
A thousand windows and a thousand doors:
Not one of them was ours, my dear, not one of them was ours.

Stood on a great plain in the falling snow;
Ten thousand soldiers marched to and fro:
Looking for you and me, my dear, looking for you and me.

March 1939

46

The Unknown Citizen

To JS/07/M/378
This Marble Monument is Erected by the State

He was found by the Bureau of Statistics to be
One against whom there was no official complaint,
And all the reports on his conduct agree
That, in the modern sense of an old-fashioned word,
he was a saint,
For in everything he did he served the Greater Community.
Except for the War till the day he retired
He worked in a factory and never got fired,
But satisfied his employers, Fudge Motors Inc.
Yet he wasn't a scab or odd in his views,
For his Union reports that he paid his dues,
(Our report on his Union shows it was sound)
And our Social Psychology workers found
That he was popular with his mates and liked a drink.
The Press are convinced that he bought a paper every day
And that his reactions to advertisements were normal in
every way.
Policies taken out in his name prove that he was fully insured,
And his Health-card shows he was once in hospital but
left it cured.
Both Producers Research and High-Grade Living declare
He was fully sensible to the advantages of the Installment Plan
And had everything necessary to the Modern Man,
A gramophone, a radio, a car and a frigidaire.
Our researchers into Public Opinion are content
That he held the proper opinions for the time of year;
When there was peace, he was for peace; when there
was war, he went.
He was married and added five children to the population,
Which our Eugenist says was the right number for a parent of
his generation,

And our teachers report that he never interfered with
their education.

Was he free? Was he happy? The question is absurd:
Had anything been wrong, we should certainly have heard.

March 1939

47

September 1, 1939

I sit in one of the dives
On Fifty-Second Street
Uncertain and afraid
As the clever hopes expire
Of a low dishonest decade:
Waves of anger and fear
Circulate over the bright
And darkened lands of the earth,
Obsessing our private lives;
The unmentionable odour of death
Offends the September night.

Accurate scholarship can
Unearth the whole offence
From Luther until now
That has driven a culture mad,
Find what occurred at Linz,
What huge imago made
A psychopathic god:
I and the public know
What all schoolchildren learn,
Those to whom evil is done
Do evil in return.

Exiled Thucydides knew
All that a speech can say
About Democracy,
And what dictators do,
The elderly rubbish they talk
To an apathetic grave;
Analysed all in his book,
The enlightenment driven away,
The habit-forming pain,
Mismanagement and grief:
We must suffer them all again.

Into this neutral air
Where blind skyscrapers use
Their full height to proclaim
The strength of Collective Man,
Each language pours its vain
Competitive excuse:
But who can live for long
In an euphoric dream;
Out of the mirror they stare,
Imperialism's face
And the international wrong.

Faces along the bar
Cling to their average day:
The lights must never go out,
The music must always play,
All the conventions conspire
To make this fort assume
The furniture of home;
Lest we should see where we are,
Lost in a haunted wood,
Children afraid of the night
Who have never been happy or good.

The windiest militant trash
Important Persons shout
Is not so crude as our wish:
What mad Nijinsky wrote
About Diaghilev
Is true of the normal heart;
For the error bred in the bone
Of each woman and each man
Craves what it cannot have,
Not universal love
But to be loved alone.

From the conservative dark
Into the ethical life
The dense commuters come,
Repeating their morning vow,
"I *will* be true to the wife,
I'll concentrate more on my work,"
And helpless governors wake
To resume their compulsory game:
Who can release them now,
Who can reach the deaf,
Who can speak for the dumb?

All I have is a voice
To undo the folded lie,
The romantic lie in the brain
Of the sensual man-in-the-street
And the lie of Authority
Whose buildings grope the sky:
There is no such thing as the State
And no one exists alone;
Hunger allows no choice
To the citizen or the police;
We must love one another or die.

Defenceless under the night
Our world in stupor lies;
Yet, dotted everywhere,
Ironic points of light
Flash out wherever the Just
Exchange their messages:
May I, composed like them
Of Eros and of dust,
Beleaguered by the same
Negation and despair,
Show an affirming flame.

September 1939

48

Law, say the gardeners, is the sun,
Law is the one
All gardeners obey
To-morrow, yesterday, to-day.

Law is the wisdom of the old
The impotent grandfathers shrilly scold;
The grandchildren put out a treble tongue,
Law is the senses of the young.

Law, says the priest with a priestly look,
Expounding to an unpriestly people,
Law is the words in my priestly book,
Law is my pulpit and my steeple.

Law, says the judge as he looks down his nose,
Speaking clearly and most severely,
Law is as I've told you before,

Law is as you know I suppose,
Law is but let me explain it once more,
Law is The Law.

Yet law-abiding scholars write:
Law is neither wrong nor right,
Law is only crimes
Punished by places and by times,
Law is the clothes men wear
Anytime, anywhere,
Law is Good-morning and Good-night.

Others say, Law is our Fate;
Others say, Law is our State;
Others say, others say
Law is no more
Law has gone away.

And always the loud angry crowd
Very angry and very loud
Law is We,
And always the soft idiot softly Me.

If we, dear, know we know no more
Than they about the law,
If I no more than you
Know what we should and should not do
Except that all agree
Gladly or miserably
That the law is
And that all know this,
If therefore thinking it absurd
To identify Law with some other word,
Unlike so many men
I cannot say Law is again,
No more than they can we suppress
The universal wish to guess
Or slip out of our own position
Into an unconcerned condition.

Although I can at least confine
Your vanity and mine
To stating timidly
A timid similarity,
We shall boast anyway:
Like love I say.

Like love we don't know where or why
Like love we can't compel or fly
Like love we often weep
Like love we seldom keep.

September 1939

49

In Memory of Sigmund Freud

(d. September 1939)

When there are so many we shall have to mourn,
When grief has been made so public, and exposed
To the critique of a whole epoch
The frailty of our conscience and anguish,

Of whom shall we speak? For every day they die
Among us, those who were doing us some good,
And knew it was never enough but
Hoped to improve a little by living.

Such was this doctor: still at eighty he wished
To think of our life, from whose unruliness
So many plausible young futures
With threats or flattery ask obedience.

But his wish was denied him; he closed his eyes
Upon that last picture common to us all,
Of problems like relatives standing
Puzzled and jealous about our dying.

For about him at the very end were still
Those he had studied, the nervous and the nights,
And shades that still waited to enter
The bright circle of his recognition

Turned elsewhere with their disappointment as he
Was taken away from his old interest
To go back to the earth in London,
An important Jew who died in exile.

Only Hate was happy, hoping to augment
His practice now, and his shabby clientele
Who think they can be cured by killing
And covering the gardens with ashes.

They are still alive but in a world he changed
Simply by looking back with no false regrets;
All that he did was to remember
Like the old and be honest like children.

He wasn't clever at all: he merely told
The unhappy Present to recite the Past
Like a poetry lesson till sooner
Or later it faltered at the line where

Long ago the accusations had begun,
And suddenly knew by whom it had been judged,
How rich life had been and how silly,
And was life-forgiven and more humble,

Able to approach the Future as a friend
Without a wardrobe of excuses, without
A set mask of rectitude or an
Embarrassing over-familiar gesture.

No wonder the ancient cultures of conceit
In his technique of unsettlement foresaw
The fall of princes, the collapse of
Their lucrative patterns of frustration.

If he succeeded, why, the Generalised Life
Would become impossible, the monolith
Of State be broken and prevented
The co-operation of avengers.

Of course they called on God: but he went his way,
Down among the Lost People like Dante, down
To the stinking fosse where the injured
Lead the ugly life of the rejected.

And showed us what evil is: not as we thought
Deeds that must be punished, but our lack of faith,
Our dishonest mood of denial,
The concupiscence of the oppressor.

And if something of the autocratic pose,
The paternal strictness he distrusted, still
Clung to his utterance and features,
It was a protective imitation

For one who lived among enemies so long:
If often he was wrong and at times absurd,
To us he is no more a person
Now but a whole climate of opinion

Under whom we conduct our differing lives:
Like weather he can only hinder or help,
The proud can still be proud but find it
A little harder, and the tyrant tries

To make him do but doesn't care for him much.
He quietly surrounds all our habits of growth;
He extends, till the tired in even
The remotest most miserable duchy

Have felt the change in their bones and are cheered,
And the child unlucky in his little State,
    Some hearth where freedom is excluded,
    A hive whose honey is fear and worry,

Feels calmer now and somehow assured of escape;
While as they lie in the grass of our neglect,
    So many long-forgotten objects
    Revealed by his undiscouraged shining

Are returned to us and made precious again;
Games we had thought we must drop as we grew up,
    Little noises we dared not laugh at,
    Faces we made when no one was looking.

But he wishes us more than this: to be free
Is often to be lonely; he would unite
    The unequal moieties fractured
    By our own well-meaning sense of justice,

Would restore to the larger the wit and will
The smaller possesses but can only use
    For arid disputes, would give back to
    The son the mother's richness of feeling.

But he would have us remember most of all
To be enthusiastic over the night
    Not only for the sense of wonder
    It alone has to offer, but also

Because it needs our love: for with sad eyes
Its delectable creatures look up and beg
    Us dumbly to ask them to follow;
    They are exiles who long for the future

That lies in our power. They too would rejoice
If allowed to serve enlightenment like him,
    Even to bear our cry of "Judas,"
    As he did and all must bear who serve it.

One rational voice is dumb: over a grave
The household of Impulse mourns one dearly loved.
Sad is Eros, builder of cities,
And weeping anarchic Aphrodite.

November 1939

50

Lady, weeping at the crossroads
Would you meet your love
In the twilight with his greyhounds,
And the hawk on his glove?

Bribe the birds then on the branches,
Bribe them to be dumb,
Stare the hot sun out of heaven
That the night may come.

Starless are the nights of travel,
Bleak the winter wind;
Run with terror all before you
And regret behind.

Run until you hear the ocean's
Everlasting cry;
Deep though it may be and bitter
You must drink it dry.

Wear out patience in the lowest
Dungeons of the sea,
Searching through the stranded shipwrecks
For the golden key.

Push on to the world's end, pay the
Dread guard with a kiss;
Cross the rotten bridge that totters
Over the abyss.

There stands the deserted castle
Ready to explore;
Enter, climb the marble staircase
Open the locked door.

Cross the silent empty ballroom,
Doubt and danger past;
Blow the cobwebs from the mirror
See yourself at last.

Put your hand behind the wainscot,
You have done your part;
Find the penknife there and plunge it
Into your false heart.

1940

51

Song for St. Cecilia's Day

I

In a garden shady this holy lady
With reverent cadence and subtle psalm,
Like a black swan as death came on
Poured forth her song in perfect calm:
And by ocean's margin this innocent virgin
Constructed an organ to enlarge her prayer,
And notes tremendous from her great engine
Thundered out on the Roman air.

Blonde Aphrodite rose up excited,
Moved to delight by the melody,
White as an orchid she rode quite naked
In an oyster shell on top of the sea;
At sounds so entrancing the angels dancing
Came out of their trance into time again,
And around the wicked in Hell's abysses
The huge flame flickered and eased their pain.

Blessed Cecilia, appear in visions
To all musicians, appear and inspire:
Translated Daughter, come down and startle
Composing mortals with immortal fire.

II

I cannot grow;
I have no shadow
To run away from,
I only play

I cannot err;
There is no creature
Whom I belong to,
Whom I could wrong.

I am defeat
When it knows it
Can now do nothing
By suffering.

All you lived through,
Dancing because you
No longer need it
For any deed.

I shall never be
Different. Love me.

III

O ear whose creatures cannot wish to fall,
O calm of spaces unafraid of weight,
Where Sorrow is herself, forgetting all
The gaucheness of her adolescent state,
Where Hope within the altogether strange
From every outworn image is released,
And Dread born whole and normal like a beast
Into a world of truths that never change:
Restore our fallen day; O re-arrange.

O dear white children casual as birds,
Playing among the ruined languages,
So small beside their large confusing words,
So gay against the greater silences
Of dreadful things you did: O hang the head,
Impetuous child with the tremendous brain,
O weep, child, weep, O weep away the stain,
Lost innocence who wished your lover dead,
Weep for the lives your wishes never led.

O cry created as the bow of sin
Is drawn across our trembling violin.
O weep, child, weep, O weep away the stain.
O law drummed out by hearts against the still
Long winter of our intellectual will.
That what has been may never be again.
O flute that throbs with the thanksgiving breath
Of convalescents on the shores of death.
O bless the freedom that you never chose.
O trumpets that unguarded children blow
About the fortress of their inner foe.
O wear your tribulation like a rose.

July 1940

52

The Quest

The Door

Out of it steps the future of the poor,
Enigmas, executioners and rules,
Her Majesty in a bad temper or
The red-nosed Fool who makes a fool of fools.

Great persons eye it in the twilight for
A past it might so carelessly let in,
A widow with a missionary grin,
The foaming inundation at a roar.

We pile our all against it when afraid,
And beat upon its panels when we die:
By happening to be open once, it made

Enormous Alice see a wonderland
That waited for her in the sunshine, and,
Simply by being tiny, made her cry.

The Preparations

All had been ordered weeks before the start
From the best firms at such work; instruments
To take the measure of all queer events,
And drugs to move the bowels or the heart.

A watch, of course, to watch impatience fly,
Lamps for the dark and shades against the sun;
Foreboding, too, insisted on a gun
And coloured beads to soothe a savage eye.

In theory they were sound on Expectation
Had there been situations to be in;
Unluckily they were their situation:

One should not give a poisoner medicine,
A conjurer fine apparatus, nor
A rifle to a melancholic bore.

The Crossroads

The friends who met here and embraced are gone,
Each to his own mistake; one flashes on
To fame and ruin in a rowdy lie,
A village torpor holds the other one,
Some local wrong where it takes time to die:
The empty junction glitters in the sun.

So at all quays and crossroads: who can tell,
O places of decision and farewell,
To what dishonour all adventure leads,
What parting gift could give that friend protection,
So orientated, his salvation needs
The Bad Lands and the sinister direction?

All landscapes and all weathers freeze with fear,
But none have ever thought, the legends say,
The time allowed made it impossible;
For even the most pessimistic set
The limit of their errors at a year.
What friends could there be left then to betray,
What joy take longer to atone for? Yet
Who would complete without the extra day
The journey that should take no time at all?

The Traveller

No window in his suburb lights that bedroom where
A little fever heard large afternoons at play:
His meadows multiply; that mill, though, is not there
Which went on grinding at the back of love all day.

Nor all his weeping ways through weary wastes have found
The castle where his Greater Hallows are interned;
For broken bridges halt him, and dark thickets round
Some ruin where an evil heritage was burned.

Could he forget a child's ambition to be old
And institutions where it learned to wash and lie,
He'd tell the truth for which he thinks himself too young,

That everywhere on the horizon of his sigh
Is now, as always, only waiting to be told
To be his father's house and speak his mother tongue.

The City

In villages from which their childhoods came
Seeking Necessity, they had been taught
Necessity by nature is the same,
No matter how or by whom it be sought.

The city, though, assumed no such belief,
But welcomed each as if he came alone,
The nature of Necessity like grief
Exactly corresponding to his own.

And offered them so many, every one
Found some temptation fit to govern him;
And settled down to master the whole craft

Of being nobody; sat in the sun
During the lunch-hour round the fountain rim;
And watched the country kids arrive and laughed.

The First Temptation

Ashamed to be the darling of his grief
He joined a gang of rowdy stories where
His gift for magic quickly made him chief
Of all these boyish powers of the air;

Who turned his hungers into Roman food.
The town's asymmetry into a park;
All hours took taxis; any solitude
Became his flattered duchess in the dark.

But if he wished for anything less grand,
The nights came padding after him like wild
Beasts that meant harm, and all the doors cried Thief;

And when Truth met him and put out her hand.
He clung in panic to his tall belief
And shrank away like an ill-treated child.

The Second Temptation

The library annoyed him with its look
Of calm belief in being really there;
He threw away a rival's silly book,
And clattered panting up the spiral stair.

Swaying upon the parapet he cried:
"O Uncreated Nothing, set me free,
Now let Thy perfect be identified,
Unending passion of the Night, with Thee."

And his long suffering flesh, that all the time
Had felt the simple cravings of the stone
And hoped to be rewarded for her climb,

Took it to be a promise when he spoke
That now at last she would be left alone,
And plunged into the college quad, and broke.

The Third Temptation

He watched with all his organs of concern
How princes walk, what wives and children say;
Re-opened old graves in his heart to learn
What laws the dead had died to disobey.

And came reluctantly to his conclusion:
"All the arm-chair philosophers are false;
To love another adds to the confusion;
The song of pity is the Devil's Waltz."

And bowed to fate and was successful so
That soon he was the king of all the creatures:
Yet, shaking in an autumn nightmare, saw,

Approaching down a ruined corridor,
A figure with his own distorted features
That wept, and grew enormous, and cried Woe.

The Tower

This is an architecture for the odd;
Thus heaven was attacked by the afraid,
So once, unconsciously, a virgin made
Her maidenhead conspicuous to a god.

Here on dark nights while worlds of triumph sleep
Lost Love in abstract speculation burns,
And exiled Will to politics returns
In epic verse that lets its traitors weep.

Yet many come to wish their tower a well;
For those who dread to drown of thirst may die,
Those who see all become invisible:

Here great magicians caught in their own spell
Long for a natural climate as they sigh
"Beware of Magic" to the passer-by.

The Presumptuous

They noticed that virginity was needed
To trap the unicorn in every case,
But not that, of those virgins who succeeded,
A high percentage had an ugly face.

The hero was as daring as they thought him,
But his peculiar boyhood missed them all;
The angel of a broken leg had taught him
The right precautions to avoid a fall.

So in presumption they set forth alone
On what, for them, was not compulsory:
And stuck halfway to settle in some cave
With desert lions to domesticity;

Or turned aside to be absurdly brave,
And met the ogre and were turned to stone.

The Average

His peasant parents killed themselves with toil
To let their darling leave a stingy soil
For any of those smart professions which
Encourage shallow breathing, and grow rich.

The pressure of their fond ambition made
Their shy and country-loving child afraid
No sensible career was good enough,
Only a hero could deserve such love.

So here he was without maps or supplies,
A hundred miles from any decent town;
The desert glared into his blood-shot eyes;

The silence roared displeasure: looking down,
He saw the shadow of an Average Man
Attempting the Exceptional, and ran.

Vocation

Incredulous, he stared at the amused
Official writing down his name among
Those whose request to suffer was refused.

The pen ceased scratching: though he came too late
To join the martyrs, there was still a place
Among the tempters for a caustic tongue

To test the resolution of the young
With tales of the small failings of the great,
And shame the eager with ironic praise.

Though mirrors might be hateful for a while,
Women and books should teach his middle age
The fencing wit of an informal style
To keep the silences at bay and cage
His pacing manias in a worldly smile.

The Useful

The over-logical fell for the witch
Whose argument converted him to stone;
Thieves rapidly absorbed the over-rich;
The over-popular went mad alone,
And kisses brutalised the over-male.

As agents their effectiveness soon ceased;
Yet, in proportion as they seemed to fail,
Their instrumental value was increased
To those still able to obey their wish.

By standing stones the blind can feel their way,
Wild dogs compel the cowardly to fight,
Beggars assist the slow to travel light,
And even madmen manage to convey
Unwelcome truths in lonely gibberish.

The Way

Fresh addenda are published every day
To the encyclopedia of the Way.

Linguistic notes and scientific explanations,
And texts for schools with modernised spelling and illustrations.

Now everyone knows the hero must choose the old horse,
Abstain from liquor and sexual intercourse

And look out for a stranded fish to be kind to:
Now everyone thinks he could find, had he a mind to,

The way through the waste to the chapel in the rock
For a vision of the Triple Rainbow or the Astral Clock.

Forgetting his information comes mostly from married men
Who liked fishing and a flutter on the horses now and then.

And how reliable can any truth be that is got
By observing oneself and then just inserting a Not?

The Lucky

Suppose he'd listened to the erudite committee,
He would have only found where not to look;
Suppose his terrier when he whistled had obeyed,
It would not have unearthed the buried city;
Suppose he had dismissed the careless maid,
The cryptogram would not have fluttered from the book.

"It was not I", he cried as, healthy and astounded,
He stepped across a predecessor's skull;
"A nonsense jingle simply came into my head
And left the intellectual Sphinx dumbfounded;
I won the Queen because my hair was red;
The terrible adventure is a little dull."

Hence Failure's torment: "Was I doomed in any case,
Or would I not have failed had I believed in Grace?"

The Hero

He parried every question that they hurled:
"What did the Emperor tell you?" "Not to push."
"What is the greatest wonder of the world?"
"The bare man Nothing in the Beggar's Bush."

Some muttered, "He is cagey for effect.
A hero owes a duty to his fame.
He looks too like a grocer for respect."
Soon they slipped back into his Christian name.

The only difference that could be seen
From those who'd never risked their lives at all
Was his delight in details and routine.

For he was always glad to mow the grass,
Pour liquids from large bottles into small,
Or look at clouds through bits of coloured glass.

Adventure

Others had swerved off to the left before,
But only under protest from outside;
Embittered robbers outlawed by the Law,
Lepers in terror of the terrified.

Now no one else accused these of a crime;
They did not look ill: old friends, overcome,
Stared as they rolled away from talk and time
Like marbles out into the blank and dumb.

The crowd clung all the closer to convention,
Sunshine and horses, for the sane know why
The even numbers should ignore the odd:

The Nameless is what no free people mention;
Successful men know better than to try
To see the face of their Absconded God.

The Adventurers

Spinning upon their central thirst like tops,
They went the Negative Way toward the Dry;
By empty caves beneath an empty sky
They emptied out their memories like slops

Which made a foul marsh as they dried to death,
Where monsters bred who forced them to forget
The lovelies their consent avoided; yet,
Still praising the Absurd with their last breath,

They seeded out into their miracles:
The images of each grotesque temptation
Became some painter's happiest inspiration;

And barren wives and burning virgins came
To drink the pure cold water of their wells,
And wish for beaux and children in their name.

The Waters

Poet, oracle and wit
Like unsuccessful anglers by
The ponds of apperception sit,
Baiting with the wrong request
The vectors of their interest;
At nightfall tell the angler's lie.

With time in tempest everywhere,
To rafts of frail assumption cling
The saintly and the insincere;
Enraged phenomena bear down
In overwhelming waves to drown
Both sufferer and suffering.

The waters long to hear our question put
Which would release their longed-for answer, but.

The Garden

Within these gates all opening begins:
White shouts and flickers through its green and red,
Where children play at seven earnest sins
And dogs believe their tall conditions dead.

Here adolescence into number breaks
The perfect circle time can draw on stone,
And flesh forgives division as it makes
Another's moment of consent its own.

All journeys die here; wish and weight are lifted:
Where often round some old maid's desolation
Roses have flung their glory like a cloak,

The gaunt and great, the famed for conversation
Blushed in the stare of evening as they spoke,
And felt their centre of volition shifted.

Summer 1940

53

But I Can't

Time will say nothing but I told you so,
Time only knows the price we have to pay;
If I could tell you I would let you know.

If we should weep when clowns put on their show,
If we should stumble when musicians play,
Time will say nothing but I told you so.

There are no fortunes to be told, although,
Because I love you more than I can say,
If I could tell you I would let you know.

The winds must come from somewhere when they blow,
There must be reasons why the leaves decay;
Time will say nothing but I told you so.

Perhaps the roses really want to grow,
The vision seriously intends to stay;
If I could tell you I would let you know.

Suppose the lions all get up and go,
And all the brooks and soldiers run away;
Will Time say nothing but I told you so?
If I could tell you I would let you know.

October 1940

54

In Sickness and in Health

(FOR MAURICE AND GWEN MANDELBAUM)

Dear, all benevolence of fingering lips
That does not ask forgiveness is a noise
  At drunken feasts where Sorrow strips
To serve some glittering generalities:
Now, more than ever, we distinctly hear
The dreadful shuffle of a murderous year
And all our senses roaring as the Black
Dog leaps upon the individual back.

Whose sable genius understands too well
What code of famine can administrate
  Those inarticulate wastes where dwell
Our howling appetites: dear heart, do not
Think lightly to contrive his overthrow;
O promise nothing, nothing, till you know

The kingdom offered by the love-lorn eyes
A land of condors, sick cattle, and dead flies.

And how contagious is its desolation,
What figures of destruction unawares
  Jump out on Love's imagination
And chase away the castles and the bears;
How warped the mirrors where our worlds are made;
What armies burn up honour, and degrade
Our will-to-order into thermal waste;
How much lies smashed that cannot be replaced.

O let none say I Love until aware
What huge resources it will take to nurse
  One ruining speck, one tiny hair
That casts a shadow through the universe:
We are the deaf immured within a loud
And foreign language of revolt, a crowd
Of poaching hands and mouths who out of fear
Have learned a safer life than we can bear.

Nature by nature in unnature ends:
Echoing each other like two waterfalls,
  Tristan, Isolde, the great friends,
Make passion out of passion's obstacles;
Deliciously postponing their delight,
Prolong frustration till it lasts all night,
Then perish lest Brangaene's worldly cry
Should sober their cerebral ecstasy.

But, dying, conjure up their opposite,
Don Juan, so terrified of death he hears
  Each moment recommending it,
And knows no argument to counter theirs;
Trapped in their vile affections, he must find
Angels to keep him chaste; a helpless, blind,
Unhappy spook, he haunts the urinals,
Existing solely by their miracles.

That syllogistic nightmare must reject
The disobedient phallus for the sword;
  The lovers of themselves collect,
And Eros is politically adored:
New Machiavellis flying through the air
Express a metaphysical despair,
Murder their last voluptuous sensation,
All passion in one passionate negation.

Beloved, we are always in the wrong,
Handling so clumsily our stupid lives,
  Suffering too little or too long,
Too careful even in our selfish loves:
The decorative manias we obey
Die in grimaces round us every day,
Yet through their tohu-bohu comes a voice
Which utters an absurd command—Rejoice.

Rejoice. What talent for the makeshift thought
A living corpus out of odds and ends?
  What pedagogic patience taught
Pre-occupied and savage elements
To dance into a segregated charm?
Who showed the whirlwind how to be an arm,
And gardened from the wilderness of space
The sensual properties of one dear face?

Rejoice, dear love, in Love's peremptory word;
All chance, all love, all logic, you and I,
  Exist by grace of the Absurd,
And without conscious artifice we die:
O, lest we manufacture in our flesh
The lie of our divinity afresh,
Describe round our chaotic malice now,
The arbitrary circle of a vow.

The scarves, consoles, and fauteuils of the mind
May be composed into a picture still,
The matter of corrupt mankind
Resistant to the dream that makes it ill,
Not by our choice but our consent: beloved, pray
That Love, to Whom necessity is play,
Do what we must yet cannot do alone
And lay your solitude beside my own.

That reason may not force us to commit
That sin of the high-minded, sublimation,
Which damns the soul by praising it,
Force our desire, O Essence of creation,
To seek Thee always in Thy substances,
Till the performance of those offices
Our bodies, Thine opaque enigmas, do,
Configure Thy transparent justice too.

Lest animal bias should decline our wish
For Thy perfection to identify
Thee with Thy things, to worship fish,
Or solid apples, or the wavering sky,
Our intellectual motions with Thy light
To such intense vibration, Love, excite,
That we give forth a quiet none can tell
From that in which the lichens live so well.

That this round O of faithfulness we swear
May never wither to an empty nought
Nor petrify into a square,
Mere habits of affection freeze our thought
In their inert society, lest we
Mock virtue with its pious parody
And take our love for granted, Love, permit
Temptations always to endanger it.

Lest, blurring with old moonlight of romance
The landscape of our blemishes, we try
   To set up shop on Goodwin Sands,
That we, though lovers, may love soberly,
O Fate, *O Felix Osculum*, to us
Remain nocturnal and mysterious:
Preserve us from presumption and delay;
O hold us to the voluntary way.

? Autumn 1940

55

Jumbled in the common box
Of their dark stupidity,
Orchid, swan, and Caesar lie;
Time that tires of everyone
Has corroded all the locks,
Thrown away the key for fun.

In its cleft the torrent mocks
Prophets who in days gone by
Made a profit on each cry,
Persona grata now with none;
And a jackass language shocks
Poets who can only pun.

Silence settles on the clocks;
Nursing mothers point a sly
Index finger at a sky,
Crimson with the setting sun;
In the valley of the fox
Gleams the barrel of a gun.

Once we could have made the docks,
Now it is too late to fly;
Once too often you and I
Did what we should not have done;
Round the rampant rugged rocks
Rude and ragged rascals run.

January 1941

56

Atlantis

Being set on the idea
  Of getting to Atlantis,
You have discovered of course
  Only the Ship of Fools is
Making the voyage this year,
As gales of abnormal force
  Are predicted, and that you
  Must therefore be ready to
Behave absurdly enough
  To pass for one of The Boys,
At least appearing to love
  Hard liquor, horseplay and noise.

Should storms, as may well happen,
  Drive you to anchor a week
In some old harbour-city
  Of Ionia, then speak
With her witty scholars, men
Who have proved there cannot be
  Such a place as Atlantis:
  Learn their logic, but notice

How its subtlety betrays
   Their enormous simple grief;
Thus they shall teach you the ways
   To doubt that you may believe.

If, later, you run aground
   Among the headlands of Thrace,
Where with torches all night long
   A naked barbaric race
Leaps frenziedly to the sound
Of conch and dissonant gong;
   On that stony savage shore
   Strip off your clothes and dance, for
Unless you are capable
   Of forgetting completely
About Atlantis, you will
   Never finish your journey.

Again, should you come to gay
   Carthage or Corinth, take part
In their endless gaiety;
   And if in some bar a tart,
As she strokes your hair, should say
"This is Atlantis, dearie,"
   Listen with attentiveness
   To her life-story: unless
You become acquainted now
   With each refuge that tries to
Counterfeit Atlantis, how
   Will you recognise the true?

Assuming you beach at last
   Near Atlantis, and begin
The terrible trek inland
   Through squalid woods and frozen
Tundras where all are soon lost;

If, forsaken then, you stand,
  Dismissal everywhere,
  Stone and snow, silence and air,
O remember the great dead
  And honour the fate you are,
Travelling and tormented,
  Dialectic and bizarre.

Stagger onward rejoicing;
  And even then if, perhaps
Having actually got
  To the last col, you collapse
With all Atlantis shining
Below you yet you cannot
  Descend, you should still be proud
  Even to have been allowed
Just to peep at Atlantis
  In a poetic vision:
Give thanks and lie down in peace,
  Having seen your salvation.

All the little household gods
  Have started crying, but say
Good-bye now, and put to sea.
  Farewell, my dear, farewell: may
Hermes, master of the roads,
And the four dwarf Kabiri,
  Protect and serve you always;
  And may the Ancient of Days
Provide for all you must do
  His invisible guidance,
Lifting up, dear, upon you
  The light of His countenance.

January 1941

57

At the Grave of Henry James

The snow, less intransigeant than their marble,
Has left the defence of whiteness to these tombs;
  For all the pools at my feet
Accommodate blue now, and echo such clouds as occur
To the sky, and whatever bird or mourner the passing
  Moment remarks they repeat

While the rocks, named after singular spaces
Within which images wandered once that caused
  All to tremble and offend,
Stand here in an innocent stillness, each marking the spot
Where one more series of errors lost its uniqueness
  And novelty came to an end.

To whose real advantage were such transactions
When worlds of reflection were exchanged for trees?
  What living occasion can
Be just to the absent? O noon but reflects on itself,
And the small taciturn stone that is the only witness
  To a great and talkative man

Has no more judgement than my ignorant shadow
Of odious comparisons or distant clocks
  Which challenge and interfere
With the heart's instantaneous reading of time, time that is
A warm enigma no longer in you for whom I
  Surrender my private cheer.

Startling the awkward footsteps of my apprehension,
The flushed assault of your recognition is
  The *donnée* of this doubtful hour:
O stern proconsul of intractable provinces,
O poet of the difficult, dear addicted artist,
  Assent to my soil and flower.

As I stand awake on our solar fabric,
That primary machine, the earth, which gendarmes, banks,
  And aspirin pre-suppose,
On which the clumsy and sad may all sit down,
                                        and any who will
Say their a-ha to the beautiful, the common locus
  Of the master and the rose.

Our theatre, scaffold, and erotic city
Where all the infirm species are partners in the act
  Of encroachment bodies crave,
Though solitude in death is *de rigueur* for their flesh
And the self-denying hermit flies as it approaches
  Like the carnivore to a cave.

That its plural numbers may unite in meaning,
Its vulgar tongues unravel the knotted mass
  Of the improperly conjunct,
Open my eyes now to all its hinted significant forms,
Sharpen my ears to detect amid its brilliant uproar
  The low thud of the defunct.

O dwell, ironic at my living centre,
Half ancestor, half child; because the actual self
  Round whom time revolves so fast
Is so afraid of what its motions might possibly do
That the actor is never there when his really important
  Acts happen. Only the past

Is present, no one about but the dead as,
Equipped with a few inherited odds and ends,
  One after another we are
Fired into life to seek that unseen target where all
Our equivocal judgements are judged and resolved in
  One whole Alas or Hurrah.

And only the unborn remark the disaster
When, though it makes no difference to the pretty airs
  The bird of Appetite sings,

And Amour Propre is his usual amusing self,
Out from the jungle of an undistinguished moment
   The flexible shadow springs.

Now more than ever, when torches and snare-drum
Excite the squat women of the saurian brain
   Till a milling mob of fears
Breaks in insultingly on anywhere, when in our dreams
Pigs play on the organs and the blue sky runs shrieking
   As the Crack of Doom appears,

Are the good ghosts needed with the white magic
Of their subtle loves. War has no ambiguities
   Like a marriage; the result
Required of its *affaire fatale* is simple and sad,
The physical removal of all human objects
   That conceal the Difficult.

Then remember me that I may remember
The test we have to learn to shudder for is not
   An historical event,
That neither the low democracy of a nightmare nor
An army's primitive tidiness may deceive me
   About our predicament,

That catastrophic situation which neither
Victory nor defeat can annul; to be
   Deaf yet determined to sing,
To be lame and blind yet burning for the Great Good Place,
To be radically corrupt yet mournfully attracted
   By the Real Distinguished Thing.

And shall I not specially bless you as, vexed with
My little inferior questions, to-day I stand
   Beside the bed where you rest
Who opened such passionate arms to your *Bon* when It ran
Towards you with Its overwhelming reasons pleading
   All beautifully in Its breast?

O with what innocence your hand submitted
To those formal rules that help a child to play,
While your heart, fastidious as
A delicate nun, remained true to the rare noblesse
Of your lucid gift and, for its own sake, ignored the
Resentful muttering Mass,

Whose ruminant hatred of all which cannot
Be simplified or stolen is still at large;
No death can assuage its lust
To vilify the landscape of Distinction and see
The heart of the Personal brought to a systolic standstill,
The Tall to diminished dust.

Preserve me, Master, from its vague incitement;
Yours be the disciplinary image that holds
Me back from agreeable wrong
And the clutch of eddying muddle, lest Proportion shed
The alpine chill of her shrugging editorial shoulder
On my loose impromptu song.

Suggest; so may I segregate my disorder
Into districts of prospective value: approve;
Lightly, lightly, then, may I dance
Over the frontier of the obvious and fumble no more
In the old limp pocket of the minor exhibition,
Nor riot with irrelevance,

And no longer shoe geese or water stakes, but
Bolt in my day my grain of truth to the barn
Where tribulations may leap
With their long-lost brothers at last in the festival
Of which not one has a dissenting image, and the
Flushed immediacy sleep.

Into this city from the shining lowlands
Blows a wind that whispers of uncovered skulls
And fresh ruins under the moon,

Of hopes that will not survive the secousse of this spring
Of blood and flames, of the terror that walks by night and
  The sickness that strikes at noon.

All will be judged. Master of nuance and scruple,
Pray for me and for all writers living or dead;
  Because there are many whose works
Are in better taste than their lives; because there is no end
To the vanity of our calling: make intercession
  For the treason of all clerks.

Because the darkness is never so distant,
And there is never much time for the arrogant
  Spirit to flutter its wings,
Or the broken bone to rejoice, or the cruel to cry
For Him whose property is always to have mercy, the author
  And giver of all good things.

? Spring 1941

58

Mundus et Infans

(FOR ALBERT AND ANGELYN STEVENS)

Kicking his mother until she let go of his soul
Has given him a healthy appetite: clearly, her rôle
  In the New Order must be
To supply and deliver his raw materials free;
  Should there be any shortage,
She will be held responsible; she also promises
To show him all such attentions as befit his age.
  Having dictated peace,

With one fist clenched behind his head, heel drawn up to thigh,
The cocky little ogre dozes off, ready,
  Though, to take on the rest
Of the world at the drop of a hat or the mildest
  Nudge of the impossible,
Resolved, cost what it may, to seize supreme power and
Sworn to resist tyranny to the death with all
  Forces at his command.

A pantheist not a solipsist, he co-operates
With a universe of large and noisy feeling-states
  Without troubling to place
Them anywhere special, for, to his eyes, Funnyface
  Or Elephant as yet
Mean nothing. His distinction between Me and Us
Is a matter of taste; his seasons are Dry and Wet;
  He thinks as his mouth does.

Still his loud iniquity is still what only the
Greatest of saints become—someone who does not lie:
  He because he cannot
Stop the vivid present to think, they by having got
  Past reflection into
A passionate obedience in time. We have our Boy-
Meets-Girl era of mirrors and muddle to work through,
  Without rest, without joy.

Therefore we love him because his judgements are so
Frankly subjective that his abuse carries no
  Personal sting. We should
Never dare offer our helplessness as a good
  Bargain, without at least
Promising to overcome a misfortune we blame
History or Banks or the Weather for: but this beast
  Dares to exist without shame.

Let him praise our Creator with the top of his voice,
Then, and the motions of his bowels; let us rejoice
  That he lets us hope, for
He may never become a fashionable or
  Important personage:
However bad he may be, he has not yet gone mad;
Whoever we are now, we were no worse at his age;
  So of course we ought to be glad

When he bawls the house down. Has he not a perfect right
To remind us at every moment how we quite
  Rightly expect each other
To go upstairs or for a walk if we must cry over
  Spilt milk, such as our wish
That, since, apparently, we shall never be above
Either or both, we had never learned to distinguish
  Between hunger and love?

? August 1942

59

The Lesson

The first time that I dreamed, we were in flight,
And fagged with running; there was civil war,
A valley full of thieves and wounded bears.

Farms blazed behind us; turning to the right,
We came at once to a tall house, its door
Wide open, waiting for its long-lost heirs.

An elderly clerk sat on the bedroom stairs
Writing; but we had tiptoed past him when
He raised his head and stuttered—"Go away."
We wept and begged to stay:

He wiped his pince-nez, hesitated, then
Said no, he had no power to give us leave;
Our lives were not in order; we must leave.

* * *

The second dream began in a May wood;
We had been laughing; your blue eyes were kind,
Your excellent nakedness without disdain.

Our lips met, wishing universal good;
But on their impact sudden flame and wind
Fetched you away and turned me loose again

To make a focus for a wide wild plain,
Dead level and dead silent and bone dry,
Where nothing could have suffered, sinned, or grown.
On a high chair alone
I sat, a little master, asking why
The cold and solid object in my hands
Should be a human hand, one of your hands.

* * *

And the last dream was this: we were to go
To a great banquet and a Victory Ball
After some tournament or dangerous test.

Only our seats had velvet cushions, so
We must have won; though there were crowns for all,
Ours were of gold, of paper all the rest.

O fair or funny was each famous guest.
Love smiled at Courage over priceless glass,
And rockets died in hundreds to express
Our learned carelessness.
A band struck up; all over the green grass
A sea of paper crowns rose up to dance:
Ours were too heavy; we did not dance.

* * *

I woke. You were not there. But as I dressed
Anxiety turned to shame, feeling all three
Intended one rebuke. For had not each
In its own way tried to teach
My will to love you that it cannot be,
As I think, of such consequence to want
What anyone is given, if they want?

October 1942

60

The Sea and the Mirror

A Commentary on Shakespeare's The Tempest

(TO JAMES AND TANIA STERN)

And am I wrong to worship where
Faith cannot doubt nor Hope despair
Since my own soul can grant my prayer?
Speak, God of Visions, plead for me
And tell why I have chosen thee.

Emily Brontë

Preface

(The Stage Manager to the Critics)

The aged catch their breath,
For the nonchalant couple go
Waltzing across the tightrope
As if there were no death
Or hope of falling down;

The wounded cry as the clown
Doubles his meaning, and O
How the dear little children laugh
When the drums roll and the lovely
Lady is sawn in half.

O what authority gives
Existence its surprise?
Science is happy to answer
That the ghosts who haunt our lives
Are handy with mirrors and wire,
That song and sugar and fire,
Courage and come-hither eyes
Have a genius for taking pains.
But how does one think up a habit?
Our wonder, our terror remains.

Art opens the fishiest eye
To the Flesh and the Devil who heat
The Chamber of Temptation
Where heroes roar and die.
We are wet with sympathy now;
Thanks for the evening; but how
Shall we satisfy when we meet,
Between Shall-I and I-Will,
The lion's mouth whose hunger
No metaphors can fill?

Well, who in his own backyard
Has not opened his heart to the smiling
Secret he cannot quote?
Which goes to show that the Bard
Was sober when he wrote
That this world of fact we love
Is unsubstantial stuff:
All the rest is silence
On the other side of the wall;
And the silence ripeness,
And the ripeness all.

I Prospero to Ariel

Stay with me, Ariel, while I pack, and with your first free act
  Delight my leaving; share my resigning thoughts
As you have served my revelling wishes: then, brave spirit,
  Ages to you of song and daring, and to me
Briefly Milan, then earth. In all, things have turned out better
  Than I once expected or ever deserved;
I am glad that I did not recover my dukedom till
  I do not want it; I am glad that Miranda
No longer pays me any attention; I am glad I have freed you,
  So at last I can really believe I shall die.
For under your influence death is inconceivable:
  On walks through winter woods, a bird's dry carcass
Agitates the retina with novel images,
  A stranger's quiet collapse in a noisy street
Is the beginning of much lively speculation,
  And every time some dear flesh disappears
What is real is the arriving grief; thanks to your service,
  The lonely and unhappy are very much alive.
But now all these heavy books are no use to me any more, for
  Where I go, words carry no weight: it is best,
Then, I surrender their fascinating counsel
  To the silent dissolution of the sea
Which misuses nothing because it values nothing;
  Whereas man overvalues everything
Yet, when he learns the price is pegged to his valuation,
  Complains bitterly he is being ruined which, of course, he is.
So kings find it odd they should have a million subjects
  Yet share in the thoughts of none, and seducers
Are sincerely puzzled at being unable to love
  What they are able to possess; so, long ago,
In an open boat, I wept at giving a city,
  Common warmth and touching substance, for a gift
In dealing with shadows. If age, which is certainly
  Just as wicked as youth, look any wiser,
It is only that youth is still able to believe

It will get away with anything, while age
Knows only too well that it has got away with nothing:
The child runs out to play in the garden, convinced
That the furniture will go on with its thinking lesson,
Who, fifty years later, if he plays at all,
Will first ask its kind permission to be excused.

When I woke into my life, a sobbing dwarf
Whom giants served only as they pleased,
I was not what I seemed;
Beyond their busy backs I made a magic
To ride away from a father's imperfect justice,
Take vengeance on the Romans for their grammar,
Usurp the popular earth and blot out for ever
The gross insult of being a mere one among many:
Now, Ariel, I am that I am, your late and lonely master,
Who knows now what magic is:—the power to enchant
That comes from disillusion. What the books can teach one
Is that most desires end up in stinking ponds,
But we have only to learn to sit still and give no orders,
To make you offer us your echo and your mirror;
We have only to believe you, then you dare not lie;
To ask for nothing, and at once from your calm eyes,
With their lucid proof of apprehension and disorder,
All we are not stares back at what we are. For all things,
In your company, can be themselves: historic deeds
Drop their hauteur and speak of shabby childhoods
When all they longed for was to join in the gang of doubts
Who so tormented them; sullen diseases
Forget their dreadful appearance and make silly jokes;
Thick-headed goodness for once is not a bore.
No one but you had sufficient audacity and eyesight
To find those clearings where the shy humiliations
Gambol on sunny afternoons, the waterhole to which
The scarred rogue sorrow comes quietly in the small hours:
And no one but you is reliably informative on hell;
As you whistle and skip past, the poisonous

Resentments scuttle over your unrevolted feet,
  And even the uncontrollable vertigo,
Because it can scent no shame, is unobliged to strike.

Could he but once see Nature as
  In truth she is for ever,
What oncer would not fall in love?
Hold up your mirror, boy, to do
  Your vulgar friends this favour:
One peep, though, will be quite enough;
  To those who are not true,
A statue with no figleaf has
  A pornographic flavour.

Inform my hot heart straight away
  Its treasure loves another,
But turn to neutral topics then,
Such as the pictures in this room,
  Religion or the Weather;
Pure scholarship in Where and When,
  How Often and With Whom,
Is not for Passion that must play
  The Jolly Elder Brother.

Be frank about our heathen foe,
  For Rome will be a goner
If you soft-pedal the loud beast;
Describe in plain four-letter words
  This dragon that's upon her:
But should our beggars ask the cost,
  Just whistle like the birds;
Dare even Pope or Caesar know
  The price of faith and honour?

  To-day I am free and no longer need your freedom:
You, I suppose, will be off now to look for likely victims;
  Crowds chasing ankles, lone men stalking glory,

Some feverish young rebel among amiable flowers
In consultation with his handsome envy,
A punctual plump judge, a fly-weight hermit in a dream
Of gardens that time is for ever outside—
To lead absurdly by their self-important noses.
Are you malicious by nature? I don't know.
Perhaps only incapable of doing nothing or of
Being by yourself, and, for all your wry faces,
May secretly be anxious and miserable without
A master to need you for the work you need.
Are all your tricks a test? If so, I hope you find, next time,
Someone in whom you cannot spot the weakness
Through which you will corrupt him with your charm. Mine you did
And me you have: thanks to us both, I have broken
Both of the promises I made as an apprentice:—
To hate nothing and to ask nothing for its love.
All by myself I tempted Antonio into treason;
However that could be cleared up; both of us know
That both were in the wrong, and neither need be sorry:
But Caliban remains my impervious disgrace.
We did it, Ariel, between us; you found on me a wish
For absolute devotion; result—his wreck
That sprawls in the weeds and will not be repaired:
My dignity discouraged by a pupil's curse,
I shall go knowing and incompetent into my grave.

The extravagant children, who lately swaggered
Out of the sea like gods, have, I think, been soundly hunted
By their own devils into their human selves:
To all, then, but me, their pardons. Alonso's heaviness
Is lost; and weak Sebastian will be patient
In future with his slothful conscience—after all, it pays;
Stephano is contracted to his belly, a minor
But a prosperous kingdom; stale Trinculo receives,
Gratis, a whole fresh repertoire of stories, and
Our younger generation its independent joy.
Their eyes are big and blue with love; its lighting

Makes even us look new: yes, to-day it all looks so easy.
  Will Ferdinand be as fond of a Miranda
Familiar as a stocking? Will a Miranda who is
  No longer a silly lovesick little goose,
When Ferdinand and his brave world are her profession,
  Go into raptures over existing at all?
Probably I over-estimate their difficulties;
  Just the same, I am very glad I shall never
Be twenty and have to go through that business again,
  The hours of fuss and fury, the conceit, the expense.

Sing first that green remote Cockaigne
  Where whiskey-rivers run,
And every gorgeous number may
  Be laid by anyone;
For medicine and rhetoric
  Lie mouldering on shelves,
While sad young dogs and stomach-aches
  Love no one but themselves.

Tell then of witty angels who
  Come only to the beasts,
Of Heirs Apparent who prefer
  Low dives to formal feasts;
For shameless Insecurity
  Prays for a boot to lick,
And many a sore bottom finds
  A sorer one to kick.

Wind up, though, on a moral note:—
  That Glory will go bang,
Schoolchildren shall co-operate,
  And honest rogues must hang;
Because our sound committee man
  Has murder in his heart:
But should you catch a living eye,
  Just wink as you depart.

Now our partnership is dissolved, I feel so peculiar:
  As if I had been on a drunk since I was born
And suddenly now, and for the first time, am cold sober,
  With all my unanswered wishes and unwashed days
Stacked up all around my life; as if through
the ages I had dreamed
  About some tremendous journey I was taking,
Sketching imaginary landscapes, chasms and cities,
  Cold walls, hot spaces, wild mouths, defeated backs,
Jotting down fictional notes on secrets overheard
  In theatres and privies, banks and mountain inns,
And now, in my old age, I wake, and this journey really exists,
  And I have actually to take it, inch by inch,
Alone and on foot, without a cent in my pocket,
  Through a universe where time is not foreshortened,
No animals talk, and there is neither floating nor flying.

  When I am safely home, oceans away in Milan, and
Realise once and for all I shall never see you again,
  Over there, maybe, it won't seem quite so dreadful
Not to be interesting any more, but an old man
  Just like other old men, with eyes that water
Easily in the wind, and a head that nods in the sunshine,
  Forgetful, maladroit, a little grubby,
And to like it. When the servants settle me into a chair
  In some well-sheltered corner of the garden,
And arrange my muffler and rugs, shall I ever be able
  To stop myself from telling them what I am doing,—
Sailing alone, out over seventy thousand fathoms—?
  Yet if I speak, I shall sink without a sound
Into unmeaning abysses. Can I learn to suffer
  Without saying something ironic or funny
On suffering? I never suspected the way of truth
  Was a way of silence where affectionate chat
Is but a robbers' ambush and even good music
  In shocking taste; and you, of course, never told me.
If I peg away at it honestly every moment,
  And have luck, perhaps by the time death pounces

His stumping question, I shall just be getting to know
   The difference between moonshine and daylight. . . .
I see you starting to fidget. I forgot. To you
   That doesn't matter. My dear, here comes Gonzalo
With a solemn face to fetch me. O Ariel, Ariel,
   How I shall miss you. Enjoy your element. Good-bye.

Sing, Ariel, sing,
Sweetly, dangerously
Out of the sour
And shiftless water,
Lucidly out
Of the dozing tree,
Entrancing, rebuking
The raging heart
With a smoother song
Than this rough world,
Unfeeling god.

O brilliantly, lightly,
Of separation,
Of bodies and death,
Unanxious one, sing
To man, meaning me,
As now, meaning always,
In love or out,
Whatever that mean,
Trembling he takes
The silent passage
Into discomfort.

II The Supporting Cast, Sotto Voce

ANTONIO

As all the pigs have turned back into men
And the sky is auspicious and the sea
Calm as a clock, we can all go home again.

Yes, it undoubtedly looks as if we
Could take life as easily now as tales
Write ever-after: not only are the

Two heads silhouetted against the sails
—And kissing, of course—well-built, but the lean
Fool is quite a person, the fingernails

Of the dear old butler for once quite clean,
And the royal passengers quite as good
As rustics, perhaps better, for they mean

What they say, without, as a rustic would,
Casting reflections on the courtly crew.
Yes, Brother Prospero, your grouping could

Not be more effective: given a few
Incomplete objects and a nice warm day,
What a lot a little music can do.

Dotted about the deck they doze or play,
Your loyal subjects all, grateful enough
To know their place and believe what you say.

Antonio, sweet brother, has to laugh.
How easy you have made it to refuse
Peace to your greatness! Break your wand in half,

The fragments will join; burn your books or lose
Them in the sea, they will soon reappear,
Not even damaged: as long as I choose

To wear my fashion, whatever you wear
Is a magic robe; while I stand outside
Your circle, the will to charm is still there.

As I exist so you shall be denied,
Forced to remain our melancholy mentor,
The grown-up man, the adult in his pride,

Never have time to curl up at the centre
Time turns on when completely reconciled,
Never become and therefore never enter
The green occluded pasture as a child.

Your all is partial, Prospero;
  My will is all my own:
Your need to love shall never know
Me: I am I, Antonio,
  By choice myself alone.

FERDINAND

Flesh, fair, unique, and you, warm secret that my kiss
Follows into meaning Miranda, solitude
Where my omissions are, still possible, still good,
Dear Other at all times, retained as I do this,

From moment to moment as you enrich them so
Inherit me, my cause, as I would cause you now
With mine your sudden joy, two wonders as one vow
Pre-empting all, here, there, for ever, long ago.

I would smile at no other promise than touch, taste, sight,
Were there not, my enough, my exaltation, to bless
As world is offered world, as I hear it to-night

Pleading with ours for us, another tenderness
That neither without either could or would possess,
The Right Required Time, The Real Right Place, O Light.

One bed is empty, Prospero,
My person is my own;
Hot Ferdinand will never know
The flame with which Antonio
Burns in the dark alone.

STEPHANO

Embrace me, belly, like a bride;
Dear daughter, for the weight you drew
From humble pie and swallowed pride,
Believe the boast in which you grew:
Where mind meets matter, both should woo;
Together let us learn that game
The high play better than the blue:
A lost thing looks for a lost name.

Behind your skirts your son must hide
When disappointments bark and boo;
Brush my heroic ghosts aside,
Wise nanny, with a vulgar pooh:
Exchanging cravings we pursue
Alternately a single aim:
Between the bottle and the "loo"
A lost thing looks for a lost name.

Though in the long run satisfied,
The will of one by being two
At every moment is denied;
Exhausted glasses wonder who
Is self and sovereign, I or You?
We cannot both be what we claim,
The real Stephano—Which is true?
A lost thing looks for a lost name.

Child? Mother? Either grief will do;
The need for pardon is the same,
The contradiction is not new:
A lost thing looks for a lost name.

One glass is untouched, Prospero,
My nature is my own;
Inert Stephano does not know
The feast at which Antonio
Toasts One and One alone.

GONZALO

Evening, grave, immense, and clear,
Overlooks our ship whose wake
Lingers undistorted on
Sea and silence; I look back
For the last time as the sun
Sets behind that island where
All our loves were altered: yes,
My prediction came to pass,
Yet I am not justified,
And I weep but not with pride.
Not in me the credit for
Words I uttered long ago
Whose glad meaning I betrayed;
Truths to-day admitted, owe
Nothing to the councillor
In whose booming eloquence
Honesty became untrue.
Am I not Gonzalo who
By his self-reflection made
Consolation an offence?

There was nothing to explain:
Had I trusted the Absurd
And straightforward note by note

Sung exactly what I heard,
Such immediate delight
Would have taken there and then
Our common welkin by surprise,
All would have begun to dance
Jigs of self-deliverance.
It was I prevented this,
Jealous of my native ear,
Mine the art which made the song
Sound ridiculous and wrong,
I whose interference broke
The gallop into jog-trot prose
And by speculation froze
Vision into an idea,
Irony into a joke,
Till I stood convicted of
Doubt and insufficient love.

Farewell, dear island of our wreck:
All have been restored to health,
All have seen the Commonwealth,
There is nothing to forgive.
Since a storm's decision gave
His subjective passion back
To a meditative man,
Even reminiscence can
Comfort ambient troubles like
Some ruined tower by the sea
Whence boyhoods growing and afraid
Learn a formula they need
In solving their mortality,
Even rusting flesh can be
A simple locus now, a bell
The Already There can lay
Hands on if at any time
It should feel inclined to say
To the lonely—"Here I am,"
To the anxious—"All is well."

One tongue is silent, Prospero,
My language is my own;
Decayed Gonzalo does not know
The shadow that Antonio
Talks to, at noon, alone.

ADRIAN AND FRANCISCO

Good little sunbeams must learn to fly,
But it's madly ungay when the goldfish die.

One act is censored, Prospero,
My audience is my own;
Nor Adrian nor Francisco know
The drama that Antonio
Plays in his head alone.

ALONSO

Dear Son, when the warm multitudes cry,
Ascend your throne majestically,
But keep in mind the waters where fish
See sceptres descending with no wish
To touch them; sit regal and erect,
But imagine the sands where a crown
Has the status of a broken-down
Sofa or mutilated statue:
Remember as bells and cannon boom
The cold deep that does not envy you,
The sunburnt superficial kingdom
Where a king is an object.

Expect no help from others, for who
Talk sense to princes or refer to
The scorpion in official speeches
As they unveil some granite Progress
Leading a child and holding a bunch
Of lilies? In their Royal Zoos the

Shark and the octopus are tactfully
Omitted; synchronised clocks march on
Within their powers: without, remain
The ocean flats where no subscription
Concerts are given, the desert plain
Where there is nothing for lunch.

Only your darkness can tell you what
A prince's ornate mirror dare not,
Which you should fear more—the sea in which
A tyrant sinks entangled in rich
Robes while a mistress turns a white back
Upon his splutter, or the desert
Where an emperor stands in his shirt
While his diary is read by sneering
Beggars, and far off he notices
A lean horror flapping and hopping
Toward him with inhuman swiftness:
Learn from your dreams what you lack,

For as your fears are, so must you hope.
The Way of Justice is a tightrope
Where no prince is safe for one instant
Unless he trust his embarrassment,
As in his left ear the siren sings
Meltingly of water and a night
Where all flesh had peace, and on his right
The efreet offers a brilliant void
Where his mind could be perfectly clear
And all his limitations destroyed:
Many young princes soon disappear
To join all the unjust kings.

So, if you prosper, suspect those bright
Mornings when you whistle with a light
Heart. You are loved; you have never seen
The harbour so still, the park so green,
So many well-fed pigeons upon

Cupolas and triumphal arches,
So many stags and slender ladies
Beside the canals. Remember when
Your climate seems a permanent home
For marvellous creatures and great men,
What griefs and convulsions startled Rome,
Ecbatana, Babylon.

How narrow the space, how slight the chance
For civil pattern and importance
Between the watery vagueness and
The triviality of the sand,
How soon the lively trip is over
From loose craving to sharp aversion,
Aimless jelly to paralysed bone:
At the end of each successful day
Remember that the fire and the ice
Are never more than one step away
From the temperate city; it is
But a moment to either.

But should you fail to keep your kingdom
And, like your father before you, come
Where thought accuses and feeling mocks,
Believe your pain: praise the scorching rocks
For their desiccation of your lust,
Thank the bitter treatment of the tide
For its dissolution of your pride,
That the whirlwind may arrange your will
And the deluge release it to find
The spring in the desert, the fruitful
Island in the sea, where flesh and mind
Are delivered from mistrust.

Blue the sky beyond her humming sail
As I sit to-day by our ship's rail
Watching exuberant porpoises
Escort us homeward and writing this

For you to open when I am gone:
Read it, Ferdinand, with the blessing
Of Alonso, your father, once King
Of Naples, now ready to welcome
Death, but rejoicing in a new love,
A new peace, having heard the solemn
Music strike and seen the statue move
To forgive our illusion.

One crown is lacking, Prospero,
My empire is my own;
Dying Alonso does not know
The diadem Antonio
Wears in his world alone.

MASTER AND BOATSWAIN

At Dirty Dick's and Sloppy Joe's
We drank our liquor straight,
Some went upstairs with Margery,
And some, alas, with Kate;
And two by two like cat and mouse
The homeless played at keeping house.

There Wealthy Meg, the Sailor's Friend,
And Marion, cow-eyed,
Opened their arms to me but I
Refused to step inside;
I was not looking for a cage
In which to mope in my old age.

The nightingales are sobbing in
The orchards of our mothers,
And hearts that we broke long ago
Have long been breaking others;
Tears are round, the sea is deep:
Roll them overboard and sleep.

One gaze points elsewhere, Prospero,
My compass is my own;
Nostalgic sailors do not know
The waters where Antonio
Sails on and on alone.

SEBASTIAN

My rioters all disappear, my dream
Where Prudence flirted with a naked sword,
Securely vicious, crumbles; it is day;
Nothing has happened; we are all alive:
I am Sebastian, wicked still, my proof
Of mercy that I wake without a crown.

What sadness signalled to our children's day
Where each believed all wishes wear a crown
And anything pretended is alive,
That one by one we plunged into that dream
Of solitude and silence where no sword
Will ever play once it is called a proof?

The arrant jewel singing in his crown
Persuaded me my brother was a dream
I should not love because I had no proof,
Yet all my honesty assumed a sword;
To think his death I thought myself alive
And stalked infected through the blooming day.

The lie of Nothing is to promise proof
To any shadow that there is no day
Which cannot be extinguished with some sword,
To want and weakness that the ancient crown
Envies the childish head, murder a dream
Wrong only while its victim is alive.

O blessed be bleak Exposure on whose sword,
Caught unawares, we prick ourselves alive!
Shake Failure's bruising fist! Who else would crown
Abominable error with a proof?
I smile because I tremble, glad to-day
To be ashamed, not anxious, not a dream.

Children are playing, brothers are alive,
And not a heart or stomach asks for proof
That all this dearness is no lovers' dream;
Just Now is what it might be every day,
Right Here is absolute and needs no crown,
Ermine or trumpets, protocol or sword.

In dream all sins are easy, but by day
It is defeat gives proof we are alive;
The sword we suffer is the guarded crown.

One face cries nothing, Prospero,
My conscience is my own;
Pallid Sebastian does not know
The dream in which Antonio
Fights the white bull alone.

TRINCULO

Mechanic, merchant, king,
Are warmed by the cold clown
Whose head is in the clouds
And never can get down.

Into a solitude
Undreamed of by their fat
Quick dreams have lifted me;
The north wind steals my hat.

On clear days I can see
Green acres far below,
And the red roof where I
Was Little Trinculo.

There lies that solid world
These hands can never reach;
My history, my love,
Is but a choice of speech.

A terror shakes my tree,
A flock of words fly out,
Whereat a laughter shakes
The busy and devout.

Wild images, come down
Out of your freezing sky,
That I, like shorter men,
May get my joke and die.

One note is jarring, Prospero,
My humour is my own;
Tense Trinculo will never know
The paradox Antonio
Laughs at, in woods, alone.

MIRANDA

My Dear One is mine as mirrors are lonely,
As the poor and sad are real to the good king,
And the high green hill sits always by the sea.

Up jumped the Black Man behind the elder tree,
Turned a somersault and ran away waving;
My Dear One is mine as mirrors are lonely.

The Witch gave a squawk; her venomous body
Melted into light as water leaves a spring
And the high green hill sits always by the sea.

At his crossroads, too, the Ancient prayed for me;
Down his wasted cheeks tears of joy were running:
My Dear One is mine as mirrors are lonely.

He kissed me awake, and no one was sorry;
The sun shone on sails, eyes, pebbles, anything,
And the high green hill sits always by the sea.

So, to remember our changing garden, we
Are linked as children in a circle dancing:
My Dear One is mine as mirrors are lonely,
And the high green hill sits always by the sea.

One link is missing, Prospero,
My magic is my own;
Happy Miranda does not know
The figure that Antonio,
The Only One, Creation's O
Dances for Death alone.

III Caliban to the Audience

If now, having dismissed your hired impersonators with verdicts ranging from the laudatory orchid to the disgusted and disgusting egg, you ask and, of course, notwithstanding the conscious fact of his irrevocable absence, you instinctively *do* ask for our so good, so great, so dead author to stand before the finally lowered curtain and take his shyly responsible bow for this, his latest, ripest production, it is I—my reluctance is, I can assure you, co-equal with your dismay—who will always loom thus wretchedly into your confused picture, for, in default of the all-wise, all-explaining master you would speak *to*, who else at least can, who else indeed must respond to your bewildered cry, but its very echo, the begged question you would speak to him *about.*

*   *   *

We must own [*for the present I speak your echo*] to a nervous perplexity not unmixed, frankly, with downright resentment. How *can* we grant the indulgence for which in his epilogue your personified type of the creative so lamely, tamely pleaded? Imprisoned, by you, in the mood doubtful, loaded, by you, with distressing embarrassments, we are, we submit, in no position to set *anyone* free.

Our native Muse, heaven knows and heaven be praised, is not exclusive. Whether out of the innocence of a childlike heart to whom all things are pure, or with the serenity of a status so majestic that the mere keeping up of tones and appearances, the suburban wonder as to what the strait-laced Unities might possibly think, or sad sour Probability possibly say, are questions for which she doesn't because she needn't, she hasn't in her lofty maturity any longer to care a rap, she invites, dear generous-hearted creature that she is, just *tout le monde* to drop in at any time so that her famous, memorable, sought-after evenings present to the speculative eye an ever-shining, never-tarnished proof of her amazing unheard-of power to combine and happily contrast, to make *every* shade of the social and moral palette contribute to the general richness, of the skill, unapproached and unattempted by Grecian aunt or Gallic sister, with which she can skate full tilt toward the forbidden incoherence and then, in the last split second, on the shuddering edge of the bohemian standardless abyss effect her breathtaking triumphant turn.

No timid segregation by rank or taste for her, no prudent listing into those who will, who might, who certainly would not get on, no nicely graded scale of invitations to heroic formal Tuesdays, young comic Thursdays, al fresco farcical Saturdays. No, the real, the only test of the theatrical as of the gastronomic, her practice confidently wagers, is the mixed perfected brew.

As he looks in on her, so marvellously at home with all her cosy swarm about her, what accents will not assault the new arrival's ear, the magnificent tropes of tragic defiance and despair, the repartee of the high humour, the pun of the very low, cultured drawl and manly illiterate bellow, yet all of them gratefully doing their huge or tiny best to make the party go?

And if, assured by her smiling wave that of course he may, he should presently set out to explore her vast and rambling mansion, to do honour to its dear odd geniuses of local convenience and proportion, its multiplied deities of mysterious stair and interesting alcove, not one of the laughing groups and engrossed warmed couples that he keeps "surprising"—the never-ending surprise for him is that he doesn't seem to—but affords some sharper instance of relations he would have been the last to guess at, choleric prince at his ease with lymphatic butler, moist hand taking so to dry, youth getting on quite famously with stingy cold old age, some stranger vision of the large loud liberty violently rocking yet never, he is persuaded, finally upsetting the jolly crowded boat.

What, he may well ask, has the gracious goddess done to all these people that, at her most casual hint, they should so trustingly, so immediately take off those heavy habits one thinks of them as having for their health and happiness day and night to wear, without in this unfamiliar unbuttoned state—the notable absence of the slightest shiver or not-quite-inhibited sneeze is indication positive—for a second feeling the draught? Is there, could there be, *any* miraculous suspension of the wearily historic, the dingily geographic, the dully drearily sensible beyond her faith, her charm, her love, to command? Yes, there could be, yes, alas, indeed yes, O there is, right here, right now before us, the situation present.

How *could* you, you who are one of the oldest habitues at these delightful functions, one, possibly the closest, of her trusted inner circle, how could you be guilty of the incredible unpardonable treachery of bringing along the one creature, as you above all men must have known, whom she cannot and will not under any circumstances stand, the solitary exception she is not at any hour of the day or night at home to, the unique case that her attendant spirits have absolute instructions never, neither at the front door nor at the back, to admit?

At Him and at Him only does she draw the line, not because there are any limits to her sympathy but precisely because there are none. Just because of all she is and all she means to be, she cannot conceivably tolerate in her presence the represented principle of *not* sympathising, *not* associating, *not* amusing, the only child of her Awful Enemy, the rival whose real name she will never sully her lips with—"that envious witch" is sign sufficient—who does not rule but defiantly is the unrectored chaos.

All along and only too well she has known what would happen if, by any careless mischance—of conscious malice she never dreamed till now—He should ever manage to get in. She foresaw what He would do to the conversation, lying in wait for its vision of private love or public justice to warm to an Egyptian brilliance and then with some fishlike odour or *bruit insolite* snatching the visionaries back tongue-tied and blushing to the here and now; she foresaw what He would do to the arrangements, breaking, by a refusal to keep in step, the excellent order of the dancing ring, and ruining supper by knocking over the loaded appetising tray; worst of all, she foresaw, she dreaded what He would end up by doing to her, that, not content with upsetting her guests, with spoiling their fun, His progress from outrage to outrage would not relent before the gross climax of His making, horror unspeakable, a pass at her virgin self.

Let us suppose, even, that in your eyes she is by no means as we have always fondly imagined, your dear friend, that what we have just witnessed was not what it seemed to us, the inexplicable betrayal of a life-long sacred loyalty, but your long-premeditated just revenge, the final evening up of some ancient never-forgotten score, then even so, why make us suffer who have never, in all conscience, done you harm? Surely the theatrical relation, no less than the marital, is governed by the sanely decent general law that, before visitors, in front of the children or the servants, there shall be no indiscreet revelation of animosity, no "scenes," that, no matter to what intolerable degrees of internal temperature and pressure restraint may raise both the injured and the guilty, nevertheless such restraint is applied to tones and topics, the exhibited picture must be still as always the calm and smiling one the most malicious observer can see nothing wrong with, and not until the last of those whom manifested anger or mistrust would embarrass or amuse or not be good for have gone away or out or up, is the voice raised, the table thumped, the suspicious letter snatched at or the outrageous bill furiously waved.

For we, after all—you cannot have forgotten this—are strangers to her. We have never claimed her acquaintance, knowing as well as she that we do not and never could belong on her side of the curtain. All we have ever asked for is that for a few hours the curtain should be left undrawn, so as to allow our humble ragged selves the privilege of craning and gaping at the splendid goings-on inside. We most emphatically do *not* ask that she should speak to us, or try to understand us; on the contrary our one desire has always been that she should preserve for ever her old high strangeness, for what delights us about her world is just that it neither is nor possibly could become one in which we could breathe or behave, that in her house the right of innocent passage should remain so universal that the same neutral space accommodates the conspirator and his victim; the generals of both armies, the chorus of patriots and the choir of nuns, palace and farmyard, cathedral and smugglers' cave, that time should never revert to that intransigent element we are so ineluctably and only too familiarly in, but remain the passive good-natured creature she and her friends can by common consent do anything they like with—(it is not surprising that they should take advantage of their strange power and so frequently skip hours and days and even years: the dramatic mystery is that they should always so unanimously agree upon exactly how many hours and days and years to skip)—that upon their special constitutions the moral law should continue to operate so exactly that the timid not only deserve but actually win the fair, and it is the socially and physically unemphatic David who lays low the gorilla-chested Goliath with one well-aimed custard pie, that in their blessed climate, the manifestation of the inner life should always remain so easy and habitual that a sudden eruption of musical and metaphorical power is instantly recognised as standing for grief and disgust, an elegant *contrapposto* for violent death, and that consequently the picture which they in there present to us out here is always that of the perfectly tidiable case of disorder, the beautiful and serious problem exquisitely set without a single superflous datum and insoluble with less, the expert landing of all the passengers with all their luggage safe and sound in the best of health and spirits and without so much as a scratch or a bruise.

Into that world of freedom without anxiety, sincerity without loss of vigour, feeling that loosens rather than ties the tongue, we are not, we reiterate, so blinded by presumption to our proper status and interest as to expect or even wish at any time to enter, far less to dwell there.

Must we—it seems oddly that we must—remind you that our existence does not, like hers, enjoy an infinitely indicative mood, an eternally present tense, a limitlessly active voice, for in our shambling, slovenly makeshift world any two persons whether domestic first or neighbourly second, require and necessarily presuppose, in both their numbers and in all their cases, the whole inflected gamut of an alien third since, without a despised or dreaded Them to turn the back *on*, there could be no intimate or affectionate Us to turn the eye *to;* that, *chez nous*, space is never the whole uninhibited circle but always some segment, its eminent domain upheld by two co-ordinates. There always has been and always will be not only the vertical boundary, the river on this side of which initiative and honesty stroll arm in arm wearing sensible clothes, and beyond which is a savage elsewhere swarming with contagious diseases, but also its horizontal counterpart, the railroad above which houses stand in their own grounds, each equipped with a garage and a beautiful woman, sometimes with several, and below which huddled shacks provide a squeezing shelter to collarless herds who eat blancmange and have never said anything witty. Make the case as special as you please; take the tamest congregation or the wildest faction; take, say, a college. What river and railroad did for the grosser instance, lawn and corridor do for the more refined, dividing the tender who value from the tough who measure, the superstitious who still sacrifice to causation from the heretics who have already reduced the worship of truth to bare description, and so creating the academic fields to be guarded with umbrella and learned periodical against the trespass of any unqualified stranger, not a whit less jealously than the game-preserve is protected from the poacher by the unamiable shot-gun. For without these prohibitive frontiers we should never know who we were or what we wanted. It is they who donate to neighbourhood all its accuracy and vehemence. It is thanks to them that we do know with whom to associate, make love, exchange recipes and jokes, go mountain climbing or sit side by side fishing from piers. It is thanks to them, too, that we know against whom to rebel. We *can* shock our parents by visiting the dives below the railroad tracks, we *can* amuse ourselves on what would otherwise have been a very dull evening indeed, in plotting to seize the post office across the river.

Of course, these several private regions must together comprise one public whole—we would never deny that logic and instinct require that—of course, We and They are united in the candid glare of the same commercial hope by day, and the soft refulgence of the same erotic nostalgia by night but—and this is our point—without our privacies of situation, our local idioms of triumph and mishap, our different doctrines concerning the transubstantiation of the larger pinker bun on the terrestrial dish for which the mature sense may reasonably water and the adult fingers furtively or unabashedly go for, our specific choices of which hill it would be romantic to fly away over or what sea it would be exciting to run away to, our peculiar visions of the absolute stranger with a spontaneous longing for the lost who will adopt our misery not out of desire but pure compassion, without, in short, our devoted pungent expression of the partial and contrasted, the Whole would have no importance and its Day and Night no interest.

So, too, with Time who, in our auditorium, is not her dear old buffer so anxious to please everybody, but a prim magistrate whose court never adjourns, and from whose decisions, as he laconically sentences one to loss of hair and talent, another to seven days' chastity, and a third to boredom for life, there is no appeal. We should not be sitting here now, washed, warm, well-fed, in seats we have paid for, unless there were others who are not here; our liveliness and good-humour, such as they are, are those of survivors, conscious that there are others who have not been so fortunate, others who did not succeed in navigating the narrow passage or to whom the natives were not friendly, others whose streets were chosen by the explosion or through whose country the famine turned aside from ours to go, others who failed to repel the invasion of bacteria or to crush the insurrection of their bowels, others who lost their suit against their parents or were ruined by wishes they could not adjust or murdered by resentments they could not control; aware of some who were better and bigger but from whom, only the other day, Fortune withdrew her hand in sudden disgust, now nervously playing chess with drunken sea-captains in sordid cafés on the equator or the Arctic Circle, or lying, only a few blocks away, strapped and screaming on iron beds or dropping to naked pieces in damp graves. And shouldn't you too, dear master, reflect—forgive us for mentioning it—that we might very well not have been attending a production of yours this evening, had not some other and maybe—who can tell?—brighter talent married a barmaid or turned religious and shy or gone down in a liner with all his manuscripts, the loss recorded only in the corner of some country newspaper below A Poultry Lover's Jottings?

You yourself, we seem to remember, have spoken of the conjured spectacle as "a mirror held up to nature," a phrase misleading in its aphoristic sweep but indicative at least of one aspect of the relation between the real and the imagined, their mutual reversal of value, for isn't the essential artistic strangeness to which your citation of the sinisterly biassed image would point just this: that on the far side of the mirror the general will to compose, to form at all costs a felicitous pattern becomes the *necessary cause* of any particular effort to live or act or love or triumph or vary, instead of being as, in so far as it emerges at all, it is on this side, their *accidental effect*?

Does Ariel—to nominate the spirit of reflection in your terms—call for manifestation? Then neither modesty nor fear of reprisals excuses the one so called on from publicly confessing that she cheated at croquet or that he committed incest in a dream. Does He demand concealment? Then their nearest and dearest must be deceived by disguises of sex and age which anywhere else would at once attract the attention of the police or the derisive whistle of the awful schoolboy. That is the price asked, and how promptly and gladly paid, for universal reconciliation and peace, for the privilege of all galloping together past the finishing post neck and neck.

How then, we continue to wonder, knowing all this, could you act as if you did not, as if you did not realise that the embarrassing compresence of the absolutely natural, incorrigibly right-handed, and, to any request for co-operation, utterly negative, with the enthusiastically self-effacing would be a simultaneous violation of both worlds, as if you were not perfectly well aware that the magical musical condition, the orphic spell that turns the fierce dumb greedy beasts into grateful guides and oracles who will gladly take one anywhere and tell one everything free of charge, is precisely and simply that of His finite immediate note *not*, under any circumstances, being struck, of its not being tentatively whispered, far less positively banged.

Are we not bound to conclude, then, that, whatever snub to the poetic you may have intended incidentally to administer, your profounder motive in so introducing Him to them among whom, because He doesn't belong, He couldn't appear as anything but His distorted parody, a deformed and savage slave, was to deal a mortal face-slapping insult to us among whom He does and is, moreover, all grossness turned to glory, no less a person than the nude august elated archer of our heaven, the darling single son of Her who, in her right milieu, is certainly no witch but the most sensible of all the gods, whose influence is as sound as it is pandemic, on the race-track no less than in the sleeping cars of the Orient Express, our great white Queen of Love herself?

But even that is not the worst we suspect you of. If your words have not buttered any parsnips, neither have they broken any bones.

He, after all, can come back to us now to be comforted and respected, perhaps, after the experience of finding Himself for a few hours and for the first time in His life not wanted, more fully and freshly appreciative of our affection than He has always been in the past; as for His dear mother, She is far too grand and far too busy to hear or care what you say or think. If only we were certain that your malice was confined to the verbal affront, we should long ago have demanded our money back and gone whistling home to bed. Alas, in addition to resenting what you have openly said, we fear even more what you may secretly have done. Is it possible that, not content with inveigling Caliban into Ariel's kingdom, you have also let loose Ariel in Caliban's? We note with alarm that when the other members of the final tableau were dismissed, He was not returned to His arboreal confinement as He should have been. Where is He now? For if the intrusion of the real has disconcerted and incommoded the poetic, that is a mere bagatelle compared to the damage which the poetic would inflict if it ever succeeded in intruding upon the real. We want no Ariel here, breaking down our picket fences in the name of fraternity, seducing our wives in the name of romance, and robbing us of our sacred pecuniary deposits in the name of justice. Where is Ariel? What have you done with Him? For we won't, we daren't leave until you give us a satisfactory answer.

* * *

Such (*let me cease to play your echo and return to my officially natural role*)—such are your questions, are they not, but before I try to deal with them, I must ask for your patience, while I deliver a special message for our late author to those few among you, if indeed there be any—I have certainly heard no comment yet from them—who have come here, not to be entertained but to learn; that is, to any gay apprentice in the magical art who may have chosen this specimen of the prestidigitatory genus to study this evening in the hope of grasping more clearly just how the artistic contraption works, of observing some fresh detail in the complex process by which the heady wine of amusement is distilled from the grape of composition. The rest of you I must beg for a little while to sit back and relax as the remarks I have now to make do not concern you; your turn will follow later.

* * *

So, strange young man,—it is at his command, remember, that I say this to you; whether I agree with it or not is neither here nor there—you have decided on the conjurer's profession. Somewhere, in the middle of a salt marsh or at the bottom of a kitchen garden or on the top of a bus, you heard imprisoned Ariel call for help, and it is now a liberator's face that congratulates you from your shaving mirror every morning. As you walk the cold streets hatless, or sit over coffee and doughnuts in the corner of a cheap restaurant, your secret has already set you apart from the howling merchants and transacting multitudes to watch with fascinated distaste the bellowing barging banging passage of the awkward profit-seeking elbow, the dazed eye of the gregarious acquisitive condition. Lying awake at night in your single bed you are conscious of a power by which you will survive the wallpaper of your boardinghouse or the expensive bourgeois horrors of your home. Yes, Ariel is grateful; He does come when you call, He does tell you all the gossip He overhears on the stairs, all the goings-on He observes through the keyhole; He really is willing to arrange anything you care to ask for, and you are rapidly finding out the right orders to give—who should be killed in the hunting accident, which couple to send into the cast-iron shelter, what scent will arouse a Norwegian engineer, how to get the young hero from the country lawyer's office to the Princess' reception, when to mislay the letter, where the cabinet minister should be reminded of his mother, why the dishonest valet must be a martyr to indigestion but immune from the common cold.

As the gay productive months slip by, in spite of fretful discouraged days, of awkward moments of misunderstanding or rather, seen retrospectively as happily cleared up and got over, verily because of them, you are definitely getting the hang of this, at first so novel and bewildering, relationship between magician and familiar, whose duty it is to sustain your infinite conceptual appetite with vivid concrete experiences. And, as the months turn into years, your wonder-working romance into an economic habit, the encountered case of good or evil in our wide world of property and boredom which leaves you confessedly and unsympathetically at a loss, the aberrant phase in the whole human cycle of ecstasy and exhaustion with which you are imperfectly familiar, become increasingly rare. No perception however petite, no notion however subtle, escapes your attention or baffles your understanding: on entering any room you immediately distinguish the wasters who throw away their fruit half-eaten from the preservers who bottle all the summer; as the passengers file down the ship's gangway you unerringly guess which suitcase contains indecent novels; a five-minute chat about the weather or the coming elections is all you require to diagnose any distemper, however self-assured, for by then your eye has already spotted the tremor of the lips in that infinitesimal moment while the lie was getting its balance, your ear already picked up the heart's low whimper which the capering legs were determined to stifle, your nose detected on love's breath the trace of ennui which foretells his early death, or the despair just starting to smoulder at the base of the scholar's brain which years hence will suddenly blow it up with one appalling laugh: in every case you can prescribe the saving treatment called for, knowing at once when it may be gentle and remedial, when all that is needed is soft music and a pretty girl, and when it must be drastic and surgical, when nothing will do any good but political disgrace or financial and erotic failure. If I seem to attribute these powers to you when the eyes, the ears, the nose, the putting two and two together are, of course, all His, and yours only the primitive wish to know, it is a rhetorical habit I have caught from your, in the main juvenile and feminine, admirers whose naive unawareness of whom they ought properly to thank and praise you see no point in, for mere accuracy's stuffy sake, correcting.

Anyway, the partnership is a brilliant success. On you go together to ever greater and faster triumphs; ever more major grows the accumulated work, ever more masterly the manner, sound even at its pale sententious worst, and at its best the rich red personal flower of the grave and grand, until one day which you can never either at the time or later identify exactly, your strange fever reaches its crisis and from now on begins, ever so slowly, maybe to subside. At first you cannot tell what or why is the matter; you have only a vague feeling that it is no longer between you so smooth and sweet as it used to be. Sour silences appear, at first only for an occasional moment, but progressively more frequently and more prolonged, curdled moods in which you cannot for the life of you think of any request to make, and His dumb standing around, waiting for orders gets inexplicably but maddeningly on your nerves, until presently, to your amazement, you hear yourself asking Him if He wouldn't like a vacation and are shocked by your feeling of intense disappointment when He who has always hitherto so immediately and recklessly taken your slightest hint, says gauchely "No." So it goes on from exasperated bad to desperate worst until you realise in despair that there is nothing for it but you two to part. Collecting all your strength for the distasteful task, you finally manage to stammer or shout "You are free. Good-bye," but to your dismay He whose obedience through all the enchanted years has never been less than perfect, now refuses to budge. Striding up to Him in fury, you glare into His unblinking eyes and stop dead, transfixed with horror at seeing reflected there, not what you had always expected to see, a conqueror smiling at a conqueror, both promising mountains and marvels, but a gibbering fist-clenched creature with which you are all too unfamiliar, for this is the first time indeed that you have met the only subject that you have, who is not a dream amenable to magic but the all too solid flesh you must acknowledge as your own; at last you have come face to face with me, and are appalled to learn how far I am from being, in any sense, your dish; how completely lacking in that poise and calm and all-forgiving because all-understanding good nature which to the critical eye is so wonderfully and domestically present on every page of your published inventions.

But where, may I ask, should I have acquired them, when, like a society mother who, although she is, of course, as she tells everyone, absolutely *devoted* to her child, simply *cannot* leave the dinner table just now and really *must* be in Le Touquet to-morrow, and so leaves him in charge of servants she doesn't know or boarding schools she has never seen, you have never in all these years taken the faintest personal interest in me? "Oh!" you protestingly gasp, "but how can you say such a thing, after I've toiled and moiled and worked my fingers to the bone, trying to give you a good home, after all the hours I've spent planning wholesome nourishing meals for you, after all the things I've gone without so that you should have swimming lessons and piano lessons and a new bicycle. Have I ever let you go out in summer without your sun hat, or come in in winter without feeling your stockings and insisting, if they were the least bit damp, on your changing them at once? Haven't you always been allowed to do everything, in reason, that you liked?

Exactly: even deliberate ill-treatment would have been less unkind. Gallows and battlefields are, after all, no less places of mutual concern than sofa and bridal-bed; the dashing flirtations of fighter pilots and the coy tactics of twirled moustache and fluttered fan, the gasping mudcaked wooing of the coarsest foes and the reverent rage of the highest-powered romance, the lover's nip and the grip of the torturer's tongs are all,—ask Ariel,—variants of one common type, the bracket within which life and death with such passionate gusto cohabit, to be distinguished solely by the plus or minus sign which stands before them, signs which He is able at any time and in either direction to switch, but the one exception, the sum no magic of His can ever transmute, is the indifferent zero. Had you tried to destroy me, had we wrestled through long dark hours, we might by daybreak have learnt something from each other; in some panting pause to recover breath for further more savage blows or in the moment before your death or mine, we might both have heard together that music which explains and pardons all.

Had you, on the other hand, really left me alone to go my whole free-wheeling way to disorder, to be drunk every day before lunch, to jump stark naked from bed to bed, to have a fit every week or a major operation every other year, to forge checks or water the widow's stock, I might, after countless skids and punctures have come by the bumpy third-class road of guilt and remorse, smack into that very same truth which you were meanwhile admiring from your distant comfortable veranda but would never point out to me.

Such genuine escapades, though, might have disturbed the master at his meditations and even involved him in trouble with the police. The strains of oats, therefore, that you prudently permitted me to sow were each and all of an unmitigatedly minor wildness: a quick cold clasp now and then in some *louche* hotel to calm me down while you got on with the so thorough documentation of your great unhappy love for one who by being bad or dead or married provided you with the Good Right Subject that would never cease to bristle with importance; one bout of flu per winter, an occasional twinge of toothache, and enough tobacco to keep me in a good temper while you composed your melting eclogues of rustic piety; licence to break my shoelaces, spill soup on my tie, burn cigarette holes in the tablecloth, lose letters and borrowed books, and generally keep myself busy while you polished to a perfection your lyric praises of the more candid, more luxurious world to come.

Can you wonder then, when, as was bound to happen sooner or later, your charms, because they no longer amuse you, have cracked and your spirits, because you are tired of giving orders, have ceased to obey, and you are left alone with me, the dark thing you could never abide to be with, if I do not yield you kind answer or admire you for the achievements I was never allowed to profit from, if I resent hearing you speak of your neglect of me as your "exile," of the pains you never took with me as "all lost"?

But why continue? From now on we shall have, as we both know only too well, no company but each other's, and if I have had, as I consider, a good deal to put up with from you, I must own that, after all, I am not just the person I would have chosen for a life companion myself; so the only chance, which in any case is slim enough, of my getting a tolerably new master and you a tolerably new man, lies in our both learning, if possible and as soon as possible, to forgive and forget the past, and to keep our respective hopes for the future within moderate, very moderate, limits.

* * *

And now at last it is you, assorted, consorted specimens of the general popular type, the major flock who have trotted trustingly hither but found, you reproachfully baah, no grazing, that I turn to and address on behalf of Ariel and myself. To your questions I shall attempt no direct reply, for the mere fact that you have been able so anxiously to put them is in itself sufficient proof that you possess their answers. All your clamour signifies is this: that your first big crisis, the breaking of the childish spell in which, so long as it enclosed you, there was, for you, no mirror, no magic, for everything that happened was a miracle—it was just as extraordinary for a chair to be a chair as for it to turn into a horse; it was no more absurd that the girding on of coal-scuttle and poker should transform you into noble Hector than that you should have a father and mother who called you Tommy—and it was therefore only necessary for you to presuppose one genius, one unrivalled I to wish these wonders in all their endless plenitude and novelty to be, is, in relation to your present, behind, that your singular transparent globes of enchantment have shattered one by one, and you have now all come together in the larger colder emptier room on this side of the mirror which *does* force your eyes to recognise and reckon with the two of us, your ears to detect the irreconcilable difference between my reiterated affirmation of what your furnished circumstances categorically are, and His successive propositions as to everything else which they conditionally might be. You have, as I say, taken your first step.

The Journey of life—the down-at-heels disillusioned figure can still put its characterisation across—is infinitely long and its possible destinations infinitely distant from one another, but the time spent in actual travel is infinitesimally small. The hours the traveller measures are those in which he is at rest between the three or four decisive instants of transportation which are all he needs and all he gets to carry him the whole of his way; the scenery he observes is the view, gorgeous or drab, he glimpses from platform and siding; the incidents he thrills or blushes to remember take place in waiting and washrooms, ticket queues and parcels offices: it is in those promiscuous places of random association, in that air of anticipatory fidget, that he makes friends and enemies, that he promises, confesses, kisses, and betrays until, either because it is the one he has been expecting, or because, losing his temper, he has vowed to take the first to come along, or because he has been given a free ticket, or simply by misdirection or mistake, a train arrives which he does get into: it whistles—at least he thinks afterwards he remembers it whistling—but before he can blink, it has come to a standstill again and there he stands clutching his battered bags, surrounded by entirely strange smells and noises—yet in their smelliness and noisiness how familiar—one vast important stretch the nearer Nowhere, that still smashed terminus at which he will, in due course, be deposited, seedy and by himself.

Yes, you have made a definite start; you *have* left your homes way back in the farming provinces or way out in the suburban tundras, but whether you have been hanging around for years or have barely and breathlessly got here on one of those locals which keep arriving minute after minute, this is still only the main depot, the Grandly Average Place from which at odd hours the expresses leave seriously and sombrely for Somewhere, and where it is still possible for me to posit the suggestion that you go no farther. You will never, after all, feel better than in your present shaved and breakfasted state which there are restaurants and barber shops here indefinitely to preserve; you will never feel more secure than you do now in your knowledge that you *have* your ticket, your passport *is* in order, you have *not* forgotten to pack your pyjamas and an extra clean shirt; you will never have the same opportunity of learning about *all* the holy delectable spots of current or historic interest—an insistence on reaching *one* will necessarily exclude the others—than you have in these bepostered halls; you will never meet a jollier, more various crowd than you see around you here, sharing with you the throbbing, suppressed excitement of those to whom the exciting thing is still, perhaps, to happen. But once you leave, no matter in which direction, your next stop will be far outside this land of habit that so democratically stands up for your right to stagestruck hope, and well inside one of those, all equally foreign, uncomfortable and despotic, certainties of failure or success. Here at least I, and Ariel too, are free to warn you not, should we meet again there, to speak to either of us, not to engage either of us as your guide, but there we shall no longer be able to refuse you; then, unfortunately for you, we shall be compelled to say nothing and obey your fatal foolish commands. Here, whether you listen to me or not, and it's highly improbable that you will, I can at least warn you what will happen if at our next meeting you should insist—and that is all too probable—on putting one of us in charge.

* * *

"Release us," you will beg, then, supposing it is I whom you make for,—oh how awfully uniform, once one translates them out of your private lingoes of expression, all your sorrows are and how awfully well I know them—"release us from our minor roles. Carry me back, Master, to the cathedral town where the canons run through the water meadows with butterfly nets and the old women keep sweetshops in the cobbled side streets, or back to the upland mill town (gunpowder and plush) with its grope-movie and its poolroom lit by gas, carry me back to the days before my wife had put on weight, back to the years when beer was cheap and the rivers really froze in winter. Pity me, Captain, pity a poor old stranded sea-salt whom an unlucky voyage has wrecked on the desolate mahogany coast of this bar with nothing left him but his big moustache. Give me my passage home, let me see that harbour once again just as it was before I learned the bad words. Patriarchs wiser than Abraham mended their nets on the modest wharf; white and wonderful beings undressed on the sand-dunes; sunset glittered on the plate-glass windows of the Marine Biological Station; far off on the extreme horizon a whale spouted. Look, Uncle, look. They have broken my glasses and I have lost my silver whistle. Pick me up, Uncle, let little Johnny ride away on your massive shoulders to recover his green kingdom, where the steam rollers are as friendly as the farm dogs and it would never become necessary to look over one's left shoulder or clench one's right fist in one's pocket. You cannot miss it. Black currant bushes hide the ruined opera house where badgers are said to breed in great numbers; an old horse-tramway winds away westward through suave foot-hills crowned with stone circles—follow it and by nightfall one would come to a large good-natured waterwheel—to the north, beyond a forest inhabited by charcoal burners, one can see the Devil's Bedposts quite distinctly, to the east the museum where for sixpence one can touch the ivory chessman. O Cupid, Cupid, howls the whole dim chorus, take us home. We have never felt really well in this climate of distinct ideas; we have never been able to follow the regulations properly; Business, Science, Religion, Art, and all the other fictitious immortal persons who matter here have, frankly, not been very kind. We're so, so tired, the rewarding soup is stone cold, and over our blue wonders the grass grew long ago. O take us home with you, strong and swelling One, home to your promiscuous pastures where the minotaur of authority is just a roly-poly ruminant and nothing is at stake, those purring sites and amusing vistas where the fluctuating arabesques of sound, the continuous eruption of colours and scents, the whole rich incoherence of a nature made up of gaps and asymmetrical events plead beautifully and bravely for our undistress."

And in that very moment when you so cry for deliverance from any and every anxious possibility, I shall have no option but to be faithful to my oath of service and instantly transport you, not indeed to any cathedral town or mill town or harbour or hillside or jungle or other specific Eden which your memory necessarily but falsely conceives of as the ultimately liberal condition, which in point of fact you have never known yet, but directly to that downright state itself. Here you are. This is it. Directly overhead a full moon casts a circle of dazzling light without any penumbra, exactly circumscribing its desolation in which every object is extraordinarily still and sharp. Cones of extinct volcanoes rise up abruptly from the lava plateau fissured by chasms and pitted with hot springs from which steam rises without interruption straight up into the windless rarefied atmosphere. Here and there a geyser erupts without warning, spouts furiously for a few seconds and as suddenly subsides. Here, where the possessive note is utterly silent and all events are tautological repetitions and no decision will ever alter the secular stagnation, at long last you are, as you have asked to be, the only subject. Who, When, Why, the poor tired little historic questions fall wilting into a hush of utter failure. Your tears splash down upon clinkers which will never be persuaded to recognise a neighbour and there is really and truly no one to appear with tea and help. You have indeed come all the way to the end of your bachelor's journey where Liberty stands with her hands behind her back, not caring, not minding *anything*. Confronted by a straight and snubbing stare to which mythology is bosh, surrounded by an infinite passivity and purely arithmetical disorder which is only open to perception, and with nowhere to go on to, your existence is indeed free at last to choose its own meaning, that is, to plunge headlong into despair and fall through silence fathomless and dry, all fact your single drop, all value your pure alas.

* * *

But what of that other, smaller, but doubtless finer group among you, important persons at the top of the ladder, exhausted lions of the season, local authorities with their tense tired faces, elderly hermits of both sexes living gloomily in the delta of a great fortune, whose *amour propre* prefers to turn for help to my more spiritual colleague.

"O yes," you will sigh, "we have had what once we would have called success. I moved the vices out of the city into a chain of re-conditioned lighthouses. I introduced statistical methods into the Liberal Arts. I revived the country dances and installed electric stoves in the mountain cottages. I saved democracy by buying steel. I gave the caesura its freedom. But this world is no better and it is now quite clear to us that there is nothing to be done with such a ship of fools, adrift on a sugarloaf sea in which it is going very soon and suitably to founder. Deliver us, dear Spirit, from the tantrums of our telephones and the whispers of our secretaries conspiring against Man; deliver us from these helpless agglomerations of dishevelled creatures with their bed-wetting, vomiting, weeping bodies, their giggling, fugitive, disappointing hearts, and scrawling, blotted, misspelt minds, to whom we have so foolishly tried to bring the light they did not want; deliver us from all the litter of *billets-doux*, empty beer bottles, laundry lists, directives, promissory notes and broken toys, the terrible mess that this particularised life, which we have so futilely attempted to tidy, sullenly insists on leaving behind it; translate us, bright Angel, from this hell of inert and ailing matter, growing steadily senile in a time for ever immature, to that blessed realm, so far above the twelve impertinent winds and the four unreliable seasons, that Heaven of the Really General Case where, tortured no longer by three dimensions and immune from temporal vertigo, Life turns into Light, absorbed for good into the permanently stationary, completely self-sufficient, absolutely reasonable One."

Obliged by the terms of His contract to gratify this other request of yours, the wish for freedom to transcend *any* condition, for direct unentailed power without *any*, however secretly immanent, obligation to inherit or transmit, what can poor shoulder-shrugging Ariel do but lead you forthwith into a nightmare which has all the wealth of exciting action and all the emotional poverty of an adventure story for boys, a state of perpetual emergency and everlasting improvisation where all is need and change.

All the phenomena of an empirically ordinary world are given. Extended objects appear to which events happen—old men catch dreadful coughs, little girls get their arms twisted, flames run whooping through woods, round a river bend, as harmless looking as a dirty old bearskin rug, comes the gliding fury of a town-effacing wave, but these are merely elements in an allegorical landscape to which mathematical measurement and phenomenological analysis have no relevance.

All the voluntary movements are possible—crawling through flues and old sewers, sauntering past shop-fronts, tiptoeing through quicksands and mined areas, running through derelict factories and across empty plains, jumping over brooks, diving into pools or swimming along between banks of roses, pulling at manholes or pushing at revolving doors, clinging to rotten balustrades, sucking at straws or wounds; all the modes of transport, letters, oxcarts, canoes, hansom cabs, trains, trolleys, cars, aeroplanes, balloons, are available, but any sense of direction, any knowledge of where on earth one has come from or where on earth one is going to is completely absent.

Religion and culture seem to be represented by a catholic belief that something is lacking which must be found, but as to what that something is, the keys of heaven, the missing heir, genius, the smells of childhood, or a sense of humour, why it is lacking, whether it has been deliberately stolen, or accidentally lost or just hidden for a lark, and who is responsible, our ancestors, ourselves, the social structure, or mysterious wicked powers, there are as many faiths as there are searchers, and clues can be found behind every clock, under every stone, and in every hollow tree to support all of them.

Again, other selves undoubtedly exist, but though everyone's pocket is bulging with birth certificates, insurance policies, passports and letters of credit, there is no way of proving whether they are genuine or planted or forged, so that no one knows whether another is his friend disguised as an enemy or his enemy disguised as a friend (there is probably no one whose real name is Brown), or whether the police who here as elsewhere are grimly busy, are crushing a criminal revolt or upholding a vicious tyranny, any more than he knows whether he himself is a victim of the theft, or the thief, or a rival thief, a professionally interested detective or a professionally impartial journalist.

Even the circumstances of the tender passion, the long-distance calls, the assignation at the aquarium, the farewell embrace under the fish-tail burner on the landing, are continually present, but since, each time it goes through its performance, it never knows whether it is saving a life, or obtaining secret information, or forgetting or spiting its real love, the heart feels nothing but a dull percussion of conceptual foreboding. Everything, in short, suggests Mind but, surrounded by an infinite extension of the adolescent difficulty, a rising of the subjective and subjunctive to ever steeper, stormier heights, the panting frozen expressive gift has collapsed under the strain of its communicative anxiety, and contributes nothing by way of meaning but a series of staccato barks or a delirious gush of glossolalia.

And from this nightmare of public solitude, this everlasting Not Yet, what relief have you but in an ever giddier collective gallop, with bisson eye and bevel course, toward the grey horizon of the bleaker vision, what landmarks but the four dead rivers, the Joyless, the Flaming, the Mournful, and the Swamp of Tears, what goal but the black stone on which the bones are cracked, for only there in its cry of agony can your existence find at last an unequivocal meaning and your refusal to be yourself become a serious despair, the love nothing, the fear all?

* * *

Such are the alternative routes, the facile glad-handed highway or the virtuous averted track, by which the human effort to make its own fortune arrives all eager at its abruptly dreadful end. I have tried—the opportunity was not to be neglected—to raise the admonitory forefinger, to ring the alarming bell, but with so little confidence of producing the right result, so certain that the open eye and attentive ear will always interpret any sight and any sound to their advantage, every rebuff as a consolation, every prohibition as a rescue—that is what they open and attend for—that I find myself almost hoping, for your sake, that I have had the futile honour of addressing the blind and the deaf.

Having learnt his language, I begin to feel something of the serio-comic embarrassment of the dedicated dramatist, who, in representing to you your condition of estrangement from the truth, is doomed to fail the more he succeeds, for the more truthfully he paints the condition, the less clearly can he indicate the truth from which it is estranged, the brighter his revelation of the truth in its order, its justice, its joy, the fainter shows his picture of your actual condition in all its drabness and sham, and, worse still, the more sharply he defines the estrangement itself—and, ultimately, what other aim and justification has he, what else exactly *is* the artistic gift which he is forbidden to hide, if not to make you unforgettably conscious of the ungarnished offended gap between what you so questionably are and what you are commanded without any question to become, of the unqualified No that opposes your every step in any direction?—the more he must strengthen your delusion that an awareness of the gap is in itself a bridge, your interest in your imprisonment a release, so that, far from your being led by him to contrition and surrender, the regarding of your defects in his mirror, your dialogue, using his words, with yourself about yourself, becomes the one activity which never, like devouring or collecting or spending, lets you down, the one game which can be guaranteed, whatever the company, to catch on, a madness of which you can only be cured by some shock quite outside his control, an unpredictable misting over of his glass or an absurd misprint in his text.

Our unfortunate dramatist, therefore, is placed in the unseemly predicament of having to give all his passion, all his skill, all his time to the task of "doing" life—consciously to give anything less than all would be a gross betrayal of his gift and an unpardonable presumption—as if it lay in *his* power to solve this dilemma—yet of having at the same time to hope that some unforeseen mishap will intervene to ruin his effect, without, however, obliterating your disappointment, the expectation aroused by him that there was an effect to ruin, that, if the smiling interest never did arrive, it must, through no fault of its own, have got stuck somewhere; that, exhausted, ravenous, delayed by fog, mobbed and mauled by a thousand irrelevancies, it has, nevertheless, not forgotten its promise but is still trying desperately to get a connection.

Beating about for some large loose image to define the original drama which aroused his imitative passion, the first performance in which the players were their own audience, the worldly stage on which their behaving flesh was really sore and sorry—for the floods of tears were not caused by onions, the deformities and wounds did not come off after a good wash, the self-stabbed heroine could not pick herself up again to make a gracious bow nor her seducer go demurely home to his plain and middle-aged spouse—the fancy immediately flushed is of the greatest grandest opera rendered by a very provincial touring company indeed.

Our performance—for Ariel and I are, you know this now, just as deeply involved as any of you—which we were obliged, all of us, to go on with and sit through right to the final dissonant chord, has been so indescribably inexcusably awful. Sweating and shivering in our moth-eaten ill-fitting stock costumes which, with only a change of hat and re-arrangement of safety-pins, had to do for the *landsknecht* and the Parisian art-student, bumping into, now a rippling palace, now a primeval forest full of holes, at cross purposes with the scraping bleating orchestra we could scarcely hear for half the instruments were missing and the cottage piano which was filling-out must have stood for too many years in some damp parlour, we floundered on from fiasco to fiasco, the schmalz tenor never quite able at his big moments to get right up nor the ham bass right down, the stud contralto gargling through her maternal grief, the ravished coloratura trilling madly off-key and the re-united lovers half a bar apart, the knock-kneed armies shuffling limply through their bloody battles, the unearthly harvesters hysterically entangled in their honest fugato.

Now it is over. No, we have not dreamt it. Here we really stand, down stage with red faces and no applause; no effect, however simple, no piece of business, however unimportant, came off; there was not a single aspect of our whole production, not even the huge stuffed bird of happiness, for which a kind word could, however patronisingly, be said.

Yet, at this very moment when we do at last see ourselves as we are, neither cosy nor playful, but swaying out on the ultimate wind-whipped cornice that overhangs the unabiding void—we have never stood anywhere else,—when our reasons are silenced by the heavy huge derision,—There is nothing to say. There never has been,—and our wills chuck in their hands—There is no way out. There never was,—it is at this moment that for the first time in our lives we hear, not the sounds which, as born actors, we have hitherto condescended to use as an excellent vehicle for displaying our personalities and looks, but the real Word which is our only *raison d'être*. Not that we have improved; everything, the massacres, the whippings, the lies, the twaddle, and all their carbon copies are still present, more obviously than ever; nothing has been reconstructed; our shame, our fear, our incorrigible staginess, all wish and no resolve, are still, and more intensely than ever, all we have: only now it is not in spite of them but with them that we are blessed by that Wholly Other Life from which we are separated by an essential emphatic gulf of which our contrived fissures of mirror and proscenium arch—we understand them at last—are feebly figurative signs, so that all our meanings are reversed and it is precisely in its negative image of Judgement that we can positively envisage Mercy; it is just here, among the ruins and the bones, that we may rejoice in the perfected Work which is not ours. Its great coherences stand out through our secular blur in all their overwhelmingly righteous obligation; its voice speaks through our muffling banks of artificial flowers and unflinchingly delivers its authentic molar pardon; its spaces greet us with all their grand old prospect of wonder and width; the working charm is the full bloom of the unbothered state; the sounded note is the restored relation.

Postscript

(Ariel to Caliban. Echo by the Prompter)

Weep no more but pity me,
Fleet persistent shadow cast
By your lameness, caught at last,
Helplessly in love with you,
Elegance, art, fascination,
  Fascinated by
  Drab mortality;
Spare me a humiliation,
  To your faults be true:
I can sing as you reply
                    . . . I

Wish for nothing lest you mar
The perfection in these eyes
Whose entire devotion lies
At the mercy of your will;
Tempt not your sworn comrade,—only
  As I am can I
  Love you as you are—
For my company be lonely
  For my health be ill:
I will sing if you will cry
                    . . . I

Never hope to say farewell,
For our lethargy is such
Heaven's kindness cannot touch
Nor earth's frankly brutal drum;
This was long ago decided,
  Both of us know why,
  Can, alas, foretell,
When our falsehoods are divided,
  What we shall become,
One evaporating sigh

. . . *I*

August 1942-February 1944

61

Noon

How still it is; the horses
Have moved into the shade, the mothers
Have followed their migrating gardens.

Curlews on kettle moraines
Foretell the end of time,
The doom of paradox.

But lovelorn sighs ascend
From wretched greedy regions
Which cannot include themselves.

And the freckled orphan flinging
Ducks and drakes at the pond
Stops looking for stones,

And wishes he were a steamboat,
Or Lugalzaggisi the loud
Tyrant of Erech and Umma.

from "The Age of Anxiety": ? 1945

62

Lament for a Lawgiver

Sob, heavy world,
Sob as you spin
Mantled in mist, remote from the happy:
The washerwomen have wailed all night,
The disconsolate clocks are crying together,
And the bells toll and toll
For tall Agrippa who touched the sky:
Shut is that shining eye
Which enlightened the lampless and lifted up
The flat and foundering, reformed the weeds
Into civil cereals and sobered the bulls;
Away the cylinder seal,
The didactic digit and dreaded voice
Which imposed peace on the pullulating
Primordial mess. Mourn for him now,
Our lost dad,
Our colossal father.

For seven cycles
For seven years
Past vice and virtue, surviving both,
Through pluvial periods, paroxysms
Of wind and wet, through whirlpools of heat,
And comas of deadly cold,
On an old white horse, an ugly nag,
In his faithful youth he followed
The black ball as it bowled downhill
On the spotted spirit's spiral journey,
Its purgative path to that point of rest
Where longing leaves it, and saw
Shimmering in the shade the shrine of gold,
The magical marvel no man dare touch,
Between the towers the tree of life
And the well of wishes,
The waters of joy.

Then he harrowed hell,
Healed the abyss
Of torpid instinct and trifling flux,
Laundered it, lighted it, made it lovable with
Cathedrals and theories; thanks to him
Brisker smells abet us,
Cleaner clouds accost our vision
And honest sounds our ears.
For he ignored the Nightmares and annexed their ranges,
Put the clawing Chimaeras in cold storage,
Berated the Riddle till it roared and fled,
Won the Battle of Whispers,
Stopped the Stupids, stormed into
The Fumblers' Forts, confined the Sulky
To their drab ditches and drove the Crashing
Bores to their bogs,
Their beastly moor.

In the high heavens,
The ageless places,
The gods are wringing their great worn hands
For their watchman is away, their world-engine
Creaking and cracking. Conjured no more
By his master music to wed
Their truths to times, the Eternal Objects
Drift about in a daze:
O the lepers are loose in Lombard Street,
The rents are rising in the river basins,
The insects are angry. Who will dust
The cobwebbed kingdoms now?
For our lawgiver lies below his people,
Bigger bones of a better kind,
Unwarped by their weight, as white limestone
Under green grass,
The grass that fades.

from "The Age of Anxiety": ? 1946

63

Under Which Lyre

A Reactionary Tract for the Times

(PHI BETA KAPPA POEM, HARVARD, 1946)

Ares at last has quit the field,
The bloodstains on the bushes yield
        To seeping showers,
And in their convalescent state
The fractured towns associate
        With summer flowers.

Encamped upon the college plain
Raw veterans already train
        As freshman forces;
Instructors with sarcastic tongue
Shepherd the battle-weary young
        Through basic courses.

Among bewildering appliances
For mastering the arts and sciences
        They stroll or run,
And nerves that never flinched at slaughter
Are shot to pieces by the shorter
        Poems of Donne.

Professors back from secret missions
Resume their proper eruditions,
        Though some regret it;
They liked their dictaphones a lot,
They met some big wheels, and do not
        Let you forget it.

But Zeus' inscrutable decree
Permits the will-to-disagree
        To be pandemic,

Ordains that vaudeville shall preach
And every commencement speech
        Be a polemic.

Let Ares doze, that other war
Is instantly declared once more
        'Twixt those who follow
Precocious Hermes all the way
And those who without qualms obey
        Pompous Apollo.

Brutal like all Olympic games,
Though fought with smiles and Christian names
        And less dramatic,
This dialectic strife between
The civil gods is just as mean,
        And more fanatic.

What high immortals do in mirth
Is life and death on Middle Earth;
        Their a-historic
Antipathy forever gripes
All ages and somatic types,
        The sophomoric

Who face the future's darkest hints
With giggles or with prairie squints
        As stout as Cortez,
And those who like myself turn pale
As we approach with ragged sail
        The fattening forties.

The sons of Hermes love to play,
And only do their best when they
        Are told they oughtn't;
Apollo's children never shrink
From boring jobs but have to think
        Their work important.

Related by antithesis,
A compromise between us is
    Impossible;
Respect perhaps but friendship never:
Falstaff the fool confronts forever
    The prig Prince Hal.

If he would leave the self alone,
Apollo's welcome to the throne,
    Fasces and falcons;
He loves to rule, has always done it;
The earth would soon, did Hermes run it,
    Be like the Balkans.

But jealous of our god of dreams,
His common-sense in secret schemes
    To rule the heart;
Unable to invent the lyre,
Creates with simulated fire
    Official art.

And when he occupies a college,
Truth is replaced by Useful Knowledge;
    He pays particular
Attention to Commercial Thought,
Public Relations, Hygiene, Sport,
    In his curricula.

Athletic, extrovert and crude,
For him, to work in solitude
    Is the offence,
The goal a populous Nirvana:
His shield bears this device: *Mens sana*
    Qui mal y pense.

Today his arms, we must confess,
From Right to Left have met success,
    His banners wave

From Yale to Princeton, and the news
From Broadway to the Book Reviews
    Is very grave.

His radio Homers all day long
In over-Whitmanated song
    That does not scan,
With adjectives laid end to end,
Extol the doughnut and commend
    The Common Man.

His, too, each homely lyric thing
On sport or spousal love or spring
    Or dogs or dusters,
Invented by some court-house bard
For recitation by the yard
    In filibusters.

To him ascend the prize orations
And sets of fugal variations
    On some folk-ballad,
While dietitians sacrifice
A glass of prune-juice or a nice
    Marsh-mallow salad.

Charged with his compound of sensational
Sex plus some undenominational
    Religious matter,
Enormous novels by co-eds
Rain down on our defenceless heads
    Till our teeth chatter.

In fake Hermetic uniforms
Behind our battle-line, in swarms
    That keep alighting,
His existentialists declare
That they are in complete despair,
    Yet go on writing.

No matter; He shall be defied;
White Aphrodite is on our side:
What though his threat
To organize us grow more critical?
Zeus willing, we, the unpolitical,
Shall beat him yet.

Lone scholars, sniping from the walls
Of learned periodicals,
Our facts defend,
Our intellectual marines,
Landing in little magazines
Capture a trend.

By night our student Underground
At cocktail parties whisper round
From ear to ear;
Fat figures in the public eye
Collapse next morning, ambushed by
Some witty sneer.

In our morale must lie our strength:
So, that we may behold at length
Routed Apollo's
Battalions melt away like fog,
Keep well the Hermetic Decalogue,
Which runs as follows:—

Thou shalt not do as the dean pleases,
Thou shalt not write thy doctor's thesis
On education,
Thou shalt not worship projects nor
Shalt thou or thine bow down before
Administration.

Thou shalt not answer questionnaires
Or quizzes upon World-Affairs,
Nor with compliance

Take any test. Thou shalt not sit
With statisticians nor commit
A social science.

Thou shalt not be on friendly terms
With guys in advertising firms,
Nor speak with such
As read the Bible for its prose,
Nor, above all, make love to those
Who wash too much.

Thou shalt not live within thy means
Nor on plain water and raw greens.
If thou must choose
Between the chances, choose the odd;
Read *The New Yorker*, trust in God;
And take short views.

1946

64

The Fall of Rome

(FOR CYRIL CONNOLLY)

The piers are pummelled by the waves;
In a lonely field the rain
Lashes an abandoned train;
Outlaws fill the mountain caves.

Fantastic grow the evening gowns;
Agents of the Fisc pursue
Absconding tax-defaulters through
The sewers of provincial towns.

Private rites of magic send
The temple prostitutes to sleep;
All the literati keep
An imaginary friend.

Cerebrotonic Cato may
Extoll the Ancient Disciplines,
But the muscle-bound Marines
Mutiny for food and pay.

Caesar's double-bed is warm
As an unimportant clerk
Writes *I DO NOT LIKE MY WORK*
On a pink official form.

Unendowed with wealth or pity,
Little birds with scarlet legs,
Sitting on their speckled eggs,
Eye each flu-infected city.

Altogether elsewhere, vast
Herds of reindeer move across
Miles and miles of golden moss,
Silently and very fast.

January 1947

65

In Praise of Limestone

If it form the one landscape that we the inconstant ones
  Are consistently homesick for, this is chiefly
Because it dissolves in water. Mark these rounded slopes
  With their surface fragrance of thyme and beneath
A secret system of caves and conduits; hear these springs
  That spurt out everywhere with a chuckle

Each filling a private pool for its fish and carving
    Its own little ravine whose cliffs entertain
The butterfly and the lizard; examine this region
    Of short distances and definite places:
What could be more like Mother or a fitter background
    For her son, for the nude young male who lounges
Against a rock displaying his dildo, never doubting
    That for all his faults he is loved, whose works are but
Extensions of his power to charm? From weathered outcrop
    To hill-top temple, from appearing waters to
Conspicuous fountains, from a wild to a formal vineyard,
    Are ingenious but short steps that a child's wish
To receive more attention than his brothers, whether
    By pleasing or teasing, can easily take.

Watch, then, the band of rivals as they climb up and down
    Their steep stone gennels in twos and threes, sometimes
Arm in arm, but never, thank God, in step; or engaged
    On the shady side of a square at midday in
Voluble discourse, knowing each other too well to think
    There are any important secrets, unable
To conceive a god whose temper-tantrums are moral
    And not to be pacified by a clever line
Or a good lay: for, accustomed to a stone that responds,
    They have never had to veil their faces in awe
Of a crater whose blazing fury could not be fixed;
    Adjusted to the local needs of valleys
Where everything can be touched or reached by walking,
    Their eyes have never looked into infinite space
Through the lattice-work of a nomad's comb; born lucky,
    Their legs have never encountered the fungi
And insects of the jungle, the monstrous forms and lives
    With which we have nothing, we like to hope, in common.
So, when one of them goes to the bad, the way his mind works
    Remains comprehensible: to become a pimp
Or deal in fake jewelry or ruin a fine tenor voice
    For effects that bring down the house could happen to all
But the best and the worst of us . . .

That is why, I suppose,
The best and worst never stayed here long but sought
Immoderate soils where the beauty was not so external,
The light less public and the meaning of life
Something more than a mad camp. "Come!" cried
the granite wastes,
"How evasive is your humor, how accidental
Your kindest kiss, how permanent is death." (Saints-to-be
Slipped away sighing.) "Come!" purred the clays and gravels,
"On our plains there is room for armies to drill; rivers
Wait to be tamed and slaves to construct you a tomb
In the grand manner: soft as the earth is mankind and both
Need to be altered." (Intendant Caesars rose and
Left, slamming the door.) But the really reckless were fetched
By an older colder voice, the oceanic whisper:
"I am the solitude that asks and promises nothing;
That is how I shall set you free. There is no love;
There are only the various envies, all of them sad."

They were right, my dear, all those voices were right
And still are; this land is not the sweet home that it looks,
Nor its peace the historical calm of a site
Where something was settled once and for all: A backward
And dilapidated province, connected
To the big busy world by a tunnel, with a certain
Seedy appeal, is that all it is now? Not quite:
It has a worldly duty which in spite of itself
It does not neglect, but calls into question
All the Great Powers assume; it disturbs our rights. The poet,
Admired for his earnest habit of calling
The sun the sun, his mind Puzzle, is made uneasy
By these solid statues which so obviously doubt
His antimythological myth; and these gamins,
Pursuing the scientist down the tiled colonnade
With such lively offers, rebuke his concern for Nature's
Remotest aspects: I, too, am reproached, for what
And how much you know. Not to lose time, not to get caught,
Not to be left behind, not, please! to resemble

The beasts who repeat themselves, or a thing like water
   Or stone whose conduct can be predicted, these
Are our Common Prayer, whose greatest comfort is music
   Which can be made anywhere, is invisible,
And does not smell. In so far as we have to look forward
   To death as a fact, no doubt we are right: But if
Sins can be forgiven, if bodies rise from the dead,
   These modifications of matter into
Innocent athletes and gesticulating fountains,
   Made solely for pleasure, make a further point:
The blessed will not care what angle they are regarded from,
   Having nothing to hide. Dear, I know nothing of
Either, but when I try to imagine a faultless love
   Or the life to come, what I hear is the murmur
Of underground streams, what I see is a limestone landscape.

May 1948

66

Song

Deftly, admiral, cast your fly
   Into the slow deep hover,
Till the wise old trout mistake and die;
   Salt are the deeps that cover
   The glittering fleets you led,
      White is your head.

Read on, ambassador, engrossed
   In your favourite Stendhal;
The Outer Provinces are lost,
   Unshaven horsemen swill
   The great wines of the Châteaux
      Where you danced long ago.

Do not turn, do not lift, your eyes
  Toward the still pair standing
On the bridge between your properties,
  Indifferent to your minding:
  In its glory, in its power,
    This is their hour.

Nothing your strength, your skill, could do
  Can alter their embrace
Or dispersuade the Furies who
  At the appointed place
  With claw and dreadful brow
    Wait for them now.

June 1948

67

A Walk After Dark

A cloudless night like this
Can set the spirit soaring;
After a tiring day
The clockwork spectacle is
Impressive in a slightly boring
Eighteenth-century way.

It soothed adolescence a lot
To meet so shameless a stare;
The things I did could not
Be as shocking as they said
If that would still be there
After the shocked were dead.

Now, unready to die
But already at the stage
When one starts to dislike the young,

I am glad those points in the sky
May also be counted among
The creatures of middle-age.

It's cosier thinking of night
As more an Old People's Home
Than a shed for a faultless machine,
That the red pre-Cambrian light
Is gone like Imperial Rome
Or myself at seventeen.

Yet however much we may like
The stoic manner in which
The classical authors wrote,
Only the young and the rich
Have the nerve or the figure to strike
The lacrimae rerum note.

For the present stalks abroad
Like the past and its wronged again
Whimper and are ignored,
And the truth cannot be hid;
Somebody chose their pain,
What needn't have happened did.

Occurring this very night
By no established rule,
Some event may already have hurled
Its first little No at the right
Of the laws we accept to school
Our post-diluvian world:

But the stars burn on overhead,
Unconscious of final ends,
As I walk home to bed,
Asking what judgement waits
My person, all my friends,
And these United States.

August 1948

68

Memorial for the City

In the self-same point that our soul is made sensual, in the self-same point is the City of God ordained to him from without beginning.

Juliana of Norwich

I

The eyes of the crow and the eye of the camera open
Onto Homer's world, not ours. First and last
They magnify earth, the abiding
Mother of gods and men; if they notice either
It is only in passing: gods behave, men die,
Both feel in their own small way, but She
Does nothing and does not care,
She alone is seriously there.

The crow on the crematorium chimney
And the camera roving the battle
Record a space where time has no place.
On the right a village is burning, in a market-town to the left
The soldiers fire, the mayor bursts into tears,
The captives are led away, while far in the distance
A tanker sinks into a dedolent sea.
That is the way things happen; for ever and ever
Plum-blossom falls on the dead, the roar of the waterfall covers
The cries of the whipped and the sighs of the lovers
And the hard bright light composes
A meaningless moment into an eternal fact
Which a whistling messenger disappears with into a defile:
One enjoys glory, one endures shame;
He may, she must. There is no one to blame.

The steady eyes of the crow and the camera's candid eye
See as honestly as they know how, but they lie.
The crime of life is not time. Even now, in this night
Among the ruins of the Post-Virgilian City
Where our past is a chaos of graves
                                        and the barbed-wire stretches ahead
Into our future till it is lost to sight,
Our grief is not Greek: As we bury our dead
We know without knowing there is reason for what we bear,
That our hurt is not a desertion, that we are to pity
Neither ourselves nor our city;
Whoever the searchlights catch,
                                whatever the loudspeakers blare,
We are not to despair.

II

Alone in a room Pope Gregory whispered his name
  While the Emperor shone on a centreless world
From wherever he happened to be; the New City rose
  Upon their opposition, the yes and no
Of a rival allegiance; the sword, the local lord
  Were not all; there was home and Rome;
Fear of the stranger was lost on the way to the shrine.

The facts, the acts of the City bore a double meaning:
  Limbs became hymns; embraces expressed in jest
A more permanent tie; infidel faces replaced
  The family foe in the choleric's nightmare;
The children of water parodied in their postures
  The infinite patience of heaven;
Those born under Saturn felt the gloom of the day of doom.

Scribes and innkeepers prospered; suspicious tribes combined
  To rescue Jerusalem from a dull god,
And disciplined logicians fought to recover thought
  From the eccentricities of the private brain
For the Sane City; framed in her windows, orchards, ports,
  Wild beasts, deep rivers and dry rocks
Lay nursed on the smile of a merciful Madonna.

In a sandy province Luther denounced as obscene
  The machine that so smoothly forgave and saved
If paid; he announced to the Sinful City a grinning gap
  No rite could cross; he abased her before the Grace:
Henceforth division was also to be her condition;
  Her conclusions were to include doubt,
Her loves were to bear with her fear; insecure, she endured.

Saints tamed, poets acclaimed the raging herod of the will;
  The groundlings wept as on a secular stage
The grand and the bad went to ruin in thundering verse;
  Sundered by reason and treason the City
Found invisible ground for concord in measured sound,
  While wood and stone learned the shameless
Games of man, to flatter, to show off, be pompous, to romp.

Nature was put to the question in the Prince's name;
  She confessed, what he wished to hear, that she had no soul;
Between his scaffold and her coldness the restrained style,
  The ironic smile became the worldly and devout,
Civility a city grown rich: in his own snob way
  The unarmed gentleman did his job
As a judge to her children, as a father to her forests.

In a national capital Mirabeau and his set
  Attacked mystery; the packed galleries roared
And history marched to the drums of a clear idea,
  The aim of the Rational City, quick to admire,
Quick to tire: she used up Napoleon and threw him away;
  Her pallid affected heroes
Began their hectic quest for the prelapsarian man.

The deserts were dangerous, the waters rough, their clothes
  Absurd but, changing their Beatrices often,
Sleeping little, they pushed on, raised the flag of the Word
  Upon lawless spots denied or forgotten
By the fear or the pride of the Glittering City;
  Guided by hated parental shades,
They invaded and harrowed the hell of her natural self.

Chimeras mauled them, they wasted away with the spleen,
  Suicide picked them off, sunk off Cape Consumption,
Lost on the Tosspot Seas, wrecked on the Gibbering Isles
  Or trapped in the ice of despair at the Soul's Pole,
They died, unfinished, alone; but now the forbidden,
  The hidden, the wild outside were known:
Faithful without faith, they died for the Conscious City.

III

Across the square,
Between the burnt-out Law Courts and Police Headquarters,
Past the Cathedral far too damaged to repair,
Around the Grand Hotel patched up to hold reporters,
  Near huts of some Emergency Committee,
  The barbed wire runs through the abolished City.

Across the plains,
Between two hills, two villages, two trees, two friends,
The barbed wire runs which neither argues nor explains
But where it likes a place, a path, a railroad ends,
  The humor, the cuisine, the rites, the taste,
  The pattern of the City, are erased.

Across our sleep
The barbed wire also runs: It trips us so we fall
And white ships sail without us though the others weep,
It makes our sorry fig-leaf at the Sneerers Ball,
  It ties the smiler to the double bed,
  It keeps on growing from the witch's head.

Behind the wire
Which is behind the mirror, our Image is the same
Awake or dreaming: It has no image to admire,
No age, no sex, no memory, no creed, no name,
  It can be counted, multiplied, employed
  In any place, at any time destroyed.

Is It our friend?
No; that is our hope; that we weep and It does not grieve,
That for It the wire and the ruins are not the end:
This is the flesh we are but never would believe,
The flesh we die but it is death to pity;
This is Adam waiting for His City.

Let Our Weakness speak

IV

Without me Adam would have fallen irrevocably with Lucifer;
he would never have been able to cry *O felix culpa.*
It was I who suggested his theft to Prometheus; my frailty
cost Adonis his life.
I heard Orpheus sing; I was not quite as moved as they say.
I was not taken in by the sheep's-eyes of Narcissus; I was
angry with Psyche when she struck a light.
I was in Hector's confidence; so far as it went.
Had he listened to me Oedipus would never have left Corinth;
I cast no vote at the trial of Orestes.
I fell asleep when Diotima spoke of love; I was not responsible
for the monsters which tempted St. Anthony.
To me the Saviour permitted His Fifth Word from the cross;
to be a stumbling-block to the stoics.
I was the unwelcome third at the meetings of Tristan with
Isolda; they tried to poison me.
I rode with Galahad on his Quest for the San Graal; without
understanding I kept his vow.
I was the just impediment to the marriage of Faustus with
Helen; I know a ghost when I see one.
With Hamlet I had no patience; but I forgave Don Quixote all
for his admission in the cart.
I was the missing entry in Don Giovanni's list; for which he
could never account.
I assisted Figaro the Barber in all his intrigues; when Prince
Tamino arrived at wisdom I too obtained my
reward.
I was innocent of the sin of the Ancient Mariner; time after
time I warned Captain Ahab to accept happiness.

As for Metropolis, that too-great city; her delusions are not
mine.
Her speeches impress me little, her statistics less; to all who
dwell on the public side of her mirrors resentments
and no peace.
At the place of my passion her photographers are gathered
together; but I shall rise again to hear her judged.

June 1949

69

Under Sirius

Yes, these are the dog-days, Fortunatus:
The heather lies limp and dead
On the mountain, the baltering torrent
Shrunk to a soodling thread;
Rusty the spears of the legion, unshaven its captain,
Vacant the scholar's brain
Under his great hat,
Drug as she may the Sibyl utters
A gush of table-chat.

And you yourself with a head-cold and upset stomach,
Lying in bed till noon,
Your bills unpaid, your much advertised
Epic not yet begun,
Are a sufferer too. All day, you tell us, you wish
Some earthquake would astonish
Or the wind of the Comforter's wing
Unlock the prisons and translate
The slipshod gathering.

And last night, you say, you dreamed
of that bright blue morning,

The hawthorn hedges in bloom,
When, serene in their ivory vessels,
The three wise Maries come,
Sossing through seamless waters, piloted in
By sea-horse and fluent dolphin:
Ah! how the cannons roar,
How jocular the bells as They
Indulge the peccant shore.

It is natural to hope and pious, of course, to believe
That all in the end shall be well,
But first of all, remember,
So the Sacred Books foretell,
The rotten fruit shall be shaken. Would your hope make sense
If today were that moment of silence
Before it break and drown
When the insurrected eagre hangs
Over the sleeping town?

How will you look and what will you do when the basalt
Tombs of the sorcerers shatter
And their guardian megalopods
Come after you pitter-patter?
How will you answer when from their qualming spring
The immortal nymphs fly shrieking
And out of the open sky
The pantocratic riddle breaks—
"Who are you and why?"

For when in a carol under the apple-trees
The reborn featly dance,
There will also, Fortunatus,
Be those who refused their chance,
Now pottering shades, querulous beside the salt-pits,
And mawkish in their wits,
To whom these dull dog-days
Between event seem crowned with olive
And golden with self-praise.

1949

70

Fleet Visit

The sailors come ashore
Out of their hollow ships,
Mild-looking middle-class boys
Who read the comic strips;
One baseball game is more
To them than fifty Troys.

They look a bit lost, set down
In this unamerican place
Where natives pass with laws
And futures of their own;
They are not here because
But only just-in-case.

The whore and ne'er-do-well
Who pester them with junk
In their grubby ways at least
Are serving the Social Beast;
They neither make nor sell—
No wonder they get drunk.

But the ships on the dazzling blue
Of the harbor actually gain
From having nothing to do;
Without a human will
To tell them whom to kill
Their structures are humane

And, far from looking lost,
Look as if they were meant
To be pure abstract design
By some master of pattern and line,
Certainly worth every cent
Of the millions they must have cost.

1951

71

The Shield of Achilles

She looked over his shoulder
  For vines and olive trees,
Marble well-governed cities,
  And ships upon untamed seas,
But there on the shining metal
  His hands had put instead
An artificial wilderness
  And a sky like lead.

A plain without a feature, bare and brown,
  No blade of grass, no sign of neighborhood,
Nothing to eat and nowhere to sit down,
  Yet, congregated on its blankness, stood
  An unintelligible multitude,
A million eyes, a million boots in line,
Without expression, waiting for a sign.

Out of the air a voice without a face
  Proved by statistics that some cause was just
In tones as dry and level as the place:
  No one was cheered and nothing was discussed;
  Column by column in a cloud of dust
They marched away enduring a belief
Whose logic brought them, somewhere else, to grief.

She looked over his shoulder
  For ritual pieties,
White flower-garlanded heifers,
  Libation and sacrifice,
But there on the shining metal
  Where the altar should have been,
She saw by his flickering forge-light
  Quite another scene.

Barbed wire enclosed an arbitrary spot
  Where bored officials lounged (one cracked a joke)
And sentries sweated, for the day was hot:
  A crowd of ordinary decent folk
  Watched from without and neither moved nor spoke
As three pale figures were led forth and bound
To three posts driven upright in the ground.

The mass and majesty of this world, all
  That carries weight and always weighs the same,
Lay in the hands of others; they were small
  And could not hope for help and no help came:
  What their foes liked to do was done, their shame
Was all the worst could wish; they lost their pride
And died as men before their bodies died.

She looked over his shoulder
  For athletes at their games,
Men and women in a dance
  Moving their sweet limbs
Quick, quick, to music,
  But there on the shining shield
His hands had set no dancing-floor
  But a weed-choked field.

A ragged urchin, aimless and alone,
  Loitered about that vacancy; a bird
Flew up to safety from his well-aimed stone:
  That girls are raped, that two boys knife a third,
  Were axioms to him, who'd never heard
Of any world where promises were kept
Or one could weep because another wept.

The thin-lipped armorer,
  Hephaestos, hobbled away;
Thetis of the shining breasts
  Cried out in dismay

At what the god had wrought
  To please her son, the strong
Iron-hearted man-slaying Achilles
  Who would not live long.

1952

72

The Willow-Wren and the Stare

A starling and a willow-wren,
  On a may-tree by a weir,
Saw them meet and heard him say:
  "Dearest of my dear,
More lively than these waters chortling
  As they leap the dam,
My sweetest duck, my precious goose,
  My white lascivious lamb."
With a smile she listened to him,
  Talking to her there:
What does he want? said the willow-wren;
  Much too much, said the stare.

"Forgive these loves who dwell in me,
  These brats of greed and fear,
The honking bottom-pinching clown,
  The snivelling sonneteer,
That so, between us, even these,
  Who till the grave are mine,
For all they fall so short of may,
  Dear heart, be still a sign."
With a smile she closed her eyes,
  Silent she lay there:
Does he mean what he says? said the willow-wren;
  Some of it, said the stare.

"Hark! Wild Robin winds his horn
And, as his notes require,
Now our laughter-loving spirits
Must in awe retire
And let their kinder partners,
Speechless with desire,
Go in their holy selfishness,
Unfunny to the fire."
Smiling, silently she threw
Her arms about him there:
Is it only that? said the willow-wren;
It's that as well, said the stare.

Waking in her arms he cried,
Utterly content:
"I have heard the high good noises,
Promoted for an instant,
Stood upon the shining outskirts
Of that Joy I thank
For you, my dog and every goody."
There on the grass bank
She laughed, he laughed, they laughed together,
Then they ate and drank:
Did he know what he meant? said the willow-wren;
God only knows, said the stare.

1953

73

Nocturne

Make this night loveable,
Moon, and with eye single
Looking down from up there,
Bless me, One especial
And friends everywhere.

With a cloudless brightness
Surround our absences;
Innocent be our sleeps,
Watched by great still spaces,
White hills, glittering deeps.

Parted by circumstance,
Grant each your indulgence
That we may meet in dreams
For talk, for dalliance,
By warm hearths, by cool streams.

Shine lest tonight any,
In the dark suddenly,
Wake alone in a bed
To hear his own fury
Wishing his love were dead.

October 1953

74

Bucolics

I Winds

(FOR ALEXIS LEGER)

  Deep below our violences,
Quite still, lie our First Dad, his watch
  And many little maids,
But the boneless winds that blow
  Round law-court and temple
Recall to Metropolis
  That Pliocene Friday when,

At His holy insufflation
  (Had He picked a teleost
Or an arthropod to inspire,
  Would our death also have come?),
One bubble-brained creature said—
  "I am loved, therefore I am"—:
And well by now might the lion
  Be lying down with the kid,
Had he stuck to that logic.

  Winds make weather; weather
Is what nasty people are
  Nasty about and the nice
Show a common joy in observing:
  When I seek an image
For our Authentic City
  (Across what brigs of dread,
Down what gloomy galleries,
  Must we stagger or crawl
Before we may cry—O look!?),
  I see old men in hallways
Tapping their barometers,
  Or a lawn over which,
The first thing after breakfast,
  A paterfamilias
Hurries to inspect his rain-gauge.

Goddess of winds and wisdom,
  When, on some windless day
Of dejection, unable
  To name or to structure,
Your poet with bodily tics,
  Scratching, tapping his teeth,
Tugging the lobe of an ear,
  Unconsciously invokes You,
Show Your good nature, allow
  Rooster or whistling maid

To fetch him Arthur O'Bower;
　Then, if moon-faced Nonsense,
That erudite forger, stalk
　Through the seven kingdoms,
Set Your poplars a-shiver
　To warn Your clerk lest he
Die like an Old Believer
　For some spurious reading:
And in all winds, no matter
　Which of Your twelve he may hear,
Equinox gales at midnight
　Howling through marram grass,
Or a faint susurration
　Of pines on a cloudless
Afternoon in midsummer,
　Let him feel You present,
That every verbal rite
　May be fittingly done,
And done in anamnesis
　Of what is excellent
Yet a visible creature,
　Earth, Sky, a few dear names.

September 1953

II Woods

(FOR NICOLAS NABOKOV)

Sylvan meant savage in those primal woods
Piero di Cosimo so loved to draw,
Where nudes, bears, lions, sows with women's heads
Mounted and murdered and ate each other raw,
Nor thought the lightning-kindled bush to tame
But, flabbergasted, fled the useful flame.

Reduced to patches owned by hunting squires
Of villages with ovens and stocks,
They whispered still of most unsocial fires,

Though Crown and Mitre warned their silly flocks
The pasture's humdrum rhythms to approve
And to abhor the license of the grove.

Guilty intention still looks for a hotel
That wants no details and surrenders none;
A wood is that, and throws in charm as well,
And many a semi-innocent, undone,
Has blamed its nightingales who round the deed
Sang with such sweetness of a happy greed.

Those birds, of course, did nothing of the sort,
And, as for sylvan nature, if you take
A snapshot at a picnic, O how short
And lower-ordersy the Gang will look
By those vast lives that never took another
And are not scared of gods, ghosts, or stepmother.

Among these coffins of its by-and-by
The Public can (it cannot on a coast)
Bridle its skirt-and-bargain-chasing eye,
And where should an austere philologist
Relax but in the very world of shade
From which the matter of his field was made.

Old sounds re-educate an ear grown coarse,
As Pan's green father suddenly raps out
A burst of undecipherable Morse,
And cuckoos mock in Welsh, and doves create
In rustic English over all they do
To rear their modern family of two.

Now here, now there, some loosened element,
A fruit in vigor or a dying leaf,
Utters its private idiom for descent,
And late man, listening through his latter grief,
Hears, close or far, the oldest of his joys,
Exactly as it was, the water noise.

A well-kempt forest begs Our Lady's grace;
Someone is not disgusted, or at least
Is laying bets upon the human race
Retaining enough decency to last;
The trees encountered on a country stroll
Reveal a lot about that country's soul.

A small grove massacred to the last ash,
An oak with heart-rot, give away the show:
This great society is going smash;
They cannot fool us with how fast they go,
How much they cost each other and the gods!
A culture is no better than its woods.

August 1952

III Mountains

(FOR HEDWIG PETZOLD)

I know a retired dentist who only paints mountains,
But the Masters seldom care
That much, who sketch them in beyond a holy face
Or a highly dangerous chair;
While a normal eye perceives them as a wall
Between worse and better, like a child, scolded in France,
Who wishes he were crying on the Italian side of the Alps:
Caesar does not rejoice when high ground
Makes a darker map,
Nor does Madam. Why should they? A serious being
Cries out for a gap.

And it is curious how often in steep places
You meet someone short who frowns,
A type you catch beheading daisies with a stick:
Small crooks flourish in big towns,
But perfect monsters—remember Dracula—
Are bred on crags in castles; those unsmiling parties,

Clumping off at dawn in the gear of their mystery
For points up, are a bit alarming;
They have the balance, nerve
And habit of the Spiritual, but what God
Does their Order serve?

A civil man is a citizen. Am I
To see in the Lake District, then,
Another bourgeois invention like the piano?
Well, I won't. How can I, when
I wish I stood now on a platform at Penrith,
Zurich, or any junction at which you leave the express
For a local that swerves off soon into a cutting? Soon
Tunnels begin, red farms disappear,
Hedges turn to walls,
Cows become sheep, you smell peat or pinewood, you hear
Your first waterfalls,

And what looked like a wall turns out to be a world
With measurements of its own
And a style of gossip. To manage the Flesh,
When angels of ice and stone
Stand over her day and night who make it so plain
They detest any kind of growth, does not encourage
Euphemisms for the effort: here wayside crucifixes
Bear witness to a physical outrage,
And serenades too
Stick to bare fact:—"O my girl has a goitre,
I've a hole in my shoe!"

Dour. Still, a fine refuge. That boy behind his goats
Has the round skull of a clan
That fled with bronze before a tougher metal.
And that quiet old gentleman
With a cheap room at the Black Eagle used to own
Three papers but is not received in Society now:

These farms can always see a panting government coming;
I'm nordic myself, but even so
I'd much rather stay
Where the nearest person who could have me hung is
Some ridges away.

To be sitting in privacy, like a cat
On the warm roof of a loft,
Where the high-spirited son of some gloomy tarn
Comes sprinting down through a green croft,
Bright with flowers laid out in exquisite splodges
Like a Chinese poem, while, near enough, a real darling
Is cooking a delicious lunch, would keep me happy for
What? Five minutes? For an uncatlike
Creature who has gone wrong,
Five minutes on even the nicest mountain
Is awfully long.

? July 1952

IV Lakes

(FOR ISAIAH BERLIN)

A lake allows an average father, walking slowly,
To circumvent it in an afternoon,
And any healthy mother to halloo the children
Back to her bedtime from their games across:
(Anything bigger than that, like Michigan or Baikal,
Though potable, is an "estranging sea").

Lake-folk require no fiend to keep them on their toes;
They leave aggression to ill-bred romantics
Who duel with their shadows over blasted heaths:
A month in a lacustrine atmosphere
Would find the fluvial rivals waltzing not exchanging
The rhyming insults of their great-great-uncles.

No wonder Christendom did not get really started
  Till, scarred by torture, white from caves and jails,
Her pensive chiefs converged on the Ascanian Lake
  And by that stork-infested shore invented
The life of Godhead, making catholic the figure
  Of three small fishes in a triangle.

Sly Foreign Ministers should always meet beside one,
  For, whether they walk widdershins or deasil,
Its path will yoke their shoulders to one liquid centre
  Like two old donkeys pumping as they plod;
Such physical compassion may not guarantee
  A marriage for their armies, but it helps.

Only a very wicked or conceited man,
  About to sink somewhere in mid-Atlantic,
Could think Poseidon's frown was meant for him in person,
  But it is only human to believe
The little lady of the glacier lake has fallen
  In love with the rare bather whom she drowns.

The drinking water of the city where one panics
  At nothing noticing how real one is
May come from reservoirs whose guards are all too conscious
  Of being followed: Webster's cardinal
Saw in a fish-pool something horrid with a hay-rake;
  I know a Sussex hammer-pond like that.

A haunted lake is sick, though; normally, they doctor
  Our tactile fevers with a visual world
Where beaks are dumb like boughs and faces safe like houses;
  The water-scorpion finds it quite unticklish,
And, if it shudder slightly when caressed by boats,
  It never asks for water or a loan.

Liking one's Nature, as lake-lovers do, benign
  Goes with a wish for savage dogs and man-traps:
One Fall, one dispossession, is enough, I'm sorry;

Why should I give Lake Eden to the Nation
Just because every mortal Jack and Jill has been
The genius of some amniotic mere?

It is unlikely I shall ever keep a swan
Or build a tower on any small tombolo,
But that's not going to stop me wondering what sort
Of lake I would decide on if I should.
Moraine, pot, oxbow, glint, sink, crater, piedmont, dimple . . . ?
Just reeling off their names is ever so comfy.

? September 1952

V Islands

(FOR GIOCONDO SACCHETTI)

Old saints on millstones float with cats
To islands out at sea,
Whereon no female pelvis can
Threaten their agape.

Beyond the long arm of the Law,
Close to a shipping road,
Pirates in their island lairs
Observe the pirate code.

Obsession with security
In Sovereigns prevails;
His Highness and The People both
Pick islands for their jails.

Once, where detected worldlings now
Do penitential jobs,
Exterminated species played
Who had not read their Hobbes.

His continental damage done,
   Laid on an island shelf,
Napoleon has five years more
   To talk about himself.

How fascinating is that class
   Whose only member is Me!
Sappho, Tiberius and I
   Hold forth beside the sea.

What is cosier than the shore
   Of a lake turned inside out?
How do all these other people
   Dare to be about?

In democratic nudity
   Their sexes lie; except
By age or weight you could not tell
   The keeping from the kept.

They go, she goes, thou goest, I go
   To a mainland livelihood:
Farmer and fisherman complain
   The other has it good.

? August 1953

VI Plains

(FOR WENDELL JOHNSON)

I can imagine quite easily ending up
   In a decaying port on a desolate coast,
Cadging drinks from the unwary, a quarrelsome,
   Disreputable old man; I can picture
A second childhood in a valley, scribbling
   Reams of edifying and unreadable verse;
But I cannot see a plain without a shudder:—
   "O God, please, please, don't ever make me live there!"

It's horrible to think what peaks come down to,
That pecking rain and squelching glacier defeat
Tall pomps of stone where goddesses lay sleeping,
Dreaming of being woken by some chisel's kiss,
That what those blind brutes leave when they are through is nothing
But a mere substance, a clay that meekly takes
The potter's cuff, a gravel that as concrete
Will unsex any space which it encloses.

And think of growing where all elsewheres are equal!
So long as there's a hill-ridge somewhere the dreamer
Can place his land of marvels; in poor valleys
Orphans can head downstream to seek a million:
Here nothing points; to choose between Art and Science
An embryo genius would have to spin a stick.
What could these farms do if set loose but drift like clouds?
What goal of unrest is there but the Navy?

Romance? Not in this weather. Ovid's charmer
Who leads the quadrilles in Arcady, boy-lord
Of hearts who can call their Yes and No their own,
Would, madcap that he is, soon die of cold or sunstroke:
These lives are in firmer hands; that old grim She
Who makes the blind dates for the hatless genera
Creates their country matters. (Woe to the child-bed,
Woe to the strawberries if She's in Her moods!)

And on these attend, greedy as fowl and harsher
Than any climate, Caesar with all his They.
If a tax-collector disappear in the hills,
If, now and then, a keeper is shot in the forest,
No thunder follows, but where roads run level,
How swift to the point of protest strides the Crown.
It hangs, it flogs, it fines, it goes. There is drink.
There are wives to beat. But Zeus is with the strong,

Born as a rule in some small place (an island,
  Quite often, where a smart lad can spot the bluff
Whence cannon would put the harbor at his mercy),
  Though it is here they chamber with Clio. At this brook
The Christian cross-bow stopped the Heathen scimitar;
  Here is a windmill whence an emperor saw
His right wing crumple; across these cabbage fields
  A pretender's Light Horse made their final charge.

If I were a plainsman I should hate us all,
  From the mechanic rioting for a cheap loaf
To the fastidious palate, hate the painter
  Who steals my wrinkles for his Twelve Apostles,
Hate the priest who cannot even make it shower.
  What could I smile at as I trudged behind my harrow
But bloodshot images of rivers screaming,
  Marbles in panic, and Don't-Care made to care?

As it is, though, I know them personally
  Only as a landscape common to two nightmares:
Across them, spotted by spiders from afar,
  I have tried to run, knowing there was no hiding and no help;
On them, in brilliant moonlight, I have lost my way
  And stood without a shadow at the dead centre
Of an abominable desolation,
  Like Tarquin ravished by his post-coital sadness.

Which goes to show I've reason to be frightened
  Not of plains, of course, but of me. I should like
—Who wouldn't?—to shoot beautifully and be obeyed
  (I should also like to own a cave with two exits);
I wish I weren't so silly. Though I can't pretend
  To think these flats poetic, it's as well at times
To be reminded that nothing is lovely,
  Not even in poetry, which is not the case.

? July 1953

VII Streams

(FOR ELIZABETH DREW)

Dear water, clear water, playful in all your streams,
As you dash or loiter through life who does not love
To sit beside you, to hear you and see you,
Pure being, perfect in music and movement?

Air is boastful at times, earth slovenly, fire rude,
But you in your bearing are always immaculate,
The most well-spoken of all the older
Servants in the household of Mrs. Nature.

Nobody suspects you of mocking him, for you still
Use the same vocables you were using the day
Before that unexpected row which
Downed every hod on half-finished Babel,

And still talk to yourself: nowhere are you disliked;
Arching your torso, you dive from a basalt sill,
Canter across white chalk, slog forward
Through red marls, the aboriginal pilgrim,

At home in all sections, but for whom we should be
Idolaters of a single rock, kept apart
By our landscapes, excluding as alien
The tales and diets of all other strata.

How could we love the absent one if you did not keep
Coming from a distance, or quite directly assist,
As when past Iseult's tower you floated
The willow pash-notes of wanted Tristram?

And *Homo Ludens*, surely, is your child, who make
Fun of our feuds by opposing identical banks,
Transferring the loam from Huppim
To Muppim and back each time you crankle.

Growth cannot add to your song: as unchristened brooks
Already you whisper to ants what, as Brahma's son,
Descending his titanic staircase
Into Assam, to Himalayan bears you thunder.

And not even man can spoil you: his company
Coarsens roses and dogs but, should he herd
you through a sluice
To toil at a turbine, or keep you
Leaping in gardens for his amusement,

Innocent still is your outcry, water, and there
Even, to his soiled heart raging at what it is,
Tells of a sort of world, quite other,
Altogether different from this one

With its envies and passports, a polis like that
To which, in the name of scholars everywhere,
Gaston Paris pledged his allegiance
As Bismarck's siege-guns came within earshot.

Lately, in that dale of all Yorkshire's the loveliest,
Where, off its fell-side helter-skelter, Kisdon Beck
Jumps into Swale with a boyish shouting,
Sprawled out on grass, I dozed for a second,

And found myself following a croquet tournament
In a calm enclosure with thrushes popular:
Of all the players in that cool valley
The best with the mallet was my darling.

While, on the wolds that begirdled it, wild old men
Hunted with spades and hammers, monomaniac each,
For a megalith or a fossil,
And bird-watchers stalked the mossy beech-woods.

Suddenly, over the lawn we started to run
For, lo, through the trees in a cream and golden coach
Drawn by two baby locomotives,
The god of mortal doting approached us,

Flanked by his bodyguard, those hairy armigers in green
Who laugh at thunderstorms and weep at a blue sky:
    He thanked us for our cheers of homage,
  And promised X and Y a passion undying.

With a wave of his torch he commanded a dance;
So round in a ring we flew, my dear on my right,
    When I awoke. But fortunate seemed that
  Day because of my dream and enlightened,

And dearer, water, than ever your voice, as if
Glad—though goodness knows why—to run with
                                        the human race,
    Wishing, I thought, the least of men their
  Figures of splendor, their holy places.

? July 1953

75

Horae Canonicae

"Immolatus vicerit"

I Prime

Simultaneously, as soundlessly,
  Spontaneously, suddenly
As, at the vaunt of the dawn, the kind
  Gates of the body fly open
To its world beyond, the gates of the mind,
  The horn gate and the ivory gate,
Swing to, swing shut, instantaneously
  Quell the nocturnal rummage

Of its rebellious fronde, ill-favored,
  Ill-natured and second-rate,
Disenfranchised, widowed and orphaned
  By an historical mistake:
Recalled from the shades to be a seeing being,
  From absence to be on display,
Without a name or history I wake
  Between my body and the day.

Holy this moment, wholly in the right,
  As, in complete obedience
To the light's laconic outcry, next
  As a sheet, near as a wall,
Out there as a mountain's poise of stone,
  The world is present, about,
And I know that I am, here, not alone
  But with a world, and rejoice
Unvexed, for the will has still to claim
  This adjacent arm as my own,
The memory to name me, resume
  Its routine of praise and blame,
And smiling to me is this instant while
  Still the day is intact, and I
The Adam sinless in our beginning,
  Adam still previous to any act.

I draw breath; that is of course to wish
  No matter what, to be wise,
To be different, to die and the cost,
  No matter how, is Paradise
Lost of course and myself owing a death:
  The eager ridge, the steady sea,
The flat roofs of the fishing village
  Still asleep in its bunny,
Though as fresh and sunny still, are not friends
  But things to hand, this ready flesh
No honest equal but my accomplice now,
  My assassin to be, and my name

Stands for my historical share of care
  For a lying self-made city,
Afraid of our living task, the dying
  Which the coming day will ask.

1949

II Terce

After shaking paws with his dog
(Whose bark would tell the world that he is always kind),
  The hangman sets off briskly over the heath;
He does not know yet who will be provided
  To do the high works of Justice with:
Gently closing the door of his wife's bedroom
  (Today she has one of her headaches),
With a sigh the judge descends his marble stair;
  He does not know by what sentence
He will apply on earth the Law that rules the stars:
  And the poet, taking a breather
Round his garden before starting his eclogue,
  Does not know whose Truth he will tell.

Sprites of hearth and store-room, godlings
Of professional mysteries, the Big Ones
  Who can annihilate a city,
Cannot be bothered with this moment: we are left,
  Each to his secret cult, now each of us
Prays to an image of his image of himself:
  "Let me get through this coming day
Without a dressing down from a superior,
  Being worsted in a repartee,
Or behaving like an ass in front of the girls;
  Let something exciting happen,
Let me find a lucky coin on a sidewalk,
  Let me hear a new funny story."

At this hour we all might be anyone:
It is only our victim who is without a wish,
Who knows already (that is what
We can never forgive. If he knows the answers,
Then why are we here, why is there even dust?),
Knows already that, in fact, our prayers are heard,
That not one of us will slip up,
That the machinery of our world will function
Without a hitch, that today, for once,
There will be no squabbling on Mount Olympus,
No Chthonian mutters of unrest,
But no other miracle, knows that by sundown
We shall have had a good Friday.

October 1953

III Sext

1

You need not see what someone is doing
to know if it is his vocation,

you have only to watch his eyes:
a cook mixing a sauce, a surgeon

making a primary incision,
a clerk completing a bill of lading,

wear the same rapt expression,
forgetting themselves in a function.

How beautiful it is,
that eye-on-the-object look.

To ignore the appetitive goddesses,
to desert the formidable shrines

of Rhea, Aphrodite, Demeter, Diana,
to pray instead to St. Phocas,

St. Barbara, San Saturnino,
or whoever one's patron is,

that one may be worthy of their mystery,
what a prodigious step to have taken.

There should be monuments, there should be odes,
to the nameless heroes who took it first,

to the first flaker of flints
who forgot his dinner,

the first collector of sea-shells
to remain celibate.

Where should we be but for them?
Feral still, un-housetrained, still

wandering through forests without
a consonant to our names,

slaves of Dame Kind, lacking
all notion of a city

and, at this noon, for this death,
there would be no agents.

2

You need not hear what orders he is giving
to know if someone has authority,

you have only to watch his mouth:
when a besieging general sees

a city wall breached by his troops,
when a bacteriologist

realizes in a flash what was wrong
with his hypothesis, when,

from a glance at the jury, the prosecutor
knows the defendant will hang,

their lips and the lines around them
relax, assuming an expression,

not of simple pleasure at getting
their own sweet way but of satisfaction

at being right, an incarnation
of *Fortitudo, Justicia, Nous.*

You may not like them much
(who does?) but we owe them

basilicas, divas,
dictionaries, pastoral verse,

the courtesies of the city:
without these judicial mouths

(which belong for the most part
to very great scoundrels)

how squalid existence would be,
tethered for life to some hut village,

afraid of the local snake
or the local ford demon,

speaking the local patois
of some three hundred words

(think of the family squabbles and the
poison-pens, think of the inbreeding)

and, at this noon, there would be no authority
to command this death.

3

Anywhere you like, somewhere
on broad-chested life-giving Earth,

anywhere between her thirstlands
and undrinkable Ocean,

the crowd stands perfectly still,
its eyes (which seem one) and its mouths

(which seem infinitely many)
expressionless, perfectly blank.

The crowd does not see (what everyone sees)
a boxing match, a train wreck,

a battleship being launched,
does not wonder (as everyone wonders)

who will win, what flag she will fly,
how many will be burned alive,

is never distracted
(as everyone is always distracted)

by a barking dog, a smell of fish,
a mosquito on a bald head:

the crowd sees only one thing
(which only the crowd can see),

an epiphany of that
which does whatever is done.

Whatever god a person believes in,
in whatever way he believes

(no two are exactly alike),
as one of the crowd he believes

and only believes in that
in which there is only one way of believing.

Few people accept each other and most
will never do anything properly,

but the crowd rejects no one, joining the crowd
is the only thing all men can do.

Only because of that can we say
all men are our brothers,

superior, because of that,
to the social exoskeletons: When

have they ever ignored their queens,
for one second stopped work

on their provincial cities, to worship
The Prince of this world like us,

at this noon, on this hill,
in the occasion of this dying.

Spring 1954

IV Nones

What we know to be not possible,
  Though time after time foretold
By wild hermits, by shaman and sybil
  Gibbering in their trances,
Or revealed to a child in some chance rhyme
  Like *will* and *kill*, comes to pass
Before we realize it: we are surprised
  At the ease and speed of our deed

And uneasy: It is barely three,
  Mid-afternoon, yet the blood
Of our sacrifice is already
  Dry on the grass; we are not prepared
For silence so sudden and so soon;
  The day is too hot, too bright, too still,
Too ever, the dead remains too nothing.
  What shall we do till nightfall?

The wind has dropped and we have lost our public.
  The faceless many who always
Collect when any world is to be wrecked,
  Blown up, burnt down, cracked open,
Felled, sawn in two, hacked through, torn apart,
  Have all melted away: not one
Of these who in the shade of walls and trees
  Lie sprawled now, calmly sleeping,
Harmless as sheep, can remember why
  He shouted or what about
So loudly in the sunshine this morning;
  All if challenged would reply
—"It was a monster with one red eye,
  A crowd that saw him die, not I."—
The hangman has gone to wash, the soldiers to eat:
  We are left alone with our feat.

The Madonna with the green woodpecker,
  The Madonna of the fig-tree,
The Madonna beside the yellow dam,
  Turn their kind faces from us
And our projects under construction,
  Look only in one direction,
Fix their gaze on our completed work:
  Pile-driver, concrete-mixer,
Crane and pickaxe wait to be used again,
  But how can we repeat this?
Outliving our act, we stand where we are,
  As disregarded as some

Discarded artifact of our own,
  Like torn gloves, rusted kettles,
Abandoned branch-lines, worn lop-sided
  Grindstones buried in nettles.

This mutilated flesh, our victim,
  Explains too nakedly, too well,
The spell of the asparagus garden,
  The aim of our chalk-pit game; stamps,
Birds' eggs are not the same, behind the wonder
  Of tow-paths and sunken lanes,
Behind the rapture on the spiral stair,
  We shall always now be aware
Of the deed into which they lead, under
  The mock chase and mock capture,
The racing and tussling and splashing,
  The panting and the laughter,
Be listening for the cry and stillness
  To follow after: wherever
The sun shines, brooks run, books are written,
  There will also be this death.

Soon cool tramontana will stir the leaves,
  The shops will re-open at four,
The empty blue bus in the empty pink square
  Fill up and depart: we have time
To misrepresent, excuse, deny,
  Mythify, use this event
While, under a hotel bed, in prison,
  Down wrong turnings, its meaning
Waits for our lives: sooner than we would choose,
  Bread will melt, water will burn,
And the great quell begin, Abaddon
  Set up his triple gallows
At our seven gates, fat Belial make
  Our wives waltz naked; meanwhile
It would be best to go home, if we have a home,
  In any case good to rest.

That our dreaming wills may seem to escape
  This dead calm, wander instead
On knife edges, on black and white squares,
  Across moss, baize, velvet, boards,
Over cracks and hillocks, in mazes
  Of string and penitent cones,
Down granite ramps and damp passages,
  Through gates that will not relatch
And doors marked *Private*, pursued by Moors
  And watched by latent robbers,
To hostile villages at the heads of fjords,
  To dark châteaux where wind sobs
In the pine-trees and telephones ring,
  Inviting trouble, to a room,
Lit by one weak bulb, where our Double sits
  Writing and does not look up.

That, while we are thus away, our own wronged flesh
  May work undisturbed, restoring
The order we try to destroy, the rhythm
  We spoil out of spite: valves close
And open exactly, glands secrete,
  Vessels contract and expand
At the right moment, essential fluids
  Flow to renew exhausted cells,
Not knowing quite what has happened, but awed
  By death like all the creatures
Now watching this spot, like the hawk looking down
  Without blinking, the smug hens
Passing close by in their pecking order,
  The bug whose view is balked by grass,
Or the deer who shyly from afar
  Peer through chinks in the forest.

July 1950

V Vespers

If the hill overlooking our city has always been known as Adam's Grave, only at dusk can you see the recumbent giant, his head turned to the west, his right arm resting for ever on Eve's haunch,

can you learn, from the way he looks up at the scandalous pair, what a citizen really thinks of his citizenship,

just as now you can hear in a drunkard's caterwaul his rebel sorrows crying for a parental discipline, in lustful eyes perceive a disconsolate soul,

scanning with desperation all passing limbs for some vestige of her faceless angel who in that long ago when wishing was a help mounted her once and vanished:

For Sun and Moon supply their conforming masks, but in this hour of civil twilight all must wear their own faces.

And it is now that our two paths cross.

Both simultaneously recognize his Anti-type: that I am an Arcadian, that he is a Utopian.

He notes, with contempt, my Aquarian belly: I note, with alarm, his Scorpion's mouth.

He would like to see me cleaning latrines: I would like to see him removed to some other planet.

Neither speaks. What experience could we possibly share?

Glancing at a lampshade in a store window, I observe it is too hideous for anyone in their senses to buy: He observes it is too expensive for a peasant to buy.

Passing a slum child with rickets, I look the other way: He looks the other way if he passes a chubby one.

I hope our senators will behave like saints, provided they don't reform me: He hopes they will behave like *baritoni cattivi*, and, when lights burn late in the Citadel,

I (who have never seen the inside of a police station) am shocked and think: "Were the city as free as they say, after sundown all her bureaus would be huge black stones.":

He (who has been beaten up several times) is not shocked at all but thinks: "One fine night our boys will be working up there."

You can see, then, why, between my Eden and his New Jerusalem, no treaty is negotiable.

In my Eden a person who dislikes Bellini has the good manners not to get born: In his New Jerusalem a person who dislikes work will be very sorry he was born.

In my Eden we have a few beam-engines, saddle-tank locomotives, overshot waterwheels and other beautiful pieces of obsolete machinery to play with: In his New Jerusalem even chefs will be cucumber-cool machine minders.

In my Eden our only source of political news is gossip: In his New Jerusalem there will be a special daily in simplified spelling for non-verbal types.

In my Eden each observes his compulsive rituals and superstitious tabus but we have no morals: In his New Jerusalem the temples will be empty but all will practice the rational virtues.

One reason for his contempt is that I have only to close my eyes, cross the iron footbridge to the tow-path, take the barge through the short brick tunnel and there I stand in Eden again, welcomed back by the krumhorns, doppions, sordumes of jolly miners and a bob major from the Cathedral (romanesque) of St. Sophie (*Die Kalte*):

One reason for my alarm is that, when he closes his eyes, he arrives, not in New Jerusalem, but on some august day of outrage when hellikins cavort through ruined drawing-rooms and fish-wives intervene in the Chamber or

some autumn night of delations and noyades when the unrepentant thieves (including me) are sequestered and those he hates shall hate themselves instead.

So with a passing glance we take the other's posture: Already our steps recede, heading, incorrigible each, towards his kind of meal and evening.

Was it (as it must look to any god of cross-roads) simply a fortuitous intersection of life-paths, loyal to different fibs,

or also a rendezvous between accomplices who, in spite of themselves, cannot resist meeting

to remind the other (do both, at bottom, desire truth?) of that half of their secret which he would most like to forget,

forcing us both, for a fraction of a second, to remember our victim (but for him I could forget the blood, but for me he could forget the innocence)

on whose immolation (call him Abel, Remus, whom you will, it is one Sin Offering) arcadias, utopias, our dear old bag of a democracy, are alike founded:

For without a cement of blood (it must be human, it must be innocent) no secular wall will safely stand.

June 1954

VI Compline

Now, as desire and the things desired
  Cease to require attention,
As, seizing its chance, the body escapes,
  Section by section, to join
Plants in their chaster peace which is more
  To its real taste, now a day is its past,
Its last deed and feeling in, should come
  The instant of recollection
When the whole thing makes sense: it comes, but all
  I recall are doors banging,
Two housewives scolding, an old man gobbling,
  A child's wild look of envy,
Actions, words, that could fit any tale,
  And I fail to see either plot
Or meaning; I cannot remember
  A thing between noon and three.

Nothing is with me now but a sound,
  A heart's rhythm, a sense of stars
Leisurely walking around, and both
  Talk a language of motion
I can measure but not read: maybe
  My heart is confessing her part
In what happened to us from noon to three,
  That constellations indeed
Sing of some hilarity beyond
  All liking and happening,
But, knowing I neither know what they know
  Nor what I ought to know, scorning
All vain fornications of fancy,
  Now let me, blessing them both
For the sweetness of their cassations,
  Accept our separations.

A stride from now will take me into dream,
  Leave me, without a status,

Among its unwashed tribes of wishes
  Who have no dances and no jokes
But a magic cult to propitiate
  What happens from noon till three,
Odd rites which they hide from me—should I chance,
  Say, on youths in an oak-wood
Insulting a white deer, bribes nor threats
  Will get them to blab—and then
Past untruth is one step to nothing,
  For the end, for me as for cities,
Is total absence: what comes to be
  Must go back into non-being
For the sake of the equity, the rhythm
  Past measure or comprehending.

Can poets (can men in television)
  Be saved? It is not easy
To believe in unknowable justice
  Or pray in the name of a love
Whose name one's forgotten: *libera*
  Me, libera C (dear C)
And all poor s-o-b's who never
  Do anything properly, spare
Us in the youngest day when all are
  Shaken awake, facts are facts
(And I shall know exactly what happened
  Today between noon and three),
That we, too, may come to the picnic
  With nothing to hide, join the dance
As it moves in perichoresis,
  Turns about the abiding tree.

Spring 1954

VII Lauds

Among the leaves the small birds sing;
The crow of the cock commands awaking:
In solitude, for company.

Bright shines the sun on creatures mortal;
Men of their neighbors become sensible:
In solitude, for company.

The crow of the cock commands awaking;
Already the mass-bell goes dong-ding:
In solitude, for company.

Men of their neighbors become sensible;
God bless the Realm, God bless the People:
In solitude, for company.

Already the mass-bell goes dong-ding;
The dripping mill-wheel is again turning:
In solitude, for company.

God bless the Realm, God bless the People;
God bless this green world temporal:
In solitude, for company.

The dripping mill-wheel is again turning;
Among the leaves the small birds sing:
In solitude, for company.

1952

76

Homage to Clio

Our hill has made its submission and the green
 Swept on into the north: around me,
From morning to night, flowers duel incessantly,
 Color against color, in combats

Which they all win, and at any hour from some point else
  May come another tribal outcry
Of a new generation of birds who chirp
  Not for effect but because chirping

Is the thing to do. More lives than I perceive
  Are aware of mine this May morning
As I sit reading a book, sharper senses
  Keep watch on an inedible patch

Of unsatisfactory smell, unsafe as
  So many areas are: to observation
My book is dead, and by observations they live
  In space, as unaware of silence

As Provocative Aphrodite or her twin,
  Virago Artemis, the Tall Sisters
Whose subjects they are. That is why, in their Dual Realm,
  Banalities can be beautiful,

Why nothing is too big or too small or the wrong
  Color, and the roar of an earthquake
Rearranging the whispers of streams a loud sound
  Not a din: but we, at haphazard

And unseasonably, are brought face to face
  By ones, Clio, with your silence. After that
Nothing is easy. We may dream as we wish
  Of phallic pillar or navel-stone

With twelve nymphs twirling about it, but pictures
  Are no help: your silence already is there
Between us and any magical center
  Where things are taken in hand. Besides,

Are we so sorry? Woken at sun-up to hear
  A cock pronouncing himself himself
Though all his sons had been castrated and eaten,
  I was glad I could be unhappy: if

I don't know how I shall manage, at least I know
  The beast-with-two-backs may be a species
Evenly distributed but Mum and Dad
  Were not two other people. To visit

The grave of a friend, to make an ugly scene,
  To count the loves one has grown out of,
Is not nice, but to chirp like a tearless bird,
  As though no one dies in particular

And gossip were never true, unthinkable:
  If it were, forgiveness would be no use,
One-eye-for-one would be just and the innocent
  Would not have to suffer. Artemis,

Aphrodite, are Major Powers and all wise
  Castellans will mind their p's and q's,
But it is you, who never have spoken up,
  Madonna of silences, to whom we turn

When we have lost control, your eyes, Clio, into which
  We look for recognition after
We have been found out. How shall I describe you? They
  Can be represented in granite

(One guesses at once from the perfect buttocks,
  The flawless mouth too grand to have corners,
Whom the colossus must be), but what icon
  Have the arts for you, who look like any

Girl one has not noticed and show no special
  Affinity with a beast? I have seen
Your photo, I think, in the papers, nursing
  A baby or mourning a corpse: each time

You had nothing to say and did not, one could see,
  Observe where you were, Muse of the unique
Historical fact, defending with silence
  Some world of your beholding, a silence

No explosion can conquer but a lover's Yes
  Has been known to fill. So few of the Big
Ever listen: that is why you have a great host
  Of superfluous screams to care for and

Why, up and down like the Duke of Cumberland,
  Or round and round like the Laxey Wheel,
The Short, The Bald, The Pious, The Stammerer went,
  As the children of Artemis go,

Not yours. Lives that obey you move like music,
  Becoming now what they only can be once,
Making of silence decisive sound: it sounds
  Easy, but one must find the time. Clio,

Muse of Time, but for whose merciful silence
  Only the first step would count and that
Would always be murder, whose kindness never
  Is taken in, forgive our noises

And teach us our recollections: to throw away
  The tiniest fault of someone we love
Is out of the question, says Aphrodite,
  Who should know, yet one has known people

Who have done just that. Approachable as you seem,
  I dare not ask you if you bless the poets,
For you do not look as if you ever read them
  Nor can I see a reason why you should.

June 1955

77

First Things First

Woken, I lay in the arms of my own warmth and listened
To a storm enjoying its storminess in the winter dark
Till my ear, as it can when half-asleep or half-sober,
Set to work to unscramble that interjectory uproar,
Construing its airy vowels and watery consonants
Into a love-speech indicative of a Proper Name.

Scarcely the tongue I should have chosen, yet, as well
As harshness and clumsiness would allow, it spoke in
your praise,
Kenning you a god-child of the Moon and the West Wind
With power to tame both real and imaginary monsters,
Likening your poise of being to an upland county,
Here green on purpose, there pure blue for luck.

Loud though it was, alone as it certainly found me,
It reconstructed a day of peculiar silence
When a sneeze could be heard a mile off, and had me walking
On a headland of lava beside you, the occasion as ageless
As the stare of any rose, your presence exactly
So once, so valuable, so very now.

This, moreover, at an hour when only too often
A smirking devil annoys me in beautiful English,
Predicting a world where every sacred location
Is a sand-buried site all cultured Texans do,
Misinformed and thoroughly fleeced by their guides,
And gentle hearts are extinct like Hegelian Bishops.

Grateful, I slept till a morning that would not say
How much it believed of what I said the storm had said
But quietly drew my attention to what had been done
—So many cubic metres the more in my cistern
Against a leonine summer—putting first things first:
Thousands have lived without love, not one without water.

? 1957

78

The More Loving One

Looking up at the stars, I know quite well
That, for all they care, I can go to hell,
But on earth indifference is the least
We have to dread from man or beast.

How should we like it were stars to burn
With a passion for us we could not return?
If equal affection cannot be,
Let the more loving one be me.

Admirer as I think I am
Of stars that do not give a damn,
I cannot, now I see them, say
I missed one terribly all day.

Were all stars to disappear or die,
I should learn to look at an empty sky
And feel its total dark sublime,
Though this might take me a little time.

? September 1957

79

Friday's Child

(IN MEMORY OF DIETRICH BONHOEFFER, MARTYRED AT FLOSSENBURG, APRIL 9TH, 1945)

He told us we were free to choose
But, children as we were, we thought—
"Paternal Love will only use
Force in the last resort

On those too bumptious to repent"—
Accustomed to religious dread,
It never crossed our minds He meant
   Exactly what He said.

Perhaps He frowns, perhaps He grieves,
But it seems idle to discuss
If anger or compassion leaves
   The bigger bangs to us.

What reverence is rightly paid
To a Divinity so odd
He lets the Adam whom He made
   Perform the Acts of God?

It might be jolly if we felt
Awe at this Universal Man
(When kings were local, people knelt);
   Some try to, but who can?

The self-observed observing Mind
We meet when we observe at all
Is not alarming or unkind
   But utterly banal.

Though instruments at Its command
Make wish and counterwish come true,
It clearly cannot understand
   What It can clearly do.

Since the analogies are rot
Our senses based belief upon,
We have no means of learning what
   Is really going on,

And must put up with having learned
All proofs or disproofs that we tender
Of His existence are returned
   Unopened to the sender.

Now, did He really break the seal
And rise again? We dare not say;
But conscious unbelievers feel
  Quite sure of Judgement Day.

Meanwhile, a silence on the cross,
As dead as we shall ever be,
Speaks of some total gain or loss,
  And you and I are free

To guess from the insulted face
Just what Appearances He saves
By suffering in a public place
  A death reserved for slaves.

? 1958

80

Good-bye to the Mezzogiorno

(FOR CARLO IZZO)

Out of a gothic North, the pallid children
  Of a potato, beer-or-whiskey
Guilt culture, we behave like our fathers and come
  Southward into a sunburnt otherwhere

Of vineyards, baroque, *la bella figura,*
  To these feminine townships where men
Are males, and siblings untrained in a ruthless
  Verbal in-fighting as it is taught

In Protestant rectories upon drizzling
  Sunday afternoons—no more as unwashed
Barbarians out for gold, nor as profiteers,
  Hot for Old Masters, but for plunder

Nevertheless—some believing *amore*
  Is better down South and much cheaper
(Which is doubtful), some persuaded exposure
  To strong sunlight is lethal to germs

(Which is patently false) and others, like me,
  In middle-age hoping to twig from
What we are not what we might be next, a question
  The South seems never to raise. Perhaps

A tongue in which Nestor and Apemantus,
  Don Ottavio and Don Giovanni make
Equally beautiful sounds is unequipped
  To frame it, or perhaps in this heat

It is nonsense: the Myth of an Open Road
  Which runs past the orchard gate and beckons
Three brothers in turn to set out over the hills
  And far away, is an invention

Of a climate where it is a pleasure to walk
  And a landscape less populated
Than this one. Even so, to us it looks very odd
  Never to see an only child engrossed

In a game it has made up, a pair of friends
  Making fun in a private lingo,
Or a body sauntering by himself who is not
  Wanting, even as it perplexes

Our ears when cats are called *Cat* and dogs either
  Lupo, Nero or *Bobby*. Their dining
Puts us to shame: we can only envy people
  So frugal by nature it costs them

No effort not to guzzle and swill. Yet (if I
  Read their faces rightly after ten years)
They are without hope. The Greeks used to call the Sun
  He-who-smites-from-afar, and from here, where

Shadows are dagger-edged, the daily ocean blue,
  I can see what they meant: his unwinking
Outrageous eye laughs to scorn any notion
  Of change or escape, and a silent

Ex-volcano, without a stream or a bird,
  Echoes that laugh. This could be a reason
Why they take the silencers off their Vespas,
  Turn their radios up to full volume,

And a minim saint can expect rockets—noise
  As a countermagic, a way of saying
Boo to the Three Sisters: "Mortal we may be,
  But we are still here!" might cause them to hanker

After proximities—in streets packed solid
  With human flesh, their souls feel immune
To all metaphysical threats. We are rather shocked,
  But we need shocking: to accept space, to own

That surfaces need not be superficial
  Nor gestures vulgar, cannot really
Be taught within earshot of running water
  Or in sight of a cloud. As pupils

We are not bad, but hopeless as tutors: Goethe,
  Tapping Homeric hexameters
On the shoulder blade of a Roman girl, is
  (I wish it were someone else) the figure

Of all our stamp: no doubt he treated her well,
  But one would draw the line at calling
The Helena begotten on that occasion,
  Queen of his Second *Walpurgisnacht*,

Her baby: between those who mean by a life a
  Bildungsroman and those to whom living
Means to-be-visible-now, there yawns a gulf
  Embraces cannot bridge. If we try

To "go southern," we spoil in no time, we grow
Flabby, dingily lecherous, and
Forget to pay bills: that no one has heard of them
Taking the Pledge or turning to Yoga

Is a comforting thought—in that case, for all
The spiritual loot we tuck away,
We do them no harm—and entitles us, I think
To one little scream at *A piacere!*,

Not two. Go I must, but I go grateful (even
To a certain *Monte*) and invoking
My sacred meridian names, *Pirandello*,
Croce, *Vico*, *Verga*, *Bellini*,

To bless this region, its vendages, and those
Who call it home: though one cannot always
Remember exactly why one has been happy,
There is no forgetting that one was.

September 1958

81

Dame Kind

Steatopygous, sow-dugged
and owl-headed,
To Whom—Whom else?—the first innocent blood
was formally shed
By a chinned mammal that hard times
had turned carnivore,
From Whom his first promiscuous orgy
begged a downpour
To speed the body-building cereals
of a warmer age:
Now who put us, we should like to know,
in *Her* manage?

Strait-laced She never was
and has not grown more so
Since the skeptical academies got wind
of the *Chi-Rho*;
St. Cuckoo's wooden church for Her
where on Green Sundays
Bald hermits celebrate a wordless
cult in Her praise:
So pocket your fifty sonnets, Bud;
tell Her a myth
Of unpunishable gods and all the girls
they interfered with.

Haven't we spotted Her Picked Winners
whom She cossets, ramparts
And does the handsome by? Didn't the darlings
have cold hearts?
. . . ONE BOMB WOULD BE ENOUGH. . . . Now look
who's thinking gruesome!
Brother, you're worse than a lonesome Peeper
or a He-Virgin
Who nightly abhors the Primal Scene
in medical Latin:
She mayn't be all She might be but
She *is* our Mum.

You can't tell us your hypochondriac
Blue-Stocking from Provence
Who makes the clockwork arcadies go round
is worth twopence;
You won't find a steady in *that* museum
unless you prefer
Tea with a shapeless angel to bedtime
with a lovely monster:
Before you catch it for your mim look
and gnostic chirrup,
Ask the Kind Lady who fitted you out
to fix you up.

Supposing even (through misdirections
or your own mischief)
You do land in that anomalous duchy,
Her remotest fief,
Where four eyes encounter in two
one mirror perilous
As the clear rock-basin that stultified
frigid Narcissus,
Where tongues stammer on a First Name,
bereft of guile,
And common snub-nosed creatures are abashed
at a face in profile,

Even there, as your blushes invoke its Guardian
(whose true invocable
Name is singular for each true heart
and false to tell)
To sacre your courtship ritual so
it deserves a music
More solemn than the he-hawing
of a salesman's limerick,
Do a bow to the Coarse Old Party that wrought you
an alderliefest
Of the same verbose and sentient kidney,
grateful not least

For all the dirty work She did.
How many hundreds
Of lawful, unlawful, both equally
loveless beds,
Of lying endearments, crooked questions,
crookeder answers,
Of bawling matches, sarcastic silences,
megrims, tears,
How much half-witted horseplay and sheer
bloody misrule
It took to bring you two together
both on schedule?

1959

82

You

Really, must you,
Over-familiar
Dense companion,
Be there always?
The bond between us
Is chimerical surely:
Yet I cannot break it.

Must I, born for
Sacred play,
Turn base mechanic
So you may worship
Your secular bread,
With no thought
Of the value of time?

Thus far I have known your
Character only
From its pleasanter side,
But you know I know
A day will come
When you grow savage
And hurt me badly.

Totally stupid?
Would that you were:
But, no, you plague me
With tastes I was fool enough
Once to believe in.
Bah!, blockhead:
I know where you learned them.

Can I trust you even
On creaturely fact?

I suspect strongly
You hold some dogma
Of positive truth,
And feed me fictions:
I shall never prove it.

Oh, I know how you came by
A sinner's cranium,
How between two glaciers
The master-chronometer
Of an innocent primate
Altered its tempi:
That explains nothing.

Who tinkered and why?
Why am I certain,
Whatever your faults are,
The fault is mine,
Why is loneliness not
A chemical discomfort,
Nor Being a smell?

September 1960

83

After Reading a Child's Guide to Modern Physics

If all a top physicist knows
About the Truth be true,
Then, for all the so-and-so's,
Futility and grime,
Our common world contains,
We have a better time
Than the Greater Nebulae do,
Or the atoms in our brains.

Marriage is rarely bliss
But, surely it would be worse
As particles to pelt
At thousands of miles per sec
About a universe
In which a lover's kiss
Would either not be felt
Or break the loved one's neck.

Though the face at which I stare
While shaving it be cruel
For, year after year, it repels
An ageing suitor, it has,
Thank God, sufficient mass
To be altogether there,
Not an indeterminate gruel
Which is partly somewhere else.

Our eyes prefer to suppose
That a habitable place
Has a geocentric view,
That architects enclose
A quiet Euclidean space:
Exploded myths—but who
Would feel at home astraddle
An ever expanding saddle?

This passion of our kind
For the process of finding out
Is a fact one can hardly doubt,
But I would rejoice in it more
If I knew more clearly what
We wanted the knowledge for,
Felt certain still that the mind
Is free to know or not.

It has chosen once, it seems,
And whether our concern

For magnitude's extremes
Really becomes a creature
Who comes in a median size,
Or politicizing Nature
Be altogether wise,
Is something we shall learn.

1961

84

On the Circuit

Among pelagian travelers,
Lost on their lewd conceited way
To Massachusetts, Michigan,
Miami or L.A.,

An airborne instrument I sit,
Predestined nightly to fulfill
Columbia-Giesen-Management's
Unfathomable will,

By whose election justified,
I bring my gospel of the Muse
To fundamentalists, to nuns,
To Gentiles and to Jews,

And daily, seven days a week,
Before a local sense has jelled,
From talking-site to talking-site
Am jet-or-prop-propelled.

Though warm my welcome everywhere,
I shift so frequently, so fast,
I cannot now say where I was
The evening before last,

Unless some singular event
Should intervene to save the place,
A truly asinine remark,
A soul-bewitching face,

Or blessed encounter, full of joy,
Unscheduled on the Giesen Plan,
With, here, an addict of Tolkien,
There, a Charles Williams fan.

Since Merit but a dunghill is,
I mount the rostrum unafraid:
Indeed, 'twere damnable to ask
If I am overpaid.

Spirit is willing to repeat
Without a qualm the same old talk,
But Flesh is homesick for our snug
Apartment in New York.

A sulky fifty-six, he finds
A change of mealtime utter hell,
Grown far too crotchety to like
A luxury hotel.

The Bible is a goodly book
I always can peruse with zest,
But really cannot say the same
For Hilton's *Be My Guest*,

Nor bear with equanimity
The radio in students' cars,
Musak at breakfast, or—dear God!—
Girl-organists in bars.

Then, worst of all, the anxious thought,
Each time my plane begins to sink
And the No Smoking sign comes on:
What will there be to drink?

Is this a milieu where I must
How grahamgreeneish! How infra dig!
Snatch from the bottle in my bag
An analeptic swig?

Another morning comes: I see,
Dwindling below me on the plane,
The roofs of one more audience
I shall not see again.

God bless the lot of them, although
I don't remember which was which:
God bless the U.S.A., so large,
So friendly, and so rich.

? June 1963

85

Et in Arcadia Ego

Who, now, seeing Her so
Happily married,
Housewife, helpmate to Man,

Can imagine the screeching
Virago, the Amazon,
Earth Mother was?

Her jungle growths
Are abated, Her exorbitant
Monsters abashed,

Her soil mumbled,
Where crops, aligned precisely,
Will soon be orient:

Levant or couchant,
Well-daunted thoroughbreds
Graze on mead and pasture,

A church clock subdivides the day,
Up the lane at sundown
Geese podge home.

As for Him:
What has happened to the Brute
Epics and nightmares tell of?

No bishops pursue
Their archdeacons with axes,
In the crumbling lair

Of a robber baron
Sightseers picnic
Who carry no daggers.

I well might think myself
A humanist,
Could I manage not to see

How the autobahn
Thwarts the landscape
In godless Roman arrogance,

The farmer's children
Tiptoe past the shed
Where the gelding knife is kept.

? May 1964

86

Thanksgiving for a Habitat

Funes ceciderunt mihi in praeclaris:
etenim hereditas mea praeclara est mihi.
Psalm XVI, 6

I Prologue: The Birth of Architecture

(FOR JOHN BAYLEY)

From gallery-grave and the hunt of a wren-king
  to Low Mass and trailer camp
is hardly a tick by the carbon clock, but I
  don't count that way nor do you:
already it is millions of heartbeats ago
  back to the Bicycle Age,
before which is no *After* for me to measure,
  just a still prehistoric *Once*
where anything could happen. To you, to me,
  Stonehenge and Chartres Cathedral,
the Acropolis, Blenheim, the Albert Memorial
  are works by the same Old Man
under different names: we know what He did,
  what, even, He thought He thought,
but we don't see why. (To get that, one would have
  to be selfish in His way,
without concrete or grapefruit.) It's our turn now
  to puzzle the unborn. No world
wears as well as it should but, mortal or not,
  a world has still to be built
because of what we can see from our windows,
  that Immortal Commonwealth
which is there regardless: It's in perfect taste
  and it's never boring but
it won't quite do. Among its populations
  are masons and carpenters

who build the most exquisite shelters and safes,
but no architects, any more
than there are heretics or bounders: to take
umbrage at death, to construct
a second nature of tomb and temple, lives
must know the meaning of *If*.

? Spring 1962

II Thanksgiving for a Habitat

(FOR GEOFFREY GORER)

Nobody I know would like to be buried
with a silver cocktail shaker,
a transistor radio and a strangled
daily help, or keep his word because

of a great-great-grandmother who got laid
by a sacred beast. Only a press lord
could have built San Simeon: no unearned income
can buy us back the gait and gestures

to manage a baroque staircase, or the art
of believing footmen don't hear
human speech. (In adulterine castles
our half-strong might hang their jackets

while mending their lethal bicycle chains:
luckily, there are not enough
crags to go round.) Still, Hetty Pegler's Tump
is worth a visit, so is Schönbrunn,

to look at someone's idea of the body
that should have been his, as the flesh
Mum formulated shouldn't: that whatever
he does or feels in the mood for,

stocktaking, horseplay, worship, making love,
  he stays the same shape, disgraces
a Royal I. To be overadmired is not
  good enough: although a fine figure

is rare in either sex, others like it
  have existed before. One may
be a Proustian snob or a sound Jacksonian
  democrat, but which of us wants

to be touched inadvertently, even
  by his beloved? We know all about graphs
and Darwin, enormous rooms no longer
  superhumanize, but earnest

city planners are mistaken: a pen
  for a rational animal
is no fitting habitat for Adam's
  sovereign clone. I, a transplant

from overseas, at last am dominant
  over three acres and a blooming
conurbation of country lives, few of whom
  I shall ever meet, and with fewer

converse. Linnaeus recoiled from the Amphibia
  as a naked gruesome rabble,
Arachnids give me the shudders, but fools
  who deface their emblem of guilt

are germane to Hitler: the race of spiders
  shall be allowed their webs. I should like
to be to my water-brethren as a spell
  of fine weather: Many are stupid,

and some, maybe, are heartless, but who is not
  vulnerable, easy to scare,
and jealous of his privacy? (I am glad
  the blackbird, for instance, cannot

tell if I'm talking English, German or
just typewriting: that what he utters
I may enjoy as an alien rigmarole.) I ought
to outlast the limber dragonflies

as the muscle-bound firs are certainly
going to outlast me: I shall not end
down any esophagus, though I may succumb
to a filter-passing predator,

shall, anyhow, stop eating, surrender my smidge
of nitrogen to the World Fund
with a drawn-out *Oh* (unless at the nod
of some jittery commander

I be translated in a nano-second
to a c.c. of poisonous nothing
in a giga-death). Should conventional
blunderbuss war and its routiers

invest my balliwick, I shall of course
assume the submissive posture:
but men are not wolves and it probably
won't help. Territory, status,

and love, sing all the birds, are what matter:
what I dared not hope or fight for
is, in my fifties, mine, a toft-and-croft
where I needn't, ever, be at home *to*

those I am not at home *with*, not a cradle,
a magic Eden without clocks,
and not a windowless grave, but a place
I may go both in and out of.

August 1962

III The Cave of Making

(IN MEMORIAM LOUIS MACNEICE)

For this and for all enclosures like it the archetype
  is Weland's Stithy, an antre
more private than a bedroom even, for neither lovers nor
  maids are welcome, but without a
bedroom's secrets: from the Olivetti portable,
  the dictionaries (the very
best money can buy), the heaps of paper, it is evident
  what must go on. Devoid of
flowers and family photographs, all is subordinate
  here to a function, designed to
discourage daydreams—hence windows averted from plausible
  videnda but admitting a light one
could mend a watch by—and to sharpen hearing: reached by an
  outside staircase, domestic
noises and odors, the vast background of natural
  life are shut off. Here silence
is turned into objects.
                                I wish, Louis, I could have shown it you
  while you were still in public,
and the house and garden: lover of women and Donegal,
  from your perspective you'd notice
sights I overlook, and in turn take a scholar's interest
  in facts I could tell you (for instance,
four miles to our east, at a wood palisade, Carolingian
  Bavaria stopped, beyond it
unknowable nomads). Friends we became by personal
  choice, but fate had already
made us neighbors. For Grammar we both inherited
  good mongrel barbarian English
which never completely succumbed to the Roman rhetoric
  or the Roman gravity, that nonsense
which stood none. Though neither of our dads, like Horace's,
  wiped his nose on his forearm,
neither was porphyry-born, and our ancestors probably
  were among those plentiful subjects

it cost less money to murder. Born so, both of us
became self-conscious at a moment
when locomotives were named after knights in Malory,
Science to schoolboys was known as
Stinks, and the Manor still was politically numinous:
both watched with mixed feelings
the sack of Silence, the churches empty, the cavalry
go, the Cosmic Model
become German, and any faith, if we had it, in immanent
virtue died. More than ever
life-out-there is goodly, miraculous, lovable,
but we shan't, not since Stalin and Hitler,
trust ourselves ever again: we know that, subjectively,
all is possible.
To you, though,
ever since, last Fall, you quietly slipped out of Granusion,
our moist garden, into
the Country of Unconcern, no possibility
matters. I wish you hadn't
caught that cold, but the dead we miss are easier
to talk to: with those no longer
tensed by problems one cannot feel shy and, anyway,
when playing cards or drinking
or pulling faces are out of the question, what else is there
to do but talk to the voices
of conscience they have become? From now on, as a visitor
who needn't be met at the station,
your influence is welcome at any hour in my ubity,
especially here, where titles
from *Poems* to *The Burning Perch* offer proof positive
of the maker you were, with whom I
once collaborated, once at a weird Symposium
exchanged winks as a juggins
went on about Alienation.
Who would, for preference,
be a bard in an oral culture,
obliged at drunken feasts to improvise a eulogy
of some beefy illiterate burner,

giver of rings, or depend for bread on the moods of a
Baroque Prince, expected,
like his dwarf, to amuse? After all, it's rather a privilege
amid the affluent traffic
to serve this unpopular art which cannot be turned into
background noise for study
or hung as a status trophy by rising executives,
cannot be "done" like Venice
or abridged like Tolstoy, but stubbornly still insists upon
being read or ignored: our handful
of clients at least can rune. (It's heartless to forget about
the underdeveloped countries,
but a starving ear is as deaf as a suburban optimist's:
to stomachs only the Hindu
integers truthfully speak.) Our forerunners might envy us
our remnant still able to listen:
as Nietzsche said they would, the *plebs* have got steadily
denser, the *optimates*
quicker still on the uptake. (Today, even Talleyrand
might seem a naïf: he had so
little to cope with.) I should like to become, if possible,
a minor atlantic Goethe,
with his passion for weather and stones but without his silliness
re the Cross: at times a bore, but,
while knowing Speech can at best, a shadow echoing
the silent light, bear witness
to the Truth it is not, he wished it were, as the Francophile
gaggle of pure songsters
are too vain to. We're not musicans: to stink of Poetry
is unbecoming, and never
to be dull shows a lack of taste. Even a limerick
ought to be something a man of
honor, awaiting death from cancer or a firing squad,
could read without contempt: (at
that frontier I wouldn't dare speak to anyone
in either a prophet's bellow
or a diplomat's whisper).

Seeing you know our mystery
from the inside and therefore
how much, in our lonely dens, we need the companionship
of our good dead, to give us
comfort on dowly days when the self is a nonentity
dumped on a mound of nothing,
to break the spell of our self-enchantment when lip-smacking
imps of mawk and hooey
write with us what they will, you won't think me imposing if
I ask you to stay at my elbow
until cocktail time: dear Shade, for your elegy
I should have been able to manage
something more like you than this egocentric monologue,
but accept it for friendship's sake.

July 1964

IV Down There

(FOR IRVING WEISS)

A cellar underneath the house, though not lived in,
Reminds our warm and windowed quarters upstairs that
Caves water-scooped from limestone were our first dwellings,
A providential shelter when the Great Cold came,
Which woke our feel for somewhere fixed to come back to,
A hole by occupation made to smell human.

Self-walled, we sleep aloft, but still, at safe anchor,
Ride there on caves; lamplit we dine at street level:
But, deep in Mother Earth, beneath her key-cold cloak,
Where light and heat can never spoil what sun ripened,
In barrels, bottles, jars, we mew her kind commons,
Wine, beer, conserves and pickles, good at all seasons.

Encrust with years of clammy grime, the lair, maybe,
Of creepy-crawlies or a ghost, its flagstoned vault
Is not for girls: sometimes, to test their male courage,

A father sends the younger boys to fetch something
For Mother from down there; ashamed to whimper,
hearts pounding,
They dare the dank steps, re-emerge with proud faces.

The rooms we talk and work in always look injured
When trunks are being packed, and when, without warning,
We drive up in the dark, unlock and switch lights on,
They seem put out: a cellar never takes umbrage;
It takes us as we are, explorers, homebodies,
Who seldom visit others when we don't need them.

July 1963

V Up There

(FOR ANNE WEISS)

Men would never have come to need an attic.
Keen collectors of glass or Roman coins build
Special cabinets for them, dote on, index
Each new specimen: only women cling to
Items out of their past they have no use for,
Can't name now what they couldn't bear to part with.

Up there, under the eaves, in bulging boxes,
Hats, veils, ribbons, galoshes, programs, letters
Wait unworshiped (a starving spider spins for
The occasional fly): no clock recalls it
Once an hour to the household it's a part of,
No Saint's Day is devoted to its function.

All it knows of a changing world it has to
Guess from children, who conjure in its plenum,
Now an eyrie for two excited sisters,
Where, when Mother is bad, her rage can't reach them,
Now a schooner on which a lonely only
Boy sails north or approaches coral islands.

July 1963

VI The Geography of the House

(FOR CHRISTOPHER ISHERWOOD)

Seated after breakfast
In this white-tiled cabin
Arabs call *the House where*
Everybody goes,
Even melancholics
Raise a cheer to Mrs.
Nature for the primal
Pleasures She bestows.

Sex is but a dream to
Seventy-and-over,
But a joy proposed un-
-til we start to shave:
Mouth-delight depends on
Virtue in the cook, but
This She guarantees from
Cradle unto grave.

Lifted off the potty,
Infants from their mothers
Hear their first impartial
Words of worldly praise:
Hence, to start the morning
With a satisfactory
Dump is a good omen
All our adult days.

Revelation came to
Luther in a privy
(Crosswords have been solved there):
Rodin was no fool
When he cast his Thinker,
Cogitating deeply,
Crouched in the position
Of a man at stool.

All the Arts derive from
This ur-act of making,
Private to the artist:
Makers' lives are spent
Striving in their chosen
Medium to produce a
De-narcissus-ized en-
   -during excrement.

Freud did not invent the
Constipated miser:
Banks have letter boxes
Built in their façade,
Marked *For Night Deposits*,
Stocks are firm or liquid,
Currencies of nations
Either soft or hard.

Global Mother, keep our
Bowels of compassion
Open through our lifetime,
Purge our minds as well:
Grant us a kind ending,
Not a second childhood,
Petulant, weak-sphinctered,
In a cheap hotel.

Keep us in our station:
When we get pound-noteish,
When we seem about to
Take up Higher Thought,
Send us some deflating
Image like the pained ex-
   -pression on a Major
Prophet taken short.

(Orthodoxy ought to
Bless our modern plumbing:

Swift and St. Augustine
Lived in centuries
When a stench of sewage
Ever in the nostrils
Made a strong debating
Point for Manichees.)

Mind and Body run on
Different timetables:
Not until our morning
Visit here can we
Leave the dead concerns of
Yesterday behind us,
Face with all our courage
What is now to be.

July 1964

VII Encomium Balnei

(FOR NEIL LITTLE)

it is odd that the English
a rather dirty people
should have invented the slogan
Cleanliness is next to Godliness
meaning by that
a gentleman smells faintly of tar
persuaded themselves that constant cold hydropathy
would make the sons of gentlemen
pure in heart
(not that papa or his chilblained offspring can
hope to be gentry)
still John Bull's
hip-bath it was
that made one carnal pleasure lawful
for the first time since we quarreled

over Faith and Works
(Shakespeare probably stank
Le Grand
Monarque certainly did)
thanks to him
shrines where a subarctic fire-cult could meet and marry
a river-cult from torrid Greece
rose again
resweetened the hirsute West
a Roman though
bath addict
amphitheater fan
would be puzzled
seeing the caracallan acreage
compressed into such a few square feet
mistake them for hideouts
warrens of some outlawed sect
who mortify their flesh with strange
implements
he is not that wrong
if the tepidarium's
barrel vaulting has migrated
to churches and railroad stations
if we no longer
go there to wrestle or gossip
or make love
(you cannot purchase a conjugal tub)
St. Anthony and his wild brethren
(for them ablutions were tabu
a habit of that doomed
behavioral sink this world)
have been
just as he thought
at work
we are no more chaste
obedient
nor
if we can possibly help it

poor than he was but
enthusiasts who were have taught us
(besides showing lovers of nature
how to carry binoculars instead of a gun)
the unclassical wonder of being
all by oneself
though our dwellings may still have a master
who owns the front-door key
a bathroom
has only an inside lock
belongs today to whoever
is taking a bath
among us
to withdraw from the tribe at will
be neither Parent
Spouse nor Guest
is a sacrosanct
political right
where else shall the Average Ego
find its peace
not in sleep surely
the several worlds we invent are quite as pugnacious
as the one into which we are born
and even more public
on Oxford Street or Broadway
I may escape notice
but never
on roads I dream of
what Eden is there for the lapsed
but hot water
snug in its caul
widows
orphans
exiles may feel as self-important
as an only child
and a sage
be silly without shame
present a Lieder Abend

to a captive audience of his toes
retreat from rhyme and reason into some mallarmesque
syllabic fog
for half an hour
it is wise to forget the time
our daily peril
and each other
good for the soul
once in the twenty-four hour cycle of her body
whether according to our schedule
as we sit down to breakfast
or stand up to welcome
folk for dinner
to feel as if
the Pilgrim's Way
or as some choose to call it
the War Path
were now a square in the Holy City
that what was wrong has been put right
as if Von Hügel's
hoggers and lumpers were extinct
thinking the same as thanking
all military hardware
already slighted and submerged

April 1962

VIII Grub First, Then Ethics
—Brecht

(FOR MARGARET GARDINER)

Should the shade of Plato
visit us, anxious to know
how *anthropos* is, we could say to him: "Well,
we can read to ourselves, our use
of holy numbers would shock you, and a poet
may lament—'where is Telford

whose bridged canals are still a Shropshire glory,
where Muir who on a Douglas spruce
rode out a storm and called an earthquake noble,
where Mr. Vynyian Board,
thanks to whose lifelong fuss the hunted whale now suffers
a quicker death?'—without being
called an idiot, though none of them bore arms or
made a public splash," then "Look!"
we would point, for a dig at Athens, "Here
is the place where we cook."

Though built in Lower Austria,
do-it-yourself America
prophetically blueprinted this
palace kitchen for kingdoms
where royalty would be incognito, for an age when
Courtesy might think: "From your voice
and the back of your neck I know we shall get on
but cannot tell from your thumbs
who is to give the orders." The right note is harder
to hear than in the Age of Poise
when She talked shamelessly to her maid and sang
noble lies with Him, but struck
it can be still in New Cnossos where if I am
banned by a shrug it is my fault,
not Father's, as it is my taste whom
I put below the salt.

The prehistoric hearthstone,
round as a birthday-button
and sacred to Granny, is as old
stuff as the bowel-loosening
nasal war cry, but this all-electric room
where ghosts would feel uneasy,
a witch at a loss, is numinous and again
the center of a dwelling
not, as lately it was, an abhorrent dungeon
where the warm unlaundered meiny

belched their comic prose and from a dream of which
chaste Milady awoke blushing.
House-proud, deploring labor, extolling work,
these engines politely insist
that banausics can be liberals,
a cook a pure artist

who moves everyman
at a deeper level than
Mozart, for the subject of the verb
to-hunger is never a name:
dear Adam and Eve had different bottoms,
but the neotene who marches
upright and can subtract reveals a belly
like the serpent's with the same
vulnerable look. Jew, Gentile or pigmy,
he must get his calories
before he can consider her profile or
his own, attack you or play chess,
and take what there is however hard to get down:
then surely those in whose creed
God is edible may call a fine
omelette a Christian deed.

The sin of Gluttony
is ranked among the Deadly
Seven, but in murder mysteries
one can be sure the gourmet
didn't do it: children, brave warriors out of a job,
can weigh pounds more than they should
and one can dislike having to kiss them yet,
compared with the thin-lipped, they
are seldom detestable. Some waiter grieves
for the worst dead bore to be a good
trencherman, and no wonder chefs mature into
choleric types, doomed to observe
Beauty peck at a master-dish, their one reward
to behold the mutually hostile
mouth and eyes of a sinner married
at the first bite by a smile.

The houses of our City
are real enough but they lie
haphazardly scattered over the earth,
and her vagabond forum
is any space where two of us happen to meet
who can spot a citizen
without papers. So, too, can her foes. Where the
power lies remains to be seen,
the force, though, is clearly with them: perhaps only
by falling can She become
Her own vision, but we have sworn under four eyes
to keep Her up—all we ask for,
should the night come when comets blaze and meres break,
is a good dinner, that we
may march in high fettle, left foot first,
to hold her Thermopylae.

1958

IX For Friends Only

(FOR JOHN AND TECKLA CLARK)

Ours yet not ours, being set apart
As a shrine to friendship,
Empty and silent most of the year,
This room awaits from you
What you alone, as visitor, can bring,
A weekend of personal life.

In a house backed by orderly woods,
Facing a tractored sugar-beet country,
Your working hosts engaged to their stint,
You are unlike to encounter
Dragons or romance: were drama a craving,
You would not have come.

Books we do have for almost any
Literate mood, and notepaper, envelopes,
For a writing one (to "borrow" stamps
Is a mark of ill-breeding):
Between lunch and tea, perhaps a drive;
After dinner, music or gossip.

Should you have troubles (pets will die,
Lovers are always behaving badly)
And confession helps, we will hear it,
Examine and give our counsel:
If to mention them hurts too much,
We shall not be nosey.

Easy at first, the language of friendship
Is, as we soon discover,
Very difficult to speak well, a tongue
With no cognates, no resemblance
To the galimatias of nursery and bedroom,
Court rhyme or shepherd's prose,

And, unless often spoken, soon goes rusty.
Distance and duties divide us,
But absence will not seem an evil
If it make our re-meeting
A real occasion. Come when you can:
Your room will be ready.

In Tum-Tum's reign a tin of biscuits
On the bedside table provided
For nocturnal munching. Now weapons have changed,
And the fashion in appetites:
There, for sunbathers who count their calories,
A bottle of mineral water.

Felicissima notte! May you fall at once
Into a cordial dream, assured
That whoever slept in this bed before

Was also someone we like,
That within the circle of our affection
Also you have no double.

June 1964

X Tonight at Seven-Thirty

(FOR M. F. K. FISHER)

The life of plants
is one continuous solitary meal,
and ruminants
hardly interrupt theirs to sleep or to mate, but most
predators feel
ravenous most of the time and competitive
always, bolting such morsels as they can contrive
to snatch from the more terrified: pack-hunters do
dine *en famille*, it is true,
with protocol and placement, but none of them play host
to a stranger whom they help first. Only man,
supererogatory beast,
Dame Kind's thoroughbred lunatic, can
do the honors of a feast,

and was doing so
before the last Glaciation when he offered
mammoth-marrow
and, perhaps, Long Pig, will continue till Doomsday
when at God's board
the saints chew pickled Leviathan. In this age farms
are no longer crenellated, only cops port arms,
but the Law of the Hearth is unchanged: a brawler may not
be put to death on the spot,
but he is asked to quit the sacral dining area
instanter, and a foul-mouth gets the cold
shoulder. The right of a guest
to standing and foster is as old
as the ban on incest.

For authentic
comity the gathering should be small
and unpublic:
at mass banquets where flosculent speeches are made
in some hired hall
we think of ourselves or nothing. Christ's cenacle
seated a baker's dozen, King Arthur's rundle
the same, but today, when one's host may well be his own
chef, servitor and scullion,
when the cost of space can double in a decade,
even that holy Zodiac number is
too large a frequency for us:
in fact, six lenient semble sieges,
none of them perilous,

is now a Perfect
Social Number. But a dinner party,
however select,
is a worldly rite that nicknames or endearments
or family
diminutives would profane: two doters who wish
to tiddle and curmurr between the soup and fish
belong in restaurants, all children should be fed
earlier and be safely in bed.
Well-liking, though, is a must: married maltalents
engaged in some covert contrast can spoil
an evening like the glance
of a single failure in the toil
of his bosom grievance.

Not that a god,
immune to grief, would be an ideal guest:
he would be too odd
to talk to and, despite his imposing presence, a bore,
for the funniest
mortals and the kindest are those who are most aware
of the baffle of being, don't kid themselves our care
is consolable, but believe a laugh is less
heartless than tears, that a hostess

prefers it. Brains evolved after bowels, therefore,
great assets as fine raiment and good looks
can be on festive occasions,
they are not essential like artful cooks
and stalwart digestions.

I see a table
at which the youngest and oldest present
keep the eye grateful
for what Nature's bounty and grace of Spirit can create:
for the ear's content
one raconteur, one gnostic with amazing shop,
both in a talkative mood but knowing when to stop,
and one wide-traveled worldling to interject now and then
a sardonic comment, men
and women who enjoy the cloop of corks, appreciate
dapatical fare, yet can see in swallowing
a sign act of reverence,
in speech a work of re-presenting
the true olamic silence.

? Spring 1963

XI The Cave of Nakedness

(FOR LOUIS AND EMMIE KRONENBERGER)

Don Juan needs no bed, being far too impatient to undress,
nor do Tristan and Isolda, much too in love to care
for so mundane a matter, but unmythical
mortals require one, and prefer to take their clothes off,
if only to sleep. That is why bedroom farces
must be incredible to be funny, why Peeping Toms
are never praised, like novelists or bird watchers,
for their keenness of observation: where there's a bed,
be it a nun's restricted cot or an Emperor's
baldachined and nightly-redamselled couch, there are no
effable data. (Dreams may be repeatable,

but our deeds of errantry in the wilderness of wish
so often turn out, when told, to be less romantic
than our day's routine: besides, we cannot describe them
without faking.) Lovers don't see their embraces
as a viable theme for debate, nor a monk his prayers
(do they, in fact, remember them?): O's of passion,
interior acts of attention, not being a story
in which the names don't matter but the way of telling,
with a lawyer's wit or a nobleman's assurance,
does, need a drawing room of their own. Bed-sitting-rooms
soon drive us crazy, a dormitory even sooner
turns us to brutes: bona fide architects know
that doors are not emphatic enough, and interpose,
as a march between two realms, so alien, so disjunct,
the no-man's-land of a stair. The switch from personage,
with a state number, a first and family name,
to the naked Adam or Eve, and vice versa,
should not be off-hand or abrupt: a stair retards it
to a solemn procession.
Since my infantile entrance
at my mother's bidding into Edwardian England,
I have suffered the transit over forty thousand times,
usually, to my chagrin, by myself: about
blended flesh, those midnight colloquia of Derbies and Joans,
I know nothing therefore, about certain occult
antipathies perhaps too much. Some perks belong, though,
to all unwilling celibates: our rooms are seldom
battlefields, we enjoy the pleasure of reading in bed
(as we grow older, it's true, we may find it prudent
to get nodding drunk first), we retain the right to choose
our sacred image. (That I often start with sundry
splendors at sundry times greened after, but always end
aware of one, the same one, may be of no importance,
but I hope it is.) Ordinary human unhappiness
is life in its natural color, to cavil
putting on airs: at day-wester to think of nothing
benign to memorize is as rare as feeling
no personal blemish, and Age, despite its damage,

is well-off. When they look in their bedroom mirrors,
Fifty-plus may be bored, but Seventeen is faced by
a frowning failure, with no money, no mistress,
no manner of his own, who never got to Italy
nor met a great one: to say a few words at banquets,
to attend a cocktail party in honor of N or M,
can be severe, but Junior has daily to cope
with ghastly family meals, with dear Papa and Mama
being odd in the wrong way. (It annoys him to speak,
and it hurts him not to.)

When I disband from the world,
and entrust my future to the Gospel Makers,
I need not fear (not in neutral Austria) being called for
in the waist of the night by deaf agents, never
to be heard of on earth again: the assaults I would be spared
are none of them princely—fire, nightmare, insomnia's
Vision of Hell, when Nature's wholesome genial fabric
lies utterly discussed and from a sullen vague
wafts a contagious stench, her adamant minerals
all corrupt, each life a worthless iteration
of the general loathing (to know that, probably,
its cause is chemical can degrade the panic,
not stint it). As a rule, with pills to help them, the Holy Four
exempt my nights from nuisance, and even wake me
when I would be woken, when, audible here and there
in the half-dark, members of an avian orchestra
are already softly noodling, limbering up for
an overture at sunrise, their effort to express
in the old convention they inherit that joy in beginning
for which our species was created, and declare it
good.

We may not be obliged—though it is mannerly—to bless
the Trinity that we are corporal contraptions,
but only a villain will omit to thank Our Lady or
her henwife, Dame Kind, as he, she, or both ensemble,
emerge from a private cavity to be reborn,
reneighbored in the Country of Consideration.

June 1963

XII The Common Life

(FOR CHESTER KALLMAN)

A living room, the catholic area you
(Thou, rather) and I may enter
without knocking, leave without a bow, confronts
each visitor with a style,

a secular faith: he compares its dogmas
with his, and decides whether
he would like to see more of us. (Spotless rooms
where nothing's left lying about

chill me, so do cups used for ashtrays or smeared
with lipstick: the homes I warm to,
though seldom wealthy, always convey a feeling
of bills being promptly settled

with checks that don't bounce.) There's no *We* at an instant,
only *Thou* and *I*, two regions
of protestant being which nowhere overlap:
a room is too small, therefore,

if its occupants cannot forget at will
that they are not alone, too big
if it gives them any excuse in a quarrel
for raising their voices. What,

quizzing ours, would Sherlock Holmes infer? Plainly,
ours is a sitting culture
in a generation which prefers comfort
(or is forced to prefer it)

to command, would rather incline its buttocks
on a well-upholstered chair
than the burly back of a slave: a quick glance
at book titles would tell him

that we belong to the clerisy and spend much
  on our food. But could he read
what our prayers and jokes are about, what creatures
  frighten us most, or what names

head our roll call of persons we would least like
  to go to bed with? What draws
singular lives together in the first place,
  loneliness, lust, ambition,

or mere convenience, is obvious, why they drop
  or murder one another
clear enough: how they create, though, a common world
  between them, like Bombelli's

impossible yet useful numbers, no one
  has yet explained. Still, they do
manage to forgive impossible behavior,
  to endure by some miracle

conversational tics and larval habits
  without wincing (were you to die,
I should miss yours). It's a wonder that neither
  has been butchered by accident,

or, as lots have, silently vanished into
  History's criminal noise
unmourned for, but that, after twenty-four years,
  we should sit here in Austria

as cater-cousins, under the glassy look
  of a Naples Bambino,
the portrayed regards of Strauss and Stravinsky,
  doing British crossword puzzles,

is very odd indeed. I'm glad the builder gave
  our common-room small windows
through which no observed outsider can observe us:
  every home should be a fortress,

equipped with all the very latest engines
   for keeping Nature at bay,
versed in all ancient magic, the arts of quelling
   the Dark Lord and his hungry

animivorous chimeras. (Any brute
   can buy a machine in a shop,
but the sacred spells are secret to the kind,
   and if power is what we wish

they won't work.) *The ogre will come in any case:*
   so Joyce has warned us. Howbeit,
fasting or feasting, we both know this: without
   the Spirit we die, but life

without the Letter is in the worst of taste,
   and always, though truth and love
can never really differ, when they seem to,
   the subaltern should be truth.

? July 1963

87

Epithalamium

(FOR PETER MUDFORD AND RITA AUDEN, MAY 15, 1965)

All folk-tales mean by ending
with a State Marriage,
feast and fireworks, we wish you,
Peter and Rita,
two idiosyncrasies
who opt in this hawthorn month
to common your lives.

A diffy undertaking,
for to us, whose dreams
are odorless, what is real
seems a bit smelly:
strong nerves are an advantage,
an accurate wrist-watch too
can be a great help.

May Venus, to whose caprice
all blood must buxom,
take such a shine to you both
that, by her gifting,
your palpable substances
may re-ify those delights
they are purveyed for:

cool Hymen from Jealousy's
teratoid phantasms,
sulks, competitive headaches,
and Pride's monologue
that won't listen but demands
tautological echoes,
ever refrain you.

As genders, married or not,
who share with all flesh
a left-handed twist, your choice
reminds us to thank
Mrs. Nature for doing
(our ugly looks are our own)
the handsome by us.

We are better built to last
than tigers, our skins
don't leak like the ciliates',
our ears can detect
quarter-tones, even our most
myopic have good enough
vision for courtship:

and how uncanny it is
we're here to say so.
that life should have got to us
up through the City's
destruction layers after
surviving the inhuman
Permian purges.

Wherefore, as Mudfords, Audens,
Seth-Smiths, Bonnergees,
with civic spear and distaff
we hail a gangrel
Paleocene pseudo-rat,
the Ur-Papa of princes
and crossing-sweepers:

as Adams, Eves, commanded
to nonesuch being,
answer the One for Whom all
enantiomorphs
are super-posable, yet
Who numbers each particle
by its Proper Name.

April 1965

88

Fairground

Thumping old tunes give a voice to its whereabouts
long before one can see the dazzling archway
of colored lights, beyond which household proverbs
cease to be valid,

a ground sacred to the god of vertigo
and his cult of disarray: here jeopardy,
panic, shock, are dispensed in measured doses
by fool-proof engines.

As passive objects, packed tightly together
on Roller-Coaster or Ferris-Wheel, mortals
taste in their solid flesh the volitional
joys of a seraph.

Soon the Roundabout ends the clumsy conflict
of Right and Left: the riding mob melts into
one spinning sphere, the perfect shape performing
the perfect motion.

Mopped and mowed at, as their train worms through a tunnel,
by ancestral spooks, caressed by clammy cobwebs,
grinning initiates emerge into daylight
as tribal heroes.

Fun for Youth who knows his libertine spirit
is not a copy of Father's, but has yet to
learn that the tissues which lend it stamina,
like Mum's, are bourgeois.

Those with their wander-years behind them, who are rather
relieved that all routes of escape are spied on,
all hours of amusement counted, requiring
caution, agenda,

keep away:—to be found in coigns where, sitting
in silent synods, they play chess or cribbage,
games that call for patience, foresight, manoeuvre,
like war, like marriage.

June 1966

89

River Profile

Our body is a moulded river
Novalis

Out of a bellicose fore-time, thundering
head-on collisions of cloud and rock in an
up-thrust, crevasse-and-avalanche, troll country,
deadly to breathers,

it whelms into our picture below the melt-line,
where tarns lie frore under frowning cirques, goat-bell,
wind-breaker, fishing-rod, miner's-lamp country,
already at ease with

the mien and gestures that become its kindness,
in streams, still anonymous, still jumpable,
flows as it should through any declining country
in probing spirals.

Soon of a size to be named and the cause of
dirty in-fighting among rival agencies,
down a steep stair, penstock-and-turbine country,
it plunges ram-stam,

to foam through a wriggling gorge incised in softer
strata, hemmed between crags that nauntle heaven,
robber-baron, tow-rope, portage-way country,
nightmare of merchants.

Disembogueing from foothills, now in hushed meanders,
now in riffling braids, it vaunts across a senile
plain, well-entered, chateau-and-cider-press country,
its regal progress

gallanted for a while by quibbling poplars,
then by chimneys: led off to cool and launder
retort, steam-hammer, gasometer country,
it changes color.

Polluted, bridged by girders, banked by concrete,
now it bisects a polyglot metropolis,
ticker-tape, taxi, brothel, foot-lights country,
à la mode always.

Broadening or burrowing to the moon's phases,
turbid with pulverized wastemantle, on through
flatter, duller, hotter, cotton-gin country
it scours, approaching

the tidal mark where it puts off majesty,
disintegrates, and through swamps of a delta,
punting-pole, fowling-piece, oyster-tongs country,
wearies to its final

act of surrender, effacement, atonement
in a huge amorphous aggregate no cuddled
attractive child ever dreams of, non-country,
image of death as

a spherical dew-drop of life. Unlovely
monsters, our tales believe, can be translated
too, even as water, the selfless mother
of all especials.

July 1966

90

Prologue At Sixty

(FOR FRIEDRICH HEER)

Dark-green upon distant heights
the stationary flocks foresters tend,
blonde and fertile the fields below them:
browing a hog-back, an oak stands
post-alone, light-demanding.

Easier to hear, harder to see,
limbed lives, locomotive,
automatic and irritable,
social or solitary, seek their foods,
mates and territories while their time lasts.

Radial republics, rooted to spots,
bilateral monarchies, moving frankly,
stoic by sort and self-policing,
enjoy their rites, their realms of data,
live well by the Law of their Flesh.

All but the youngest of the yawning mammals,
Name-Giver, Ghost-Fearer,
maker of wars and wise-cracks,
a rum creature, in a crisis always,
the anxious species to which I belong,

whom chance and my own choice have arrived
to bide here yearly from bud-haze
to leaf-blush, dislodged from elsewhere,
by blood barbarian, in bias of view
a Son of the North, outside the *limes*.

Rapacious pirates my people were,
crude and cruel, but not calculating,

never marched in step nor made straight roads,
nor sank like senators to a slave's taste
for grandiose buildings and gladiators.

But the Gospel reached the unroman lands.
I can translate what onion-towers
of five parish churches preach in Baroque:
to make One, there must be Two,
Love is substantial, all Luck is good,

Flesh must fall through fated time
from birth to death, both unwilled,
but Spirit may climb counterwise
from a death, in faith freely chosen,
to resurrection, a re-beginning.

And the Greek Code got to us also:
a Mind of Honor must acknowledge
the happy eachness of all things,
distinguish even from odd numbers,
and bear witness to what-is-the-case.

East, West, on the Autobahn
motorists whoosh, on the Main Line
a far-sighted express will snake by,
through a gap granted by grace of nature:
still today, as in the Stone Age,

our sandy vale is a valued passage.
Alluvial flats, flooded often,
lands of outwash, lie to the North,
to the South litters of limestone alps
embarrass the progress of path-seekers.

Their thoughts upon ski-slope or theatre-opening,
few who pass us pay attention
to our squandered hamlets where at harvest time
chugging tractors, child-driven,
shamble away down sheltered lanes.

Quiet now but acquainted too
with unwelcome visitors, violation,
scare and scream, the scathe of battle:
Turks have been here, Boney's legions,
Germans, Russians, and no joy they brought.

Though the absence of hedge-rows is odd to me
(no Whig landlord, the landscape vaunts,
ever empired on Austrian ground),
this unenglish tract after ten years
into my love has looked itself,

added its names to my numinous map
of the *Solihull* gas-works, gazed at in awe
by a bronchial boy, the *Blue John Mine*,
the *Festiniog* railway, the *Rhayader* dams,
Cross Fell, *Keld* and *Cauldron Snout*,

of sites made sacred by something read there,
a lunch, a good lay, or sheer lightness of heart,
the Fürbringer and the *Friedrich Strasse*,
Isafjördur, *Epomeo*,
Poprad, *Basel*, *Bar-le-Duc*,

of more modern holies, *Middagh Street*,
Carnegie Hall and the Con-Ed stacks
on *First Avenue*. Who am I now?
An American? No, a New Yorker,
who opens his *Times* at the obit page,

whose dream images date him already,
awake among lasers, electric brains,
do-it-yourself sex manuals,
bugged phones, sophisticated
weapon-systems and sick jokes.

Already a helpless orbited dog
has blinked at our sorry conceited O,

where many are famished, few look good,
and my day turned out torturers
who read *Rilke* in their rest periods.

Now the Cosmocrats are crashed through time-zones
in jumbo jets to a Joint Conference:
nor sleep nor shit have our shepherds had,
and treaties are signed (with secret clauses)
by Heads who are not all there.

Can Sixty make sense to Sixteen-Plus?
What has my camp in common with theirs,
with buttons and beards and Be-Ins?
Much, I hope. In *Acts* it is written
Taste was no problem at Pentecost.

To speak is human because human to listen,
beyond hope, for an Eighth Day,
when the creatured Image shall become the Likeness:
Giver-of-Life, translate for me
till I accomplish my corpse at last.

April 1967

91

Forty Years On

Except where blast-furnaces and generating-stations
  have inserted their sharp profiles
or a Thru-Way slashes harshly across them, Bohemia's contours
  look just as amiable now
as when I saw them first (indeed, her coast is gentler,
  for tame hotels have ousted
the havocking bears), nor have her dishes lost their flavor
  since Florizel was thwacked into exile

and we and Sicily discorded, fused into rival amalgams,
  in creed and policy oppugnant.
Only to the ear is it patent something drastic has happened,
  that orators no more speak
of primogeniture, prerogatives of age and sceptre:
  (for our health we have had to learn
the fraternal shop of our new Bonzen, but that was easy.)
  For a useful technician I lacked
the schooling, for a bureaucrat the *Sitz-Fleisch*: all I had
  was the courtier's agility to adapt
my rogueries to the times. It sufficed. I survived and prosper
  better than I ever did under
the old lackadaisical economy: it is many years now
  since I picked a pocket (how deft
my hand was then!), or sang for pennies, or travelled on foot.
  (The singing I miss, but today's
audience would boo my ballads: it calls for Songs of Protest,
  and wants its bawdry straight
not surreptitious.) A pedlar still, for obvious reasons
  I no longer cry my wares,
but in ill-lit alleys coaxingly whisper to likely clients:

Anything you cannot buy
In the stores I will supply,
English foot-wear, nylon hose,
Or transistor radios;
Come to me for the Swiss Francs
Unobtainable in banks;
For a price I can invent
Any official document,
Work-Permits, Driving-Licences,
Any Certificate you please:
Believe me, I know all the tricks,
There is nothing I can't fix.

  Why, then, should I badger?
No rheum has altered my gait, as ever my cardiac muscles
  are undismayed, my cells
perfectly competent, and by now I am far too rich
  for the thought of the hangman's noose

to make me oggle. But how glib all the faces I see around me
seem suddenly to have become,
and how seldom I feel like a hay-tumble. For
three nights running
now I have had the same dream
of a suave afternoon in Fall. I am standing on high ground
looking out westward over
a plain, run smoothly by Jaguar farmers. In the eloignment,
a-glitter in the whelking sun,
a sheer bare cliff concludes the vista. At its base I see,
black, shaped like a bell-tent,
the mouth of a cave by which (I know in my dream) I am to
make my final exit,
its roof so low it will need an awkward duck to make it.
"Well, will that be so shaming?",
I ask when awake. Why should it be? When has Autolycus
ever solemned himself?

1968

92

Ode to Terminus

The High Priests of telescopes and cyclotrons
keep making pronouncements about happenings
on scales too gigantic or dwarfish
to be noticed by our native senses,

discoveries which, couched in the elegant
euphemisms of algebra, look innocent,
harmless enough but, when translated
into the vulgar anthropomorphic

tongue, will give no cause for hilarity
to gardeners or housewives: if galaxies
bolt like panicking mobs, if mesons
riot like fish in a feeding-frenzy,

it sounds too like Political History
to boost civil morale, too symbolic of
the crimes and strikes and demonstrations
we are supposed to gloat on at breakfast.

How trite, though, our fears beside the miracle
that we're here to shiver, that a Thingummy
so addicted to lethal violence
should have somehow secreted a placid

tump with exactly the right ingredients
to start and to cocker Life, that heavenly
freak for whose manage we shall have to
give account at the Judgement, our Middle-

Earth, where Sun-Father to all appearances
moves by day from orient to occident,
and his light is felt as a friendly
presence not a photonic bombardment,

where all visibles do have a definite
outline they stick to, and are undoubtedly
at rest or in motion, where lovers
recognize each-other by their surface,

where to all species except the talkative
have been allotted the niche and diet that
become them. This, whatever micro-
biology may think, is the world we

really live in and that saves our sanity,
who know all too well how the most erudite
mind behaves in the dark without a
surround it is called on to interpret,

how, discarding rhythm, punctuation, metaphor,
it sinks into a driveling monologue,
too literal to see a joke or
distinguish a penis from a pencil.

Venus and Mars are powers too natural
to temper our outlandish extravagance:
    You alone, Terminus the Mentor,
    can teach us how to alter our gestures.

God of walls, doors and reticence, nemesis
overtakes the sacrilegious technocrat,
    but blessed is the City that thanks you
    for giving us games and grammar and metres.

By whose grace, also, every gathering
of two or three in confident amity
    repeats the pentecostal marvel,
    as each in each finds his right translator.

In this world our colossal immodesty
has plundered and poisoned, it is possible
    You still might save us, who by now have
    learned this: that scientists, to be truthful,

must remind us to take all they say as a
tall story, that abhorred in the Heav'ns are all
    self-proclaimed poets who, to wow an
    audience, utter some resonant lie.

May 1968

93

August 1968

The Ogre does what ogres can,
Deeds quite impossible for Man,
But one prize is beyond his reach,
The Ogre cannot master Speech:
About a subjugated plain,
Among its desperate and slain,
The Ogre stalks with hands on hips,
While drivel gushes from his lips.

September 1968

94

A New Year Greeting

(After an Article by Mary J. Marples
in Scientific American,
January 1969)

(FOR VASSILY YANOWSKY)

On this day tradition allots
    to taking stock of our lives,
my greetings to all of you, Yeasts,
    Bacteria, Viruses,
Aerobics and Anaerobics:
    A Very Happy New Year
to all for whom my ectoderm
    is as Middle-Earth to me.

For creatures your size I offer
    a free choice of habitat,
so settle yourselves in the zone
    that suits you best, in the pools
of my pores or the tropical
    forests of arm-pit and crotch,
in the deserts of my fore-arms,
    or the cool woods of my scalp.

Build colonies: I will supply
    adequate warmth and moisture,
the sebum and lipids you need,
    on condition you never
do me annoy with your presence,
    but behave as good guests should,
not rioting into acne
    or athlete's-foot or a boil.

Does my inner weather affect
 the surfaces where you live?
Do unpredictable changes
 record my rocketing plunge
from fairs when the mind is in tift
 and relevant thoughts occur
to fouls when nothing will happen
 and no one calls and it rains.

I should like to think that I make
 a not impossible world,
but an Eden it cannot be:
 my games, my purposive acts,
may turn to catastrophes there.
 If you were religious folk,
how would your dramas justify
 unmerited suffering?

By what myths would your priests account
 for the hurricanes that come
twice every twenty-four hours,
 each time I dress or undress,
when, clinging to keratin rafts,
 whole cities are swept away
to perish in space, or the Flood
 that scalds to death when I bathe?

Then, sooner or later, will dawn
 a day of Apocalypse,
when my mantle suddenly turns
 too cold, too rancid, for you,
appetising to predators
 of a fiercer sort, and I
am stripped of excuse and nimbus,
 a Past, subject to Judgement.

May 1969

95

Moon Landing

It's natural the Boys should whoop it up for
so huge a phallic triumph, an adventure
it would not have occurred to women
to think worth while, made possible only

because we like huddling in gangs and knowing
the exact time: yes, our sex may in fairness
hurrah the deed, although the motives
that primed it were somewhat less than *menschlich*.

A grand gesture. But what does it period?
What does it osse? We were always adroiter
with objects than lives, and more facile
at courage than kindness: from the moment

the first flint was flaked this landing was merely
a matter of time. But our selves, like Adam's,
still don't fit us exactly, modern
only in this—our lack of decorum.

Homer's heroes were certainly no braver
than our Trio, but more fortunate: Hector
was excused the insult of having
his valor covered by television.

Worth *going* to see? I can well believe it.
Worth *seeing*? Mneh! I once rode through a desert
and was not charmed: give me a watered
lively garden, remote from blatherers

about the New, the von Brauns and their ilk, where
on August mornings I can count the morning
glories, where to die has a meaning,
and no engine can shift my perspective.

Unsmudged, thank God, my Moon still queens the Heavens
as She ebbs and fulls, a Presence to glop at,
    Her Old Man, made of grit not protein,
    still visits my Austrian several

with His old detachment, and the old warnings
still have power to scare me: Hybris comes to
    an ugly finish, Irreverence
    is a greater oaf than Superstition.

Our apparatniks will continue making
the usual squalid mess called History:
    all we can pray for is that artists,
    chefs and saints may still appear to blithe it.

August 1969

96

Old People's Home

    All are limitory, but each has her own
nuance of damage. The elite can dress and decent themselves,
    are ambulant with a single stick, adroit
to read a book all through, or play the slow movements of
    easy sonatas. (Yes, perhaps their very
carnal freedom is their spirit's bane: intelligent
    of what has happened and why, they are obnoxious
to a glum beyond tears.) Then come those on
                                        wheels, the average
    majority, who endure T.V. and, led by
lenient therapists, do community-singing, then
    the loners, muttering in Limbo, and last
the terminally incompetent, as improvident,
    unspeakable, impeccable as the plants
they parody. (Plants may sweat profusely but never
    sully themselves.) One tie, though, unites them: all

appeared when the world, though much was awry there,
was more
spacious, more comely to look at, its Old Ones
with an audience and secular station. Then a child,
in dismay with Mamma, could refuge with Gran
to be revalued and told a story. As of now,
we all know what to expect, but their generation
is the first to fade like this, not at home but assigned
to a numbered frequent ward, stowed out of conscience
as unpopular luggage.
As I ride the subway
to spend half-an-hour with one, I revisage
who she was in the pomp and sumpture of her hey-day,
when week-end visits were a presumptive joy,
not a good work. Am I cold to wish for a speedy
painless dormition, pray, as I know she prays,
that God or Nature will abrupt her earthly function?

April 1970

97

Talking to Myself

(FOR OLIVER SACKS)

Spring this year in Austria started off benign,
the heavens lucid, the air stable, the about
sane to all feeders, vegetate or bestial:
the deathless minerals looked pleased with their regime,
where what is not forbidden is compulsory.

Shadows of course there are, Porn-Ads, with-it clergy,
and hubby next door has taken to the bottle,
but You have preserved Your poise, strange rustic object,
whom I, made in God's Image but already warped,
a malapert will-worship, must bow to as Me.

My mortal manor, the carnal territory
alloted to my manage, my fosterling too,
I must earn cash to support, my tutor also,
but for whose neural instructions I could never
acknowledge what is or imagine what is not.

Instinctively passive, I guess, having neither
fangs nor talons nor hooves nor venom, and therefore
too prone to let the sun go down upon Your funk,
a poor smeller, or rather a censor of smells,
with an omnivore palate that can take hot food.

Unpredictably, decades ago, You arrived
among that unending cascade of creatures spewed
from Nature's maw. A random event, says Science.
Random my bottom! A true miracle, say I,
for who is not certain that he was meant to be?

As You augmented and developed a profile,
I looked at Your looks askance. *His architecture*
should have been much more imposing: I've been let down!
By now, though, I've gotten used to Your proportions
and, all things considered, I might have fared far worse.

Seldom have You been a bother. For many years
You were, I admit, a martyr to horn-colic
(it did no good to tell You—*But I'm not in love!*):
how stoutly, though, You've repelled all germ invasions,
but never chastised my tantrums with a megrim.

You are the Injured Party for, if short-sighted,
I am the book-worm who tired You, if short-winded
as cigarette addicts are, I was the pusher
who got You hooked. (Had we been both a bit younger,
I might well have mischiefed You worse with a needle.)

I'm always amazed at how little I know You.
Your coasts and outgates I know, for I govern there,
but what goes on inland, the rites, the social codes,

Your torrents, salt and sunless, remain enigmas:
what I believe is on doctors' hearsay only.

Our marriage is a drama, but no stage-play where
what is not spoken is not thought: in our theatre
all that I cannot syllable You will pronounce
in acts whose *raison-d'être* escapes me. Why secrete
fluid when I dole, or stretch Your lips when I joy?

Demands to close or open, include or eject,
must come from Your corner, are no province of mine
(all I have done is to provide the time-table
of hours when You may put them): but what is Your work
when I librate between a glum and a frolic?

For dreams I, quite irrationally, reproach You.
All I know is that I don't choose them: if I could,
they would conform to some prosodic discipline,
mean just what they say. Whatever point nocturnal
manias make, as a poet I disapprove.

Thanks to Your otherness, Your jocular concords,
so unlike my realm of dissonance and anger,
You can serve me as my emblem for the Cosmos:
for human congregations, though, as Hobbes perceived,
the apposite sign is some ungainly monster.

Whoever coined the phrase *The Body Politic*?
All States we've lived in, or historians tell of,
have had shocking health, psychosomatic cases,
physicked by sadists or glozing expensive quacks:
when I read the papers, You seem an Adonis.

Time, we both know, will decay You, and already
I'm scared of our divorce: I've seen some horrid ones.
Remember: when *Le Bon Dieu* says to You *Leave him!*,
please, please, for His sake and mine, pay no attention
to my piteous *Dont's*, but bugger off quickly.

April 1971

98

A Lullaby

The din of work is subdued,
another day has westered
and mantling darkness arrived.
Peace! Peace! Devoid your portrait
of its vexations and rest.
Your daily round is done with,
you've gotten the garbage out,
answered some tiresome letters
and paid a bill by return,
all *frettolosamente.*
Now you have licence to lie,
naked, curled like a shrimplet,
jacent in bed, and enjoy
its cosy micro-climate:
Sing, Big Baby, sing lullay.

The old Greeks got it all wrong:
Narcissus is an oldie,
tamed by time, released at last
from lust for other bodies,
rational and reconciled.
For many years you envied
the hirsute, the he-man type.
No longer: now you fondle
your almost feminine flesh
with mettled satisfaction,
imagining that you are
sinless and all-sufficient,
snug in the den of yourself,
Madonna and *Bambino:*
Sing, Big Baby, sing lullay.

Let your last thinks all be thanks:
praise your parents who gave you
a Super-Ego of strength

that saves you so much bother,
digit friends and dear them all,
then pay fair attribution
to your age, to having been
born when you were. In boyhood
you were permitted to meet
beautiful old contraptions,
soon to be banished from earth,
saddle-tank loks, beam-engines
and over-shot waterwheels.
Yes, love, you have been lucky:
Sing, Big Baby, sing lullay.

Now for oblivion: let
the belly-mind take over
down below the diaphragm,
the domain of the Mothers,
They who guard the Sacred Gates,
without whose wordless warnings
soon the verbalising I
becomes a vicious despot,
lewd, incapable of love,
disdainful, status-hungry.
Should dreams haunt you, heed them not,
for all, both sweet and horrid,
are jokes in dubious taste,
too jejune to have truck with.
Sleep, Big Baby, sleep your fill.

April 1972

99

A Thanksgiving

When pre-pubescent I felt
that moorlands and woodlands were sacred:
people seemed rather profane.

Thus, when I started to verse,
I presently sat at the feet of
Hardy and *Thomas* and *Frost*.

Falling in love altered that,
now Someone, at least, was important:
Yeats was a help, so was *Graves*.

Then, without warning, the whole
Economy suddenly crumbled:
there, to instruct me, was *Brecht*.

Finally, hair-raising things
that Hitler and Stalin were doing
forced me to think about God.

Why was I sure they were wrong?
Wild *Kierkegaard*, *Williams* and *Lewis*
guided me back to belief.

Now, as I mellow in years
and home in a bountiful landscape,
Nature allures me again.

Who are the tutors I need?
Well, *Horace*, adroitest of makers,
beeking in Tivoli, and

Goethe, devoted to stones,
who guessed that—he never could prove it—
Newton led Science astray.

Fondly I ponder You all:
without You I couldn't have managed
even my weakest of lines.

? May 1973

100

Archaeology

The archaeologist's spade
delves into dwellings
vacancied long ago,

unearthing evidence
of life-ways no one
would dream of leading now,

concerning which he has not much
to say that he can prove:
the lucky man!

Knowledge may have its purposes,
but guessing is always
more fun than knowing.

We do know that Man,
from fear or affection,
has always graved His dead.

What disastered a city,
volcanic effusion,
fluvial outrage,

or a human horde,
agog for slaves and glory,
is visually patent,

and we're pretty sure that,
as soon as palaces were built,
their rulers,

though gluttoned on sex
and blanded by flattery,
must often have yawned.

But do grain-pits signify
a year of famine?
Where a coin-series

peters out, should we infer
some major catastrophe?
Maybe. Maybe.

From murals and statues
we get a glimpse of what
the Old Ones bowed down to,

but cannot conceit
in what situations they blushed
or shrugged their shoulders.

Poets have learned us their myths,
but just how did They take them?
That's a stumper.

When Norsemen heard thunder,
did they seriously believe
Thor was hammering?

No, I'd say: I'd swear
that men have always lounged in myths
as Tall Stories,

that their real earnest
has been to grant excuses
for ritual actions.

Only in rites
can we renounce our oddities
and be truly entired.

Not that all rites
should be equally fonded:
some are abominable.

There's nothing the Crucified
would like less
than butchery to appease Him.

CODA

From Archaeology
one moral, at least, may be drawn,
to wit, that all

our school text-books lie.
What they call History
is nothing to vaunt of,

being made, as it is,
by the criminal in us:
goodness is timeless.

August 1973

A Note on the Text

The poems in this selection first appeared in Auden's published books as follows:

Poems (1930): No. 1-11
Poems (second edition 1933): No. 12-14
The Orators (1932): No. 15-16
The Dog Beneath the Skin (1935): No. 24-25
Look, Stranger! (1936, American title *On This Island*): No. 17-23, 26-30
Spain (1937): No. 34
Letters from Iceland (1937): No. 31-32
Journey to a War (1939): No. 40
Another Time (1940): No. 33, 35-39, 41-49
The Double Man (1941, British title *New Year Letter*): No. 52
For the Time Being (1944): No. 60
The Collected Poetry of W. H. Auden (1945, similar British edition *Collected Shorter Poems 1930-1944*): No. 50-51, 53-59
The Age of Anxiety (1947): No. 61-62
Nones (1951): No. 63-69 (and no. 75, parts I and IV only)
The Shield of Achilles (1955): No. 70-75
Homage to Clio (1960): No. 76-81 (and no. 86, part VIII only)
About the House (1965): No. 82-86
City Without Walls (1969): No. 87-93
Epistle to a Godson (1972): No. 94-97
Thank You, Fog (1974): No. 98-100

Auden excluded certain of his early poems from his later collections. Of the poems in this book, the following did not appear in Auden's final collected edition: no. 7, 17, 25, 34, 40 (parts IX, X, XIV, XX, XXVI only), 47. Other poems were extensively revised or abridged, notably no. 4, 10, 16, 20, 23, 24, 28, 31, 39, 40 (the remaining parts), 44, 54, 57. Most of the remaining poems have lesser revisions. The final versions may be found in *Collected Poems* (1976) or, for most of the important changes, in the paperback *Collected Shorter Poems 1927-1957* (1966).

As stated in the preface, the texts in this book are those of the first published editions, with misprints corrected on the basis of manuscripts, and with some minor revisions that Auden made shortly after first publication. Such revisions occur in only two or three poems, and only one instance amounts to more than a small adjustment in the meter. This exception is poem no. 8, where the present text adopts the cuts Auden made for the second edition (1933) of *Poems* (1930); these cuts can be dated in manuscript to about a year after the book was first published. In the same poem the present text incorporates for the first time a small change Auden made simultaneously with the cuts, but apparently forgot when preparing the new edition for the press more than a year later (the complicated textual history of this poem, published and unpublished, offers good reasons for assuming a lapse of memory on Auden's part); the revision occurs in line 17 of part IV, where "To censor the play"—clearly a superior reading in context—replaces "The intricate play".

In *About the House* some of the parts of poem no. 86 had shorter poems appended to them as "Postscripts"; these have been omitted here, as Auden omitted them in his own selections, one of which he prepared shortly after the poem first appeared.

Index of Titles and First Lines

A cellar underneath the house, though not lived in 259
A cloudless night like this 188
A lake allows an average father, walking slowly 208
A living room, the catholic area you 276
A shilling life will give you all the facts 32
A starling and a willow-wren 200
About suffering they were never wrong 79
Adrian and Francisco 141
Adventure 108
Adventurers, The 108
After Reading a Child's Guide to Modern Physics 246
After shaking paws with his dog 218
All are limitory, but each has her own 295
All folk-tales mean by ending 278
All had been ordered weeks before the start 99
Alonso 141
Always far from the centre of our names 77
Among pelagian travelers 248
Among the leaves the small birds sing 231
And the age ended, and the last deliverer died 70
And the traveller hopes: "Let me be far from any 46
Antonio 136
Archaeology 302
Ares at last has quit the field 178
Ashamed to be the darling of his grief 102
As a young child the wisest could adore him 69
As all the pigs have turned back into men 136
As I walked out one evening 60
At Dirty Dick's and Sloppy Joe's 144
At the Grave of Henry James 119
Atlantis 116

August 1968 291
Average, The 105

Being set on the idea 116
Bucolics 202
But I Can't 110
But in the evening the oppression lifted 74

Caliban to the Audience 148
Capital, The 78
Casino 45
Cave of Making, The 256
Cave of Nakedness, The 273
Certainly praise: let the song mount again and again 71
City, The 101
Common Life, The 276
Compline 230
Consider this and in our time 14
Control of the passes was, he saw, the key 3
Crossroads, The 100

Dame Kind 242
Dark-green upon distant heights 284
Dear, all benevolence of fingering lips 111
Dear Son, when the warm multitudes cry 141
Dear, though the night is gone 44
Dear water, clear water, playful in all your streams 214
Deep below our violences 202
Deftly, admiral, cast your fly 187
Don Juan needs no bed, being far too impatient to undress 273
Doom is dark and deeper than any sea-dingle 18
Door, The 99
Down There 259

Easily, my dear, you move, easily your head 33
Embrace me, belly, like a bride 138
Encomium Balnei 263
Engines bear them through the sky: they're free 72
Epitaph on a Tyrant 80
Epithalamium 278
Et in Arcadia Ego 250
Evening, grave, immense, and clear 139
Except where blast-furnaces and generating-stations 287

Fairground 280
Fall of Rome, The 183
Far from the heart of culture he was used 73
Ferdinand 137
First Temptation, The 102
First Things First 236
Fleet Visit 197
Flesh, fair, unique, and you, warm secret that my kiss 137
For Friends Only 269
For this and for all enclosures like it the archetype 256
Forty Years On 287
Fresh addenda are published every day 106
Friday's Child 237
From gallery-grave and the hunt of a wren-king 252
From the very first coming down 2

Garden, The 110
Geography of the House, The 261
Gonzalo 139
Good little sunbeams must learn to fly 141
Good-bye to the Mezzogiorno 239
Grub First, Then Ethics 266

He disappeared in the dead of winter 80
He looked in all his wisdom from the throne 70
He parried every question that they hurled 107
He stayed: and was imprisoned in possession 66
He told us we were free to choose 237
He turned his field into a meeting-place 68
He was found by the Bureau of Statistics to be 85
He was their servant–some say he was blind 68
He watched the stars and noted birds in flight 67
He watched with all his organs of concern 103
Hearing of harvests rotting in the valleys 28
Here war is simple like a monument 72
Hero, The 107
His generous bearing was a new invention 67
His peasant parents killed themselves with toil 105
Homage to Clio 232
Horae Canonicae 216
How still it is; the horses 175

I can imagine quite easily ending up 211
I know a retired dentist who only paints mountains 206
I sit in one of the dives 86
If all a top physicist knows 246
If it form the one landscape that we the inconstant ones 184
If now, having dismissed your hired impersonators 148
If the hill overlooking our city has always been known 227
In a garden shady this holy lady 96
In Memory of Sigmund Freud 91
In Memory of W. B. Yeats 80
In Praise of Limestone 184
In Sickness and in Health 111
In Time of War 64
In villages from which their childhoods came 101
Incredulous, he stared at the amused 105
Islands 210
it is odd that the English 263
It was Easter as I walked in the public gardens 7
It's natural the Boys should whoop it up for 294

Journey to Iceland 46
Jumbled in the common box 115

Kicking his mother until she let go of his soul 123

Lady, weeping at the crossroads 95
Lakes 208
Lament for a Lawgiver 176
Lauds 231
Law, say the gardeners, is the sun 89
Lay your sleeping head, my love 50
Lesson, The 125
Let me tell you a little story 55
Look, stranger, at this island now 43
Looking up at the stars, I know quite well 237
Lucky, The 107
Lullaby, A 299

Make this night loveable 201
Master and Boatswain 144
Mechanic, merchant, king 146
Memorial for the City 190

Men would never have come to need an attic 260
Miranda 147
Miss Gee 55
Moon Landing 294
More Loving One, The 237
Mountains 206
Mundus et Infans 123
Musée des Beaux Arts 79
My Dear One is mine as mirrors are lonely 147
My rioters all disappear, my dream 145

Nature is so near: the rooks in the college garden 63
New Year Greeting, A 292
No, not their names. It was the others who built 76
No window in his suburb lights that bedroom where 101
Nobody I know would like to be buried 253
Nocturne 201
Nones 223
Noon 175
Nothing is given: we must find our law 77
Now, as desire and the things desired 230
Now the leaves are falling fast 43
Now through night's caressing grip 41

O for doors to be open and an invite with gilded edges 42
O Love, the interest itself in thoughtless Heaven 25
O what is that sound which so thrills the ear 26
"O where are you going?" said reader to rider 19
"O who can ever gaze his fill" 48
Ode to Terminus 289
Old People's Home 295
Old saints on millstones float with cats 210
On the Circuit 248
On this day tradition allots 292
Only a smell had feelings to make known 66
Only the hands are living; to the wheel attracted 45
Orpheus 55
Others had swerved off to the left before 108
Our hill has made its submission and the green 232
Our hunting fathers told the story 33
Ours yet not ours, being set apart 269
Out of a bellicose fore-time, thundering 282

Out of a gothic North, the pallid children 239
Out of it steps the future of the poor 99
Out on the lawn I lie in bed 29
Oxford 63

Perfection, of a kind, was what he was after 80
Plains 211
Poet, oracle and wit 109
Postscript 174
Preparations, The 99
Presumptuous, The 104
Prime 216
Prologue At Sixty 284
Prologue: The Birth of Architecture 252
Prospero to Ariel 129

Quarter of pleasures where the rich are always waiting 78
Quest, The 99

Really, must you 245
Refugee Blues 83
River Profile 282

Say this city has ten million souls 83
Sea and the Mirror, The 127
Seated after breakfast 261
Sebastian 145
Second Temptation, The 102
September 1, 1939 86
Sext 219
She looked over his shoulder 198
Shield of Achilles, The 198
Should the shade of Plato 266
Simultaneously, as soundlessly 216
Since you are going to begin to-day 12
Sir, no man's enemy, forgiving all 7
Simple like all dream wishes, they employ 75
So from the years the gifts were showered; each 64
Sob, heavy world 176
Song 187
Song for St. Cecilia's Day 96
Spain 51

Spinning upon their central thirst like tops 108
Spring this year in Austria started off benign 296
Stay with me, Ariel, while I pack, and with your first free act 129
Steatopygous, sow-dugged 242
Stephano 138
Streams 214
Suppose he'd listened to the erudite committee 107
Sylvan meant savage in those primal woods 204

Talking to Myself 296
Taller to-day, we remember similar evenings 3
Terce 218
Thanksgiving, A 300
Thanksgiving for a Habitat 252
The aged catch their breath 127
The archaeologist's spade 302
The din of work is subdued 299
The eyes of the crow and the eye of the camera open 190
The first time that I dreamed, we were in flight 125
The friends who met here and embraced are gone 100
The High Priests of telescopes and cyclotrons 289
The library annoyed him with its look 102
The life of man is never quite completed 75
The life of plants 271
The Ogre does what ogres can 291
The over-logical fell for the witch 106
The piers are pummelled by the waves 183
The sailors come ashore 197
The snow, less intransigeant than their marble 119
The Summer holds: upon its glittering lake 36
They are and suffer; that is all they do 73
They carry terror with them like a purse 74
They died and entered the closed life like nuns 69
They noticed that virginity was needed 104
They wondered why the fruit had been forbidden 65
Third Temptation, The 103
This is an architecture for the odd 103
This lunar beauty 16
Though aware of our rank and alert to obey orders 20
Thumping old tunes gives a voice to its whereabouts 280
Time will say nothing but I told you so 110
To ask the hard question is simple 17

Tonight at Seven-Thirty 271
Tower, The 103
Traveller, The 101
Trinculo 146

Under Sirius 195
Under Which Lyre 178
Unknown Citizen, The 85
Up There 260
Useful, The 106

Vespers 227
Vocation 105

Walk After Dark, A 188
Wandering lost upon the mountains of our choice 77
Watch any day his nonchalant pauses, see 4
Waters, The 109
Way, The 106
Weep no more but pity me 174
What does the song hope for? And the moved hands 55
What we know to be not possible 223
What's in your mind, my dove, my coney 19
When all the apparatus of report 76
When pre-pubescent I felt 300
When there are so many we shall have to mourn 91
Who, now, seeing Her so 250
Who stands, the crux left of the watershed 1
Will you turn a deaf ear 5
Willow-Wren and the Stare, The 200
Winds 202
Within these gates all opening begins 110
Woken, I lay in the arms of my own warmth and listened 236
Woods 204
Wrapped in a yielding air, beside 59

Yes, these are the dog-days, Fortunatus 195
Yes, we are going to suffer, now; the sky 71
Yesterday all the past. The language of size 51
You 245
You need not see what someone is doing 219